PROGRAMMING
WITH

Alice

&

Java

PROGRAMMING
WITH

Alice
&
Java

JOHN LEWIS
Radford University

PETER DEPASQUALE
The College of New Jersey

PEARSON

Addison
Wesley

Boston   San Francisco   New York
London Toronto Sydney Tokyo Singapore Madrid
Mexico City Munich Paris Cape Town Hong Kong Montreal

Executive Editor   Michael Hirsch
Editorial Assistant   Stephanie Sellinger
Associate Managing Editor   Jeffrey Holcomb
Digital Assets Manager   Marianne Groth
Senior Media Producer   Bethany Tidd
Marketing Manager   Chris Kelly
Senior Author Support/Technology Specialist   Joe Vetere
Senior Prepress Supervisor   Caroline Fell
Senior Manufacturing Buyer   Carol Melville
Senior Media Buyer   Ginny Michaud
Text Design   Jerilyn Bockorick, Nesbitt Graphics, Inc.
Project Management   Kathy Smith, Nesbitt Graphics, Inc.
Production Coordination   Harry Druding, Nesbitt Graphics, Inc.
Composition and Art   Nesbitt Graphics, Inc.
Cover Design   Beth Paquin
Cover Image   © Shutterstock

Many of the designations used by manufacturers and sellers to distinguish their products are claimed as trademarks. Where those designations appear in this book, and Addison-Wesley was aware of a trademark claim, the designations have been printed in initial caps or all caps.

Library of Congress Cataloging-in-Publication Data

Lewis, John, 1963-
  Programming with Alice & Java / John Lewis, Peter DePasquale.-- 1st ed.
      p. cm.
  Includes index.
  ISBN 0-321-51209-X
  1. Alice (Computer file) 2. Object-oriented programming (Computer science) 3. Java (Computer program language) I. DePasquale, Peter J. (Peter Joseph) II. Title.
  QA76.64.L46 2008
  005.1'17--dc22

                                                                                    2008006538

ISBN-13: 978-0-321-51209-3
ISBN-10: 0-321-51209-X

1 2 3 4 5 6 7 8 9 10—CK—12 11 10 09 08

To Sharon, Justin, Kayla, Nathan, and Samantha.
—John

To Lisa, Lily, and Adam. All my love.
—Pete

Preface

Welcome to *Programming with Alice and Java™*. As educators, we continually wrestle with the challenge of finding the best ways to communicate computing concepts in a manner that is both effective and engaging. Traditional language-oriented textbooks work for some students, but not for all. For many students, a different approach is needed.

Yet we also must be careful not to chase after every new technology, hoping that it will magically keep our students interested and informed. All too frequently, this seems to be happening in our discipline as well.

The solution lies in the *correct* use of the *appropriate* technologies. Alice has proven to be an extremely effective tool, but it must be used appropriately. If the goal is to communicate anything beyond basic programming concepts, it is insufficient to rely upon Alice on its own.

In its coverage of technology, this book is organized into two clean sections. The first five chapters use the Alice programming environment, and the remaining seven focus on the Java programming language. Conceptually, though, the ideas of object-oriented programming are intertwined. They are revisited and reinforced. They are explored naturally in the context of examples throughout the book.

By starting with Alice, students produce interesting results immediately. Alice draws them into the world of programming without the stigma of "traditional" coding. Most importantly, correctly emphasizing the concepts involved in developing Alice worlds sets the stage for developing software in a general-purpose language such as Java.

Let's explore these ideas in more detail.

On Using Alice

For many instructors, Alice has already proven itself to be an excellent tool for introducing programming concepts. Furthermore, it's engaging. It captures and keeps the attention of students who are not satisfied with text output and dry calculations. Alice also has the benefit of appealing to both females and males—a crucial issue in today's academic setting.

Like any tool, though, Alice needs to be used correctly. There is often too much emphasis placed on teaching Alice, instead of *using* Alice to teach object-oriented programming. There's a big difference. In this book, the content in the chapters focuses on object-oriented concepts. Environment details are minimized in the chapters themselves, although they are fully explored in reference-oriented appendices. This approach clearly highlights what's important and what's not.

The whole objects-early vs. objects-late debate is largely irrelevant when you start with Alice. The objects are obvious. It's perfectly natural to discuss objects that have particular properties and behaviors. The very essence of an animation is asking objects to do things for you, such as move forward or turn right.

Our goal, though, is not to turn our students into animators—you wouldn't use Alice to do that anyway. Thus, we don't dwell on storyboarding or scene direction or hyper-detailed tricks to make the animations perfectly realistic. Alice is a terminal technology. Its lasting value comes from the programming concepts it can convey.

The other aspect of our reasoning is that, since Alice was designed to create animations, that's all we use it for. We don't use an Alice character to "say" the Fibonacci numbers, for example, or to move the camera using recursion. Such examples miss the whole point. Just because you can do something in Alice doesn't mean you should. We use Alice for the things that Alice is good at, and then *leave it behind*.

We suggest that Alice be used for approximately one-third, and certainly no more than one-half, of a semester. Then, you should apply those same concepts in a general-purpose language like Java, which doesn't have the inherent boundaries of Alice.

On Transitioning to Java

The engaging nature of Alice requires that the transition to Java be handled carefully. We don't want a student's enthusiasm to drop, and there is no reason it has to. Examples in Java can be engaging as well, especially with the foundation that Alice has provided.

The transition allows us to compare and contrast the concepts we used in Alice with the way they are embodied in Java. That repetition is pedagogical gold. The concepts sink in further and become more formalized.

In addition to smaller examples, this book introduces students to a large Java program called ThunkIt, a puzzle game that the students can play and enjoy before exploring the underlying code.

In each level of ThunkIt, the user moves a character around the screen, trying to figure out how to get to the exit. The player collects supplies, moves obstacles, and uses gadgets to solve each level. As with Alice, many of the objects in ThunkIt are obvious just by playing the game.

Another advantage of using ThunkIt is that students are *reading code as well as writing it*. We encourage them to explore the ThunkIt code without worrying about understanding it all initially. As each chapter explores particular concepts, more of the ThunkIt software is dissected to see how those concepts apply.

By using a combination of small and large examples, we expose students to a larger spectrum of the programming world. We ask them to make modifications to existing code as well as write code from scratch. We ask them to explore a large design as well as design their own smaller programs.

Unlike language-oriented texts, our goal is not to teach every nuance of a programming language. Students get a solid grounding in Java and its supporting APIs, but we don't feel obligated to make sure every single aspect of the language is covered. Instead, we explore the language as it comes up naturally in relation to core concepts.

The combination of Alice and Java, especially when a large example like ThunkIt is included, introduces students to programming in an engaging and natural way. Compared to other techniques, this approach better prepares them for future explorations in computing and makes it more likely that they will want to continue to engage them.

Supplemental Resources

Student CD

The CD in this book includes:

- Examples from the book
- "Try This" Solutions
- Java™ SE Development Kit 6
- DrJava IDE
- Eclipse™ SDK for Windows
- JCreator® LE IDE
- jGRASP™ IDE
- NetBeans™ IDE
- TextPad® Text Editor for Windows

The Alice environment can be downloaded for free from www.alice.org.

ThunkIt can be downloaded for free from www.thunkit.net.

If you can't locate your CD, you can access the Examples and "Try This" Solutions at www.aw.com/cssupport. The various pieces of software can usually be downloaded from the various websites of the organizations that develop them.

Instructor Resources

The following supplements are available to qualified instructors only:

- PowerPoint presentation slides for each chapter
- Solutions to Programming Projects
- Test Item File

Visit the Addison-Wesley Instructor Resource Center (www.aw.com/irc) or send an email to computing@aw.com for information on how to access them.

Acknowledgments

We greatly appreciate the encouragement and feedback provided by faculty and students. Questions and comments are always welcome.

We'd particularly like to thank the reviewers of this book who provided valuable feedback:

Antonia Boadi, California State University Dominguez Hills
Skip Bottom, J. Sargeant Reynolds Community College
Seth Chaiken, University at Albany
Tebring Daly, Collin County Community College
Tom Edwards, South Central College
Mary Beth Flagg, Salisbury University
Brian Hanks, Fort Lewis College
Mark C. Lewis, Trinity University
Satish Singhal, Santa Monica College
Jeffrey A. Stone, Pennsylvania State University
William Taylor, Camden County College

Producing a book like this is a group effort, and the folks at Addison-Wesley continue to amaze us. Our editor, Michael Hirsch, has wonderful insight and commitment. His assistant, Stephanie Sellinger, is a source of consistent and valuable support. Jeff Holcomb led the challenging production effort, with the help of Kathy Smith of Nesbitt Graphics. We appreciate their diligence and their patience with sometimes-cranky authors. The cover design was created with the skilled talents of Beth Paquin; for the interior design we thank Jerilyn Bockorick, also of Nesbitt Graphics. And marketing manager Chris Kelly makes sure that instructors understand the pedagogical advantages of the book. Thank you all.

We'd also like to thank our colleagues in SIGCSE, the ACM Special Interest Group on Computer Science Education. SIGCSE conferences and resources provide an opportunity for educators from all levels and all types of schools to share ideas and materials. Get involved.

Feature Walkthrough

Key Concepts. Throughout the text, the Key Concept boxes highlight fundamental ideas and important guidelines. These concepts are summarized at the end of each chapter.

2.3 Parameters

We've seen that methods can accept parameters that provide key information needed to carry out the method's purpose. For example, an object's move method accepts parameters that specify what direction to move in and how far to move (among others).

> Writing methods so that they are based on the parameter values passed to them makes them more versatile and useful.

Any method we add to an object can also be designed to accept one or more parameters. These parameters can be of any type, including objects. When you design a method, it's important to think about using parameters to make the method more versatile—that is, useful in as many situations as possible.

Consider the Jet world, shown in Figure 2.9. When the animation is played, a jet flies in a circular pattern near an airport. The jet was made using the NavyJet class from the **Vehicles** gallery and the airport was made using classes in the **Buildings** gallery.

Listings. All programming examples are presented in clearly labeled listings. The code is colored to visually distinguish between comments in green, reserved words in blue, and strings in red.

Listing 11.1

```java
//********************************************************************
//  RationalTester.java       Programming with Alice and Java
//
//  Driver to exercise the use of multiple RationalNumber objects.
//********************************************************************

public class RationalTester
{
    //-----------------------------------------------------------------
    // Creates some RationalNumber objects and performs various operations on
    // them.
    //-----------------------------------------------------------------
    public static void main (String[] args)
    {
        RationalNumber r1 = new RationalNumber (6, 8);
        RationalNumber r2 = new RationalNumber (1, 3);
        RationalNumber r3, r4, r5, r6, r7;

        System.out.println ("First rational number: " + r1);
        System.out.println ("Second rational number: " + r2);

        if (r1.isLike (r2))
            System.out.println ("r1 and r2 are equal.");
        else
            System.out.println ("r1 and r2 are NOT equal.");

        r3 = r1.reciprocal ();
        System.out.println ("The reciprocal of r1 is: " + r3);

        r4 = r1.add (r2);
        r5 = r1.subtract (r2);
        r6 = r1.multiply (r2);
        r7 = r1.divide (r2);

        System.out.println ("r1 + r2: " + r4);
        System.out.println ("r1 - r2: " + r5);
        System.out.println ("r1 * r2: " + r6);
        System.out.println ("r1 / r2: " + r7);
    }
}
```

8. Modify the `Frog` world so that the hop method accepts a parameter that specifies the jumping distance.

9. Modify the `Jet` world so that the time it takes for the jet to complete one circle is determined by a calculation based on the speed, ensuring that the jet travels the same distance each time around.

10. Modify the `Jet` world so that the `circle` method accepts a second parameter specifying the time it takes for the jet to complete that circle.

11. Modify the `Cheerleader` world so that there is a single `jump` method with a parameter of type `Pose` that determines whether the cheerleader raises her right or left arm.

TRY THIS!

◀ **Try This!** These exercises are interspersed throughout the chapters, helping you understand the material by applying it with hands-on activities. Try This! exercises are numbered consecutively within the chapters so you can track your progress as you work your way through a particular chapter.

▶ **More to Explore.** Concluding each chapter, the More to Explore sections present additional Alice and Java topics for you to research further on your own.

5.4   More to Explore

Let's conclude this last Alice chapter with a few more tips about using the Alice environment.

Saving Objects Sometime you put a lot of effort into developing the behaviors of a particular object and would like to use it or something similar in another animation. Instead of recreating the object from scratch, you'd be better off saving the object in one world and bringing it into the next. To save your object as a file, right click on it in the world view or in the object tree and choose the save object option. In another world, you can import the object using the import option on the `File` menu.

Opacity The `opacity` property of an object determines how much the user can see through it, as if it were a ghost. A value of 1.0 makes an object fully opaque (light does not pass through it), while a value of 0.0 makes an object fully invisible. One way to use this property is to make an object fade away by decreasing the `opacity` value slowly over time in a loop. Similarly, you could make an object fade in by increasing the value.

Textures A texture map is an image that is "wrapped" tightly around an object to give its surface a new look. In Alice you can import any graphic file (.gif, .jpeg, .bmp, or .tif) to use as a texture map in the properties panel of a particular object. Once uploaded, you can set the `skin  texture` property of an object to the uploaded texture map image.

Summary of Key Concepts

- Programming a computer no longer has to be a complex, arcane experience.
- In object-oriented programming, we create the objects we need and tell them to perform services for us.
- Both Alice and Java use an object-oriented approach.
- A development environment is a program used to create and run another program.
- Programming is a participation sport! The more you play, the better you'll get. Explore and experiment!
- We get an object to do something by calling one of its methods.
- A method's parameters provide additional information that tailors its behavior.
- All Alice objects have a set of built-in methods that we can use. We can also add our own.
- An object's properties describe its current state, such as its color and opacity.
- An object is created from a class. In Alice, classes are organized into galleries.
- A composite object is made up of other objects. We can control the whole object or any of its parts.

◀ **Summary of Key Concepts.** The Key Concepts presented throughout a chapter are summarized at the end of the chapter.

▶ **Exercises.** These intermediate problems require computations, the analysis or writing of code fragments, and probing questions about the chapter content. While the exercises may deal with code, they generally do not require any online activity.

Exercises

EX 7.1 Use the Java API and other references to make a list of ten different GUI components.

EX 7.2 Using just the Java API, make a list of as many GUI listener interface classes as you can find.

EX 7.3 Explain the relationship between a listener and a component.

EX 7.4 Describe how you would use a mouse event object to see whether the left or right button on the mouse was clicked.

EX 7.5 Write a sample keyListener that verifies whether the user pressed the key sequence control-5 (that is, pressed and held the control key down while the number 5 key was pressed).

EX 7.6 What is a HyperlinkListener? Which component(s) or objects can have a HyperlinkListener registered to it?

EX 7.7 Define the purpose of an inner class. What do we gain by using them?

EX 7.8 What is a MenuEvent? Which components can create MenuEvents?

EX 7.9 What would happen if the repaint method calls were removed from the mouseMoved method in the SpaceshipListener class of the SpaceshipFlight program?

◀ **Programming Projects.** These problems require the design and implementation of Alice worlds and Java programs. They vary widely in level of difficulty.

Programming Projects

PP 2.1 Create an Alice world in which a bird flies across the sky. Use an appropriate class from the **Animals** gallery to make the bird. Add a method called flap to the bird that causes both wings to move up and down in unison one full stroke while moving the bird forward a set distance.

PP 2.2 Create an Alice world that shows an astronaut bounding across the lunar landscape, then planting a flag. Create the astronaut using the Astronaut class in the **Space** gallery and the flag from the Flagpole class in the **Objects** gallery. Add a bound method to the astronaut that causes him to take an exaggerated step forward in the light gravity of the moon, and a plant flag method that shows him putting the flag in the lunar surface.

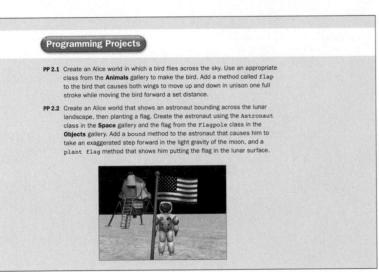

Contents

Preface   vii

Unit I   Alice

Chapter 1 ⊙ Objects   1
   1.1   **Introduction**   2
         Alice and Java   2
   1.2   **The Alice Environment**   4
   1.3   **Objects in Alice**   6
         Calling Methods   8
         Properties   11
   1.4   **Alice Classes**   12
   1.5   **Do Together and Do In Order**   13
   1.6   **Composite Objects**   15
   1.7   **More to Explore**   18

Chapter 2 ⊙ Methods and Data   25
   2.1   **Methods**   26
   2.2   **Data and Expressions**   28
         Generating Random Numbers   31
   2.3   **Parameters**   32
   2.4   **More to Explore**   34

Chapter 3 ⊙ Decisions and Loops   41
   3.1   **Making Decisions**   42
         The If/Else Statement   42
         Nested If/Else Statements   47
   3.2   **Repetition**   49
         The While Statement   49
         The Loop Statement   54
         Nested Repetition Statements   58
   3.3   **More to Explore**   60

Chapter 4 ⊙ **Events**   **67**
    4.1   **Introduction to Event Processing**   68
    4.2   **World Events**   70
    4.3   **Keyboard Events**   72
    4.4   **Mouse Events**   75
    4.5   **Condition Events**   77
    4.6   **More to Explore**   80

Chapter 5 ⊙ **Lists and Arrays**   **87**
    5.1   **Managing Multiple Objects**   88
    5.2   **Lists**   89
    5.3   **Arrays**   92
    5.4   **More to Explore**   94

Unit II   Java

Chapter 6 ⊙ **Transition to Java**   **99**
    6.1   **Comparing Alice and Java**   **100**
        Program Development   101
        Classes and Objects   102
        Data and Operators   104
        Statements   105
    6.2   **Java Classes and Objects**   **106**
    6.3   **Java Statements**   **112**
    6.4   **Introduction to ThunkIt**   **118**
    6.5   **More to Explore**   **119**

Chapter 7 ⊙ **Events**   **123**
    7.1   **Event Processing in Java**   **124**
        Buttons and Action Events   125
        Action Listeners in ThunkIt   129
    7.2   **Event Types**   **129**
    7.3   **Mouse Events**   **137**
        Mouse Listeners in ThunkIt   142
    7.4   **Keyboard Events**   **144**
        Keyboard Listeners in ThunkIt   148
    7.5   **More to Explore**   **148**

Chapter 8 ⊙ **Lists and Arrays**   **153**
    8.1   **Java Collections**   **154**
        Generic Types   154

8.2	**The ArrayList Class**	**155**
	Lists in ThunkIt	159
8.3	**Java Arrays**	**160**
	Declaring and Using Arrays	161
	Bounds Checking	161
	Initializer Lists	164
	Arrays as Parameters	167
	Arrays as Objects	168
8.4	**Two-Dimensional Arrays**	**169**
	The ThunkIt Grid	170
	Multidimensional Arrays	171
8.5	**More to Explore**	**172**

Chapter 9 ⊙ Inheritance		**177**
9.1	**Creating Subclasses**	**178**
	The protected Modifier	179
	The super Reference	180
	Overriding Methods	181
9.2	**Class Hierarchies**	**181**
	The Object Class	182
	Abstract Classes	184
	ShapeMaker	185
	Class Hierarchies in ThunkIt	191
9.3	**Polymorphism**	**192**
	Polymorphism via Inheritance	193
	ShapeMaker Revisited	194
9.4	**Threads**	**198**
9.5	**More to Explore**	**199**

Chapter 10 ⊙ Exceptions and I/O		**205**
10.1	**Exception Handling**	**206**
	Uncaught Exceptions	207
	The try-catch Statement	207
	Exception Handling in ThunkIt	210
	The finally Clause	211
10.2	**Exception Propagation**	**212**
	Checked and Unchecked Exceptions	215
10.3	**Java File I/O**	**217**
	Reading Text Files	219
	Writing Text Files	221
	File Processing in ThunkIt	223
10.4	**More to Explore**	**225**

Chapter 11 ⊙ Software Design Revisited   **231**

    11.1 The Development Process   **232**

        Software Development Models   233

        Iterative Development   234

        Identifying Classes and Objects   235

        Assigning Responsibilities   236

    11.2 UML   **237**

        Class Diagrams   237

        Sequence Diagrams   237

    11.3 Class Relationships   **239**

        Dependency   240

        Dependencies Among Objects of the Same Class 240

        Aggregation   246

    11.4 More to Explore   **247**

Chapter 12 ⊙ Recursion   **251**

    12.1 Recursive Thinking   **252**

        Infinite Recursion   253

        Recursion in Math   253

    12.2 Recursive Programming   **254**

        Recursion vs. Iteration   256

        Direct vs. Indirect Recursion   257

    12.3 Using Recursion   **257**

        Traversing a Maze   258

        The Towers of Hanoi   262

        Tiled Pictures   267

        Fractals   270

    12.4 More to Explore   **278**

Appendix A ⊙ Alice Environment Reference   **283**

Appendix B ⊙ Alice Methods and Functions   **293**

Appendix C ⊙ The Unicode Character Set   **307**

Appendix D ⊙ Java Operators   **311**

Appendix E ⊙ Java Modifiers   **317**

Appendix F ⊙ JavaDoc Documentation Generator   **321**

Index   **325**

CHAPTER 1

Objects

CHAPTER OBJECTIVES

In this chapter you will:

- ▶ Be introduced to Alice and Java and how they're used in this book.
- ▶ Create virtual worlds in Alice.
- ▶ Call methods on objects to make them behave in particular ways (such as moving and turning).
- ▶ Explore the set of methods that are available to all Alice objects.
- ▶ Set and modify the properties of an object.
- ▶ Create new objects from predefined classes.
- ▶ Cause multiple animation actions to occur at the same time.
- ▶ Explore composite objects (which are made up of other objects) and interact with a composite's individual parts.

Welcome to *Programming with Alice and Java*. If you're concerned at all about venturing into the world of computer programming, don't be. This book is designed to teach programming with intuitive and engaging techniques. And we use two of today's most exciting technologies: Alice, in which you build your own virtual worlds, and Java, the most popular programming language in use today. Jump on in—the water's warm!

1.1 Introduction

There was a time when the people who knew how to program a computer lived in a world of their own—a complex world full of arcane symbols and mathematical terms. It was the world of the geek and the nerd. Not anymore.

▶ Programming a computer no longer has to be a complex, arcane experience.

Computers are technical devices, certainly, but that doesn't mean that we have to be overwhelmed by their complexity. Almost everyone can use a computer these days because most programs are designed to be truly *usable*—much of the inherent complexity is managed for us. In a similar way, the techniques for programming a computer have become more accessible as well.

For you, this may be a one-time exploration into computing. Or you may have your sights set on continuing in this field. Either way, you're in the right place. Computing is one of the world's fastest growing disciplines, and the demand for good programmers is rising. But even if you're not looking for a career, the concepts we'll explore here are helpful in many other ways.

In this book we focus on *object-oriented programming* (OOP), which is the most popular approach to computer programming today. It has gained dominance because it is a natural, intuitive way to think about problems and their solutions. OOP is largely responsible for taking the world of programming away from the geeks and making it more accessible.

▶ In object-oriented programming, we create the objects we need and tell them to perform services for us.

As the name implies, object-oriented programming is all about managing *objects*. An object can be anything—a character in an animation, a scoreboard in a game, a list of friends, whatever. In OOP, we create the objects we need and then we tell those objects to do things for us.

Two technologies that make use of an object-oriented approach are Alice and Java, the cornerstones of this book.

Alice and Java

In the first five chapters of this book, we focus on Alice, an environment designed to introduce programming concepts in an engaging manner. In the remaining chapters we focus on Java, a popular programming language in use by professionals today. Alice will help us lay the foundation, and Java will give us the freedom to explore many other possibilities.

Alice is a computer environment in which you create virtual worlds containing three-dimensional characters and objects that move and interact. Figure 1.1 shows a screen shot from an Alice virtual world. Alice was developed at Carnegie Mellon University and is named in honor of Lewis Carroll and his wonderful books *Alice in Wonderland* and *Through the Looking Glass.*

Figure 1.1

An Alice virtual world

You can use Alice to create animations in which characters play out a scene or to create games and other interactive worlds in which objects respond to mouse clicks and keyboard input. When you create an Alice world, you are the boss. You decide which objects to include in your world and how they will behave. With Alice, you're part movie director and part choreographer. You provide the instructions, like *move forward* and *turn right*, and the objects in your world carry out those instructions.

Though it won't feel like it, when you build a virtual world in Alice and dictate the way it behaves, you are programming. After all, that's what object-oriented programming is all about—telling objects what to do.

▶ Both Alice and Java use an object-oriented approach.

Once Alice paves the way, we'll transition into developing programs in Java, which is a *general-purpose programming language.* Java can be used to create animations and games, as we can in Alice, but it is far more versatile. You wouldn't use Alice to create a social network or help manage a student organization, but you could with Java.

Java was created by James Gosling at Sun Microsystems. It's become one of the most popular programming languages in use today.

One of the ways we'll explore the capabilities of Java is by examining a program called ThunkIt, a game in which the user helps stranded students get back to their school by solving a variety of puzzles. In each level of the game a student moves obstacles and uses various gadgets to outwit the detention robots and get one step closer to school. A screen shot of ThunkIt is shown in Figure 1.2.

Figure 1.2

ThunkIt, a Java program

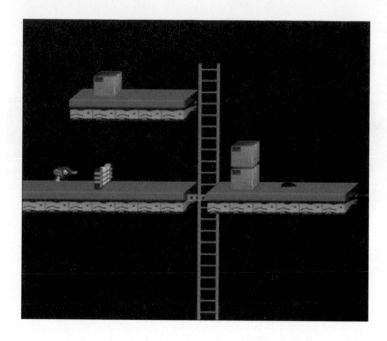

Not only will we examine the code that makes the objects in ThunkIt do what they do, but you'll create game objects of your own and then design levels of the game that use them. More on that later.

Our goal in this book is not to teach Alice or Java *per se,* but rather to use them to teach fundamental programming concepts. These concepts apply not only to Alice and Java, but also to many other popular programming languages.

No matter which programming language you use, you need a development environment in which to create and execute your programs. Let's take a look at the Alice development environment.

1.2 The Alice Environment

Alice animations are made and executed within the Alice *integrated development environment* (IDE). Versions of Alice are available for both Windows and Mac OS, and can be downloaded for free from the Alice website (www. alice.org). Appendix A contains information about installing the Alice environment.

> ▶ A development environment is a program used to create and run another program.

As shown in Figure 1.3, when you start the Alice environment, it presents a window that allows you to specify what you want to do initially. Depending on which tab you pick, you can choose to:

- run a tutorial,

- open a world you've had open recently (if any),

- start a new world using an existing template,

- explore one of several example worlds, or

- open an Alice world that was previously stored on your computer.

Figure 1.3

The Alice welcome screen

The tutorials are a good place to start, and we encourage you to use them to get acquainted with the Alice environment and its capabilities. Likewise, feel free to open and explore the various example worlds provided. Play around with them. Have fun. Don't worry if you don't understand everything you see in the tutorials and examples—we cover the key topics carefully in this book. Just don't be afraid to explore and experiment.

> ▶ Programming is a participation sport! The more you play, the better you'll get. Explore and experiment!

The primary Alice window contains several distinct areas, as shown in Figure 1.4. The *toolbar* includes a button to play the current animation, which brings up a separate window in which the animation is displayed and controlled. The *world view* shows the virtual world as it initially appears to the camera, and has controls for adjusting the camera's initial point of view. The *object tree* lists all objects in the world, allowing you to select a particular object as you develop an animation.

The *details panel* provides information about the particular object currently selected in the object tree. The *method editor* is where you make changes to the code that dictates what your animation does. Finally, the *events editor* is where you specify what will happen when particular events occur.

Figure 1.4

The Alice development
environment

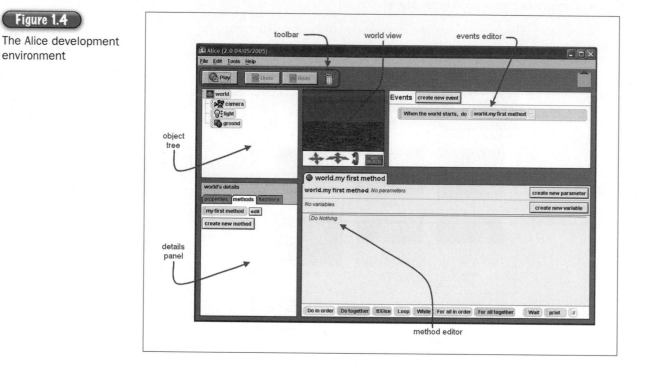

We'll explore all of these aspects of the Alice environment over time as appropriate. For now, just begin to get a feel for the layout of the environment.

Appendix A contains the details of using the Alice environment to accomplish particular tasks. Use it as needed as you progress through the chapters.

1.3 Objects in Alice

Let's start by exploring a simple Alice world called SpinningCubes (stored in the file SpinningCubes.a2w). This world contains two cubes, one red and one blue, as shown in Figure 1.5. When you play the animation, first the blue cube spins in one direction, then the red cube spins in the opposite direction. Try it! We encourage you to keep the Alice environment open while you're reading this book, experimenting with our sample worlds as you go along.

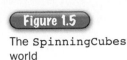
The `SpinningCubes` world

The two cubes in this animation are objects, as is everything in an Alice world. The objects contained in an Alice world are listed in the object tree, as shown in Figure 1.6. The `SpinningCubes` world contains objects that represent the camera, the light source, the ground, and the two cubes.

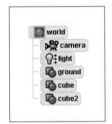

Figure 1.6

The object tree for the `SpinningCubes` world

All Alice worlds have a camera and a light source. The camera represents the point of view of the person watching the animation. Most worlds also have some kind of ground surface as well. The templates in the Alice welcome screen provide several basic ground surfaces from which to choose. The `SpinningCubes` world makes use of a ground surface covered in grass.

The camera's initial point of view of the world can be set using the camera controls, shown in Figure 1.7 and located under the world view window in the Alice environment. The camera controls may take some getting used to. The first control shifts the camera up, down, right, or left. The second control moves the camera forward or backward in the world, or rotates the camera right or left. The third control pivots the camera's view up or down. Experiment with the controls to get a feel for how they can be used to get a particular point of view on the world.

The camera controls

Once you use the camera controls to set the initial point of view, the camera will keep that orientation throughout the animation unless you dictate otherwise. As we'll see in later examples, we can set it up so that the camera's orientation changes as the animation unfolds.

TRY THIS!

1. Using the camera controls, change the camera viewpoint in `SpinningCubes` so that the blue cube is in the foreground and the red cube is behind it in the background.

2. Change the camera viewpoint in `SpinningCubes` so that it looks down on the cubes from above.

Calling Methods

A *method* is a set of statements that can be *called* (or *invoked*) whenever we want those statements to be executed. Every object has methods that define that object's

> We get an object to do something by calling one of its methods.

potential behavior. For example, most Alice objects have a method called `turn` that, when called, will rotate the object. Similarly, the `move` method will move an object in a particular direction when it is called.

The `world` object in every Alice animation has a method called `my first method` that is executed whenever the animation is played. This method often calls methods in other objects. The `my first method` method for `SpinningCubes` is shown in Figure 1.8.

Figure 1.8

The `my first method` method for the `SpinningCubes` world

● world.my first method				
world.my first method *No parameters*				create new parameter
No variables				create new variable
// SpinningCubes.a2w ▾				
Wait 0.5 seconds ▾				
cube ▾ turn left ▾ 2 revolutions ▾ more... ▾				
Wait 0.5 seconds ▾				
cube2 ▾ turn right ▾ 2 revolutions ▾ more... ▾				

In this example, the first line in `my first method` is a *comment*, in green type and beginning with two slash marks (//). Comments are included for the human reader and do not have any effect on the animation. We typically include a comment at the beginning of `my first method` to indicate the file name of the world.

The `SpinningCubes` animation makes use of the `Wait` statement, which is used to pause the animation for a particular period of time. In most of our examples we pause at the beginning of the animation just to let the human viewer see the initial state of the world before any action begins. In this example we also use a second `Wait` statement to pause in between the spinning of the two cubes. The `Wait` statement is one of several *control statements* listed below the method editor, as shown in Figure 1.9. We explore the rest of these statements at appropriate points in the next few chapters.

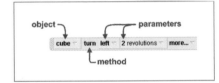

Figure 1.9

The control statements list

To make the cubes spin, we call the `turn` method of each cube. In object-oriented terms, we say we are *sending a message* to an object to request that it perform a particular service for us. In the `SpinningCubes` example, we initially ask `cube` to turn. Then, after a brief pause, we ask `cube2` to turn. Figure 1.10 shows the elements of a method call.

Figure 1.10

Calling a method of an object

Methods can accept *parameters*, which provide additional information to the method. When the `turn` method is called, we use parameters to indicate which direction to turn and how many revolutions to turn. These values can be changed using the drop-down menus in the statement. The menu labeled `more...` lets you access additional parameters, such as the statement's duration (how long it takes to execute the turn).

> ▶ A method's parameters provide additional information that tailors its behavior.

TRY THIS!

3. Modify `SpinningCubes` so that the pause between the cubes spinning is one second.

4. Modify `SpinningCubes` so that both cubes turn to the right and `cube2` turns only one revolution.

5. Modify `SpinningCubes` so that `cube` completes its turn in half a second and `cube2` completes its turn in three seconds.

To add a control statement (such as `Wait`) to a method, simply drag it up from the list into the method editor. Comments can also be added in this way. As you drag, a green line appears to indicate where you are adding the new statement. Depending on the statement, it may prompt you to set certain parameter values when you add it to the method. Consult Appendix A if needed for help with these environment operations.

The available methods for an object are listed in the details panel when that object is selected in the object tree. Figure 1.11 shows part of the methods tab of the details panel for one of the cube objects. To add a new call to a method, drag the method name from the details panel to the method editor.

Figure 1.11

Some of the methods available for `cube`

> ▶ All Alice objects have a set of built-in methods that we can use. We can also add our own.

The built-in methods for a cube object will be found in almost all other Alice objects as well. They provide several basic movement operations, including some that move relative to other objects or at a particular speed. The built-in methods also include `say` and `think`, which produce speech bubbles above the object, as in a comic strip. Another method, `play sound`, allows an object to play a sound file. A few sound effects are built into the Alice environment, but you can import any .wav or .mp3 sound file to use in your animation.

The full list of built-in methods are described in Appendix B. Feel free to experiment with these methods—we'll see many of them in use in upcoming examples. You'll learn how to add your own methods to an object in Chapter 2.

TRY THIS!

6. Make additional calls to the `turn` method in `SpinningCubes` so that each cube spins in both directions, first right then left.

7. Modify `SpinningCubes` so that the cubes float up into the air 1 meter after they spin.

8. Modify `SpinningCubes` so that `cube` makes a "pop" sound after it spins and `cube2` makes a "thud" sound after it spins.

In Alice, special methods called *functions* are used to retrieve key information about an object, such as how close it is to another object. The available functions for an object are listed in a separate tab of the details panel. We'll make use of functions in later examples as well.

Properties

In addition to methods, which represent an object's potential behaviors, an object also has *properties*, which describe its state of being at any point in time. For example, the `color` of an Alice object is one of its properties. In the `SpinningCubes` world, `cube` is blue and `cube2` is red. The values of properties can be changed as needed.

> ▶ An object's properties describe its current state, such as its color and opacity.

The properties of an object are listed in another tab in the details panel. Some standard properties are `opacity` (how much you can see through an object) and `fillingStyle` (whether an object is solid or represented as a wire frame).

The value of a property can be changed directly in the details panel using the corresponding drop-down menu. This sets the initial state of the object. A property value can also be changed during an animation using a method call. To change a property value using a method call, drag the property from the details panel into the method editor. This adds a call to a `set` method for that property.

Some object properties are not shown in the properties tab. For instance, an object's position within the world is a property of that object, but position doesn't show up in the properties list. Instead, Alice provides various methods (`move`, `turn`, `roll`, etc.) that change the object's position in a smooth, animated manner. The size of an object is another hidden property that can be changed using the `resize` method.

TRY THIS!

9. In `SpinningCubes`, use the properties drop-down menu for `fillingStyle` to show `cube` as a wire frame.

10. Modify `SpinningCubes` so that the color of `cube2` changes to yellow after both cubes finish turning.

11. Modify `SpinningCubes` so that the size of `cube` shrinks by half after it turns and the size of `cube2` doubles after it turns.

The techniques for setting the initial position and size of an object are discussed in the next section.

1.4 Alice Classes

▶ An object is created from a class. In Alice, classes are organized into galleries.

An object is created from a *class*, which serves as the blueprint, or pattern, from which all similar objects are created. For example, the two cube objects in the SpinningCubes world were created from a class called Cube. The class of an object determines the methods and properties the object will have.

The classes we use to create Alice animations are organized into *galleries*. The Alice environment has several local (built-in) galleries, and you can access several more galleries through the Web. The local galleries are generally a subset of those you can find on the Web. There may be a delay in accessing the web galleries depending on your network connection. We use classes from both sets of galleries in this book.

Pressing the Add Objects button, found next to the camera controls under the world view window, produces a window such as the one in Figure 1.12. The available class galleries are displayed along the bottom. (Local galleries are displayed by default.)

Figure 1.12

Accessing the class galleries and the object positioning controls

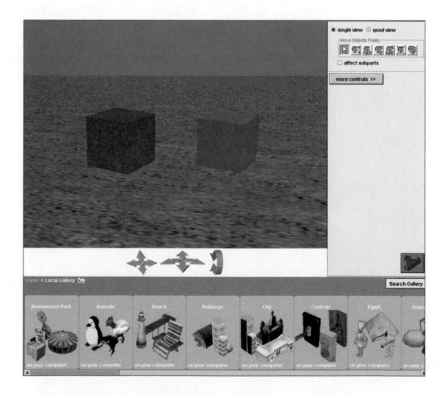

Clicking a gallery will display the classes available in that gallery. For example, clicking the **Beach** gallery provides access to the BeachChair and Lighthouse classes, among others. The Cube class used in the SpinningCubes world is found in the **Shapes** gallery. Take some time to become familiar with the various classes available in the galleries.

To add an object to an Alice world, drag the appropriate class into the world view window. Once added, you can use the controls on the right side to position, orient, resize, and copy the object as you see fit. When you're finished adding and positioning objects, press the Done button. Remember that Appendix A contains additional details about using the various environment controls.

12. Add a third cube to the `SpinningCubes` world and adjust the camera's viewpoint so you can see all three cubes. Adjust the new cube's size and orientation to be roughly equal to the others. Set its color to magenta in the properties tab of the details panel. Modify `my first method` so that the new cube spins similar to the others.

13. Add an `Anvil` object from the **Objects** gallery to the `SpinningCubes` world so that it looks like it's sitting on the red cube. Add a `StopSign` object from the **Roads and Signs** gallery between the cubes.

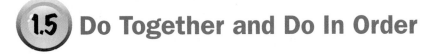

1.5 Do Together and Do In Order

Unless we indicate otherwise, the statements in a method are executed in order, one after the other. In animations, however, we often want two or more things to happen at the same time. The Alice control statements (listed below the method editor) include a statement called Do together that allows us to do two or more things simultaneously. A Do together statement contains other statements, indicating that those statements should all be executed at the same time.

Let's look at an example. The Blimps world contains two blimps floating in the sky, as shown in Figure 1.13. The blimps were created using the Blimp class found in the **Vehicles** gallery. When the animation is played, both blimps move through the sky at the same time in different directions.

Figure 1.13

The Blimps world

The my first method method for Blimps is shown in Figure 1.14. It uses a Do together statement, which contains two statements that move the two blimps. If those two statements were not contained in a Do together statement, one blimp would move, and when it was finished, the other blimp would move. By putting both statements in the Do together statement, the blimps move at the same time. Note that in this example the blimps are controlled using the move at speed method, which allows us to define how fast an object moves.

Figure 1.14

Using the Do together statement

● world.my first method
world.my first method *No parameters*
No variables
Wait 0.5 seconds ▽
⊟ Do together
blimp ▽	move at speed forward ▽	*speed* = 10 meters per second ▽	*duration* = 10 seconds ▽	more... ▽
blimp2 ▽	move at speed forward ▽	*speed* = 10 meters per second ▽	*duration* = 10 seconds ▽	more... ▽

The Do in order statement is essentially the opposite of the Do together statement. It forces the statements it contains to be executed in order, one after another. The Do in order statement is needed when you want to perform some statements sequentially within a Do together statement.

In an example world called Bugs, two bugs are shown scurrying around the ground near a tree, as depicted in Figure 1.15. The bug objects are created from the Ladybug class in the **Animals** gallery and the tree is created from the HappyTree class in the **Nature** gallery.

Figure 1.15

The Bugs world

The movement of the bugs is accomplished using various calls to their move and turn methods. We want both bugs to move at the same time, but we want each step for a bug (move, then turn, then move, etc.) to be executed in order. The method that accomplishes this coordinated movement is shown in Figure 1.16.

Figure 1.16

Using the Do in order statement

world.my first method

world.my first method *No parameters* | create new parameter

No variables | create new variable

Wait 0.5 seconds

Do together
  Do in order
    ladybug | move forward | 3 meters | *duration* = 2 seconds | more...
    ladybug | turn right | 0.125 revolutions | more...
    ladybug | move forward | 3 meters | more...
    ladybug | turn left | 0.5 revolutions | more...
    ladybug | move forward | 5 meters | *duration* = 2 seconds | more...

  Do in order
    ladybug2 | move forward | 0.5 meters | *duration* = 0.5 seconds | more...
    ladybug2 | turn left | 0.125 revolutions | more...
    ladybug2 | move forward | 2 meters | more...
    ladybug2 | turn left | 0.25 revolutions | more...
    ladybug2 | move forward | 2 meters | more...
    ladybug2 | turn left | 0.25 revolutions | more...
    ladybug2 | move forward | 2 meters | more...

The two Do in order statements are executed at the same time, one controlling the movement of one bug and the other controlling the movement of the other bug. Within each Do in order statement, the individual movements of a bug are executed sequentially.

By using a thoughtful combination of Do together and Do in order statements, it's possible to create interesting animation effects.

TRY THIS!

14. Modify SpinningCubes so that both cubes spin at the same time.

15. Add a third blimp to the Blimps world that moves half as fast as the others.

16. Add a third Ladybug object to the Bugs world that moves in its own pattern.

1.6 Composite Objects

A *composite object* is an object that contains other objects. Many objects in the Alice galleries are composite objects. Let's look at an example. The SurferWave world shows a surfer on the beach, as shown in Figure 1.17. When the animation is played, the surfer turns his head (as if noticing the viewer), turns his upper body to face the viewer, and then waves his hand.

Figure 1.17

The `SurferWave` world

The surfer was created from the `RandomGuy2` class in the **People** gallery. We modified the object's name from the default (`randomGuy2`) to something more appropriate for this example (`surfer`) in the object tree. The beach chair was created from the `BeachChair` class in the **Beach** gallery.

> ▶ A composite object is made up of other objects. We can control the whole object or any of its parts.

The surfer is a composite object. It is made up of the left leg, the right leg, and the upper body objects. Each of these parts is itself a composite object. The upper body, for instance, is made up of the left arm, the right arm, and the head. The arms and legs can be further decomposed.

A composite object has a plus sign next to it in the object tree. Clicking the plus sign expands the tree and displays its component objects, as shown in Figure 1.18. When expanded, the plus sign changes to a minus sign. When the minus sign is clicked, that section of the tree is hidden again.

Figure 1.18

Viewing the parts of the `surfer` composite object

The `Ladybug` objects from the `Bugs` world in the previous section are also composite objects. Each leg of a bug can be moved independently, as can the wings and even the antennae. In the `Bugs` world example, we simply moved the entire bug, but composite objects give you the ability to refine the animations to the level you choose.

You can send messages to (that is, call methods of) an entire object or to any component part. When referring to a component part, you access it through its containing object. In this example, the entire object is referred to as `surfer`. The entire upper body of the surfer is referred to as `surfer.upperBody`. The head of the surfer is referred to as `surfer.upperBody.head`. Figure 1.19 shows the code for the `SurferWave` world.

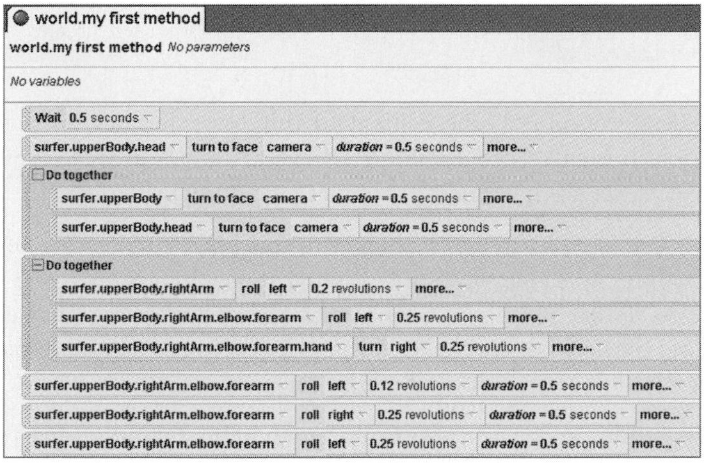

Figure 1.19

Manipulating the parts of a composite object

The `turn to face` method is used to turn the surfer's head toward the camera initially. The first `Do together` statement then turns the entire upper body toward the camera, and again turns the head. If the second head turn were not performed, the head would "ride" the upper body and turn to face away from the viewer.

The second `Do together` statement swings the arm up in preparation for the wave. To do this, it simultaneously rolls the right arm, rolls the right forearm, and turns the hand. The wave itself is accomplished with three rolls of the forearm.

TRY THIS!

17. Modify `SurferWave` so that the surfer says "Welcome to my world!" while he's waving.

18. Modify `SurferWave` so that the surfer's arm returns to its original position after finishing the wave.

19. Modify `SurferWave` so that the surfer moves his left hand to his hip during the wave.

The composite objects in the Alice galleries vary in the way they are made up. Some can be articulated down to individual fingers and others are less versatile.

Unfortunately, it is not easy to add a new class to Alice. Therefore, you can't really make your own types of objects. The process of creating a composite object is particularly tricky. It involves using additional 3D graphics software to create the pieces of the object and to define their relationships to each other, pivot points, and other details. This process is beyond the scope of this book. There is, however, a tool provided with Alice to make somewhat customized characters. We discuss that tool in the next section. In the examples in this book we constrain ourselves to using the predefined classes provided in the galleries.

1.7 More to Explore

As discussed in section 1.1, the content of this book focuses on the core ideas related to object-oriented programming. We've already introduced several in this chapter: objects, classes, methods, properties, and composite objects.

To help complete the picture, each chapter in this book ends with a section called More to Explore, in which we briefly discuss topics that you may want to look into. These issues are usually environment or language details that don't play a role in the big picture, but will help you as you develop your programs. For Alice, Appendices A and B contain further details for many of these topics.

Built-In Methods Make sure you explore the methods that are part of (almost) every Alice object by default. We've discussed a few of them in this chapter and will continue to use them as needed. Some of them have subtle but important distinctions, such as the difference between the move and move at speed methods. Appendix B contains a summary of all the built-in Alice methods.

Turn vs. Roll In a three-dimensional world, an object's orientation (the way it's facing) can be changed without changing its position. Each object has a particular pivot point around which it rotates. You can change an object's orientation by turning it right or left, turning it forward or backward (think of leaning forward or backward), or rolling it left or right (think of leaning to one side). See Figure 1.20. Keep in mind that directions are relative to an object's orientation—so changing position and orientation at the same time can cause some interesting results. For even more control, experiment with the asSeenBy parameter when making complicated movements. Like anything else, the more you experiment with the various combinations of methods and directions, the more familiar they will become.

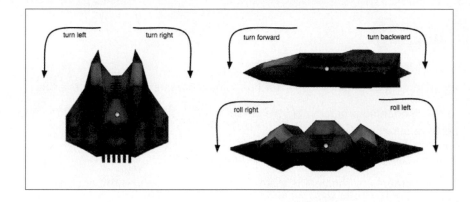

Figure 1.20

Changing an object's orientation in three dimensions

He Builder / She Builder The ability to create completely new classes of objects in Alice, using our own graphics, is not something we can tackle in this book. However, tools called `He Builder` and `She Builder` have been built into Alice to give you some control over the look of the human characters you create. You can choose skin and hair color, hair style, body type, and clothes. These tools are available at the end of the list of classes in the **People** gallery. They bring up a separate window to guide you through the character creation process, as shown in Figure 1.21.

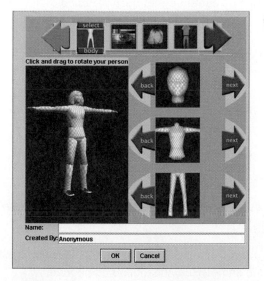

Figure 1.21

Character building

Capture Pose Getting a character to perform a particular movement (like the surfer waving his hand) can involve a complex combination of movements. One way to simplify this process is to maneuver a character into a particular pose using the mouse tools, and then capture that pose to use later. Once you have the character in the pose you want, you can right click on it and choose the `capture pose` menu option, or use the `capture pose` button on the properties tab. You can then use the `set pose` method in an animation, which causes the character to smoothly move into the specified pose. We use character poses in later examples to cut down on the amount of code otherwise required.

Summary of Key Concepts

- Programming a computer no longer has to be a complex, arcane experience.

- In object-oriented programming, we create the objects we need and tell them to perform services for us.

- Both Alice and Java use an object-oriented approach.

- A development environment is a program used to create and run another program.

- Programming is a participation sport! The more you play, the better you'll get. Explore and experiment!

- We get an object to do something by calling one of its methods.

- A method's parameters provide additional information that tailors its behavior.

- All Alice objects have a set of built-in methods that we can use. We can also add our own.

- An object's properties describe its current state, such as its color and opacity.

- An object is created from a class. In Alice, classes are organized into galleries.

- A composite object is made up of other objects. We can control the whole object or any of its parts.

Exercises

EX 1.1 Describe the following terms: object, class, method, parameter, and property.

EX 1.2 What's the difference between the move and move at speed methods? Compare the parameters and consult Appendix B as needed.

EX 1.3 What does it mean when we "send a message" to an object?

EX 1.4 Write a statement, as it would appear in an Alice program, that would cause an object called dancer to spin around three times.

EX 1.5 Write a statement that would cause an object called tree to grow to three times its current size.

EX 1.6 Write a statement that would cause an object called cheerleader to turn to face the camera.

EX 1.7 How do you get two animation steps to happen at the same time in an Alice program? Give an example.

EX 1.8 Describe the composite structure of an object created from the `Chicken` class in the **Animals** gallery.

EX 1.9 Describe the composite structure of an object created from the `Barn` class in the **Farm** gallery.

EX 1.10 How do you access a particular part of a composite object? Give an example using the `Phonograph` class in the **Objects** gallery.

Programming Projects

PP 1.1 Create an Alice world in which a penguin waddles toward a hole in a frozen lake, tips over, and falls in. The `Penguin` class can be found in the **Animals** gallery and the `FrozenLake` class is in the **Environments** gallery. Use the `Circle` class (colored gray) from the **Shapes** gallery to make the hole in the ice. In addition to the standard built-in methods, the `Penguin` class comes with a few other methods that you can call to help with this animation.

PP 1.2 Create an Alice world that shows a combination lock being dialed and then the latch opening. The combination is 15-35-5 (that is, turn right to 15, then left to 35, and right again to 5). The `CombinationLock` class is in the **Objects** gallery.

PP 1.3 Create an Alice world that shows a graveyard scene in which a casket opens and a mummy inside it sits up. Use the `Casket` and `Mummy` classes from the **Spooky** gallery, plus various others to set the mood.

PP 1.4 Using various classes from the **Vehicles** gallery, such as `Biplane`, `Blimp`, `Jet`, and `NavyJet`, create an Alice world in which several flying vehicles are moving through the air at different speeds, in different directions, and at different altitudes.

PP 1.5 Using various classes from the **Vehicles** gallery, such as `Motorboat`, `Sailboat`, and `Shakira`, create an Alice world in which several boats are moving across the water at different speeds and in different directions. Have one boat change direction at some point. Add a few colored `Sphere` objects from the **Shapes** gallery, partially submerged in the water, to represent buoys.

PP 1.6 Create an Alice world in which a `LunarLander` object from the **SciFi** gallery floats down gracefully to the moon's surface. After landing, the lander's door opens while two `AlienOnWheels` objects approach to greet the visitors.

PP 1.7 Create an Alice world depicting a moment from a fight between a troll and a wizard (created from classes in the **Medieval** gallery). As the troll swings his club down to hit the wizard, the wizard points at the club and it goes flying

out of the troll's hand. Then the wizard sinks magically into the ground and disappears, saying "Farewell" as he goes.

PP 1.8 Using various car and truck classes from the **Vehicles** gallery, such as Car, ConvertibleCorvette, DumpTruck, and Humvee, create an Alice world in which vehicles are moving right or left across the screen, going in opposite directions on a two-lane road. Use the Road class from the **City** gallery to create the road. Stagger the timing of the vehicles, starting them when needed and stopping them after they move out of the camera's view.

PP 1.9 Create an Alice world in which a chicken walks forward a few steps, pecks at the ground twice, and then clucks. Move the chicken's legs, neck, and head appropriately. Open the chicken's mouth while the clucking sound is played. The Chicken class is in the **Animals** gallery.

PP 1.10 Create an Alice world in which a helicopter lifts off the ground, flies in a wide circle, and lands. (An object can move in a circle by moving forward and turning one full rotation simultaneously.) Of course, the helicopter's propellers should be rotating whenever the helicopter is in the air. The Helicopter class can be found in the **Vehicles** gallery.

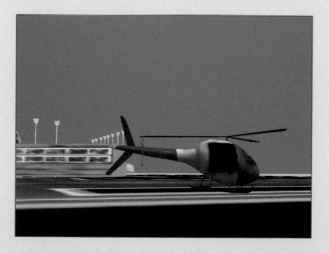

Methods and Data

CHAPTER OBJECTIVES

In this chapter you will:

- ▶ Write methods to add potential behaviors to objects.
- ▶ Declare and set the value of variables.
- ▶ Use variables in expressions to calculate new results.
- ▶ Generate random numbers in a particular range.
- ▶ Design methods to accept parameters.

We're off to a good start creating and using objects in Alice. Now we'll dive into some techniques for creating larger and more interesting animations, as well as keeping our programs well organized. This chapter explores how to define our own methods for any object and shows how to use data to refine the behavior of objects.

 Methods

As the Alice worlds we develop become more elaborate, it becomes increasingly important to organize our programs carefully. Writing one big method that controls the entire animation is not practical. It's far better to write a separate method for each logical behavior, and associate those methods with the appropriate objects.

We saw in Chapter 1 that an Alice object has several predefined methods that we can use. It's also possible to add our own methods to an object. Just as we wrote `my first method` for the `world` object, we can add any method we choose to any object we have in our world.

> ▶ We can add methods to objects to define additional behaviors for those objects.

Remember that methods define the behaviors of an object. Alice objects have basic built-in behaviors such as `move` and `turn`. By adding a method to an object, we can define more complex and interesting behaviors that are appropriate for that object. We could, for instance, add a `forehand` method to a tennis player, a `pirouette` method to a ballerina, or a `fire` method to a catapult.

Let's look at an example in the `Cheerleader` world, shown in Figure 2.1. The cheerleader object was created from the `Cheerleader` class in the **People** gallery and the gymnasium setting was created from the `Gym` class in the **High School** gallery. When the animation is played, the cheerleader first performs a preparation move, then performs two identical jumps while raising her right pompom.

Figure 2.1

The `Cheerleader` world

The `Cheerleader` world's `my first method` is shown in Figure 2.2. Amid various pauses, it calls the `ready ok` method to perform the preparation move and then calls the `right jump` method twice to perform the two jumps. We added these methods to the `cheerleader` object (as opposed to some other object, like the `world`) because they describe behaviors that this cheerleader performs. They obviously "belong" in the cheerleader object.

Figure 2.2

Calling methods of the `cheerleader` object

The `ready ok` method is shown in Figure 2.3. It consists of several calls to the `set pose` method of the `cheerleader` object to move the character smoothly into one of several preset poses. Most of the cheerleader's movements in this world are accomplished this way. Setting object poses was mentioned in Chapter 1 and is described further in Appendix A.

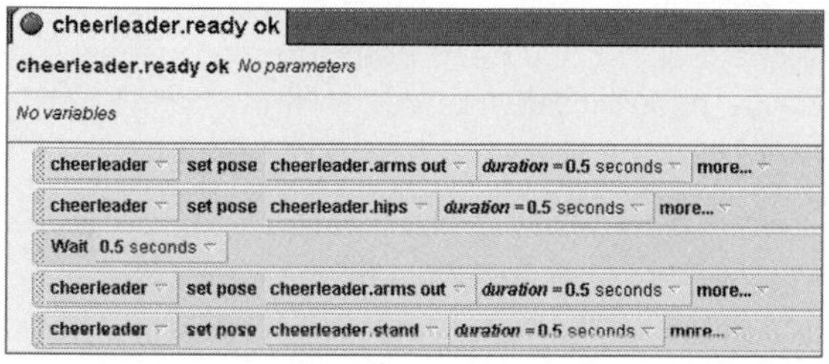

Figure 2.3

The `ready ok` method of the `cheerleader` object

The `right jump` method, which is called twice in this animation, is shown in Figure 2.4. Each call to this method causes the cheerleader to bend her knees, jump up into the air with her right arm and leg raised, return to the ground with knees bent, then stand up straight again.

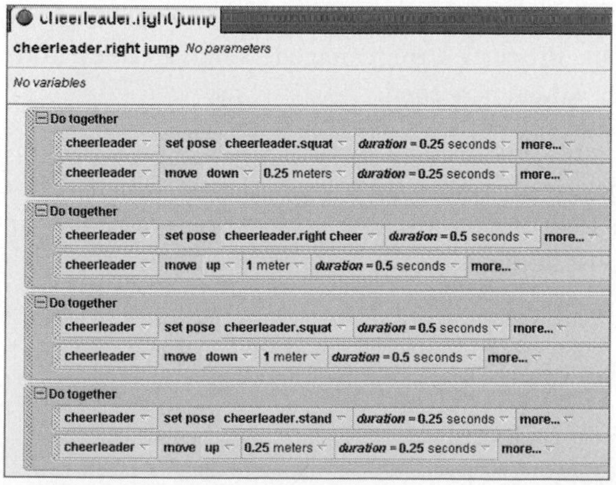

Figure 2.4

The `right jump` method of the `cheerleader` object

By adding custom methods to the cheerleader object we made it much easier to manage, modify, and extend the behaviors of that object. By defining a logical set of movements as a custom method, we can add that behavior to the animation with a single method call. Even with this short animation, the value of breaking the animation into separate behaviors is clear. The code is better organized and we are able to call those methods repeatedly, as we did with the right jump method.

> ▶ Defining appropriate methods in objects lets us organize our code and allows behaviors to be repeated easily.

To add a new method to an object, press the create new method button on the method details panel for that object (make sure the object you want to add the method to is selected in the object tree). You'll be asked to name the method, and then you'll be able to edit it in the method editor just as we've done for my first method.

TRY THIS!

1. Modify the Cheerleader world by adding a left jump method to the cheerleader that causes her to jump with her left arm and leg raised (the left cheer pose has already been created). Add calls to your new method to my first method.

2. Modify the Cheerleader world by creating a method called shake pompoms that causes the cheerleader to extend both arms and shake her pompoms. Use the arms out pose already created for the cheerleader object. Add a call to your new method to my first method.

3. Modify the Cheerleader world by duplicating the cheerleader object and having both of them cheer in unison side by side.

2.2 Data and Expressions

A *variable* is a name that represents a value. Each variable corresponds to a spot in memory when the value is stored. In Chapter 1 we discussed the properties of objects, such as color and opacity. Properties are managed using variables, and we've seen that we can change their values as needed.

We can also create and use variables inside a method to help us accomplish the purpose of the method. The variable must first be *declared*, which defines the name of the variable and the type of data it will hold. In Alice, a variable can hold one of several types of data, including:

- a number, either an integer or *floating point* (with a fractional part) value,

- a Boolean, a true or false value,

- a character string, such as a person's name, or

- any other type of object.

Unlike object properties, which are available to every method of the object, a variable declared in a method is only available in that method. Therefore a variable declared in a method is sometimes called *local data*.

An example called `Frog` world is shown in Figure 2.5. It shows a frog hopping along a fence.

> ▶ Object properties can be used by any method of the object, but a variable declared in a method can only be used in that method.

Figure 2.5

The `Frog` world

Each hop is accomplished by a call to a method called `hop` that we added to the frog object. The `Frog` world's `my first method`, which calls the `hop` method several times, is shown in Figure 2.6.

world.my first method
world.my first method *No parameters*
No variables
// Frog.a2w ▾
wait 0.5 seconds ▾
frog.hop
frog.hop
frog.hop
frog.hop

Figure 2.6

Calling the `hop` method of the `frog` object

The `hop` method is shown in Figure 2.7. It makes use of two poses for the frog, one sitting and one with its legs extended during a jump. The first `Do together` statement causes the frog to leap into the air, and the second causes it to come down and land.

● frog.hop
frog.hop *No parameters*

123 distance = 2

Wait 0.25 seconds

Do together

frog | set pose frog.extended legs | *style* = end gently | more...

frog | move up | (distance ★ 0.75) | *style* = end gently | more...

frog | move forward | (distance / 2) | *style* = end gently | more...

Do together

frog | move down | (distance ★ 0.75) | *style* = begin gently | *duration* = 0.75 seconds | more...

frog | move forward | (distance / 2) | *style* = begin gently | *duration* = 0.75 seconds | more...

frog | set pose frog.sitting | *style* = begin gently | *duration* = 0.75 seconds

At the top of the hop method, a variable called `distance` is declared and given an initial value of 2. This variable represents the total horizontal distance (in meters) that the frog will cover during its hop.

To declare a variable in a method, click the `create new variable` button on the right side of the method editor. You're then asked to specify the name and type of the variable, and give it an initial value. You can add as many variables to a method as needed.

A mathematical *expression* based on the value of `distance` is used to calculate the height of the jump. An expression is a combination of operators and operands that can be evaluated to produce a result. In this example, the height of the frog's jump is calculated to be three-quarters of the horizontal distance (the value of `distance` multiplied by 0.75). The result is passed into the method calls that move the frog up and down.

> ▶ Expressions let us calculate new values dynamically from the current value of variables.

Similarly, an expression is used to calculate the forward movement. Half the horizontal distance is covered while the frog is moving up and half is covered as it comes back down.

We could have put the literal values into each of these expressions and not used the `distance` variable at all. However, by using the variable, everything is based on one value. To change the distance covered, only one value needs to be changed—the initial value of the variable.

TRY THIS!

4. Modify the `Frog` world so that the total horizontal distance it jumps with each hop is 1.5 meters.

5. Modify the `Frog` world so that the height of the frog's jump is two-thirds of the horizontal distance of the jump.

You may have noticed that the `Frog` class comes not only with the standard built-in methods, but also with a few extra, such as `foottap`, `ribbit`, and `headnod`.

Almost all Alice objects come with the built-in methods like turn and move, but a few have some additional ones that are particular to that kind of object. Remember to explore.

Generating Random Numbers

It is often helpful to have an element of randomness in a program, so that objects don't always behave in exactly the same way every time. Alice provides a function called random number in the world object that generates a random number in a particular range.

We mentioned in Chapter 1 that functions are methods that return a value when they are called. They are not called as separate statements, but rather as part of a larger statement that does something with the value being returned, such as assigning it to a variable.

The random number function accepts parameters that allow you to specify the range (minimum and maximum) of the random value generated. It also accepts a Boolean parameter that is used to specify whether the result should be an integer or a floating point value. If this parameter is left unspecified, the function returns a floating point value.

> ▶ A function such as random number returns a value that can be used in the method that calls it.

We created a modified version of the Frog world, called Random Frog world. The only difference is in the hop method, shown in Figure 2.8. Instead of setting the distance using a literal value, an extra line of code has been added to set the value of the distance variable to the value returned by a call to the random number function. The parameters passed to random number specify that the function should return a value between 1 and 2.25.

Figure 2.8

Generating a random number to specify the distance of the hop

Note that the distance variable, when first declared, is given a value of 0. You always have to specify a value for a variable when it is created, even if you then immediately overwrite that value as we do in this example.

TRY THIS!

6. Modify the `Frog` world so that the frog turns to the left a slight amount after each hop. Create a method called `slight turn` that determines the amount of the turn randomly and executes the turn. Call `slight turn` from the `hop` method.

7. Modify the `Cheerleader` world so that the distance the cheerleader jumps is randomly determined within a reasonable range on each jump.

2.3 Parameters

We've seen that methods can accept parameters that provide key information needed to carry out the method's purpose. For example, an object's `move` method accepts parameters that specify what direction to move in and how far to move (among others).

 Writing methods so that they are based on the parameter values passed to them makes them more versatile and useful.

Any method we add to an object can also be designed to accept one or more parameters. These parameters can be of any type, including objects. When you design a method, it's important to think about using parameters to make the method more versatile—that is, useful in as many situations as possible.

Consider the `Jet` world, shown in Figure 2.9. When the animation is played, a jet flies in a circular pattern near an airport. The jet was made using the `NavyJet` class from the **Vehicles** gallery and the airport was made using classes in the **Buildings** gallery.

Figure 2.9

The `Jet` world

The my first method method of Jet world is shown in Figure 2.10. It makes three calls to the circle method of the NavyJet object. Each time the circle method is called, the jet makes one complete circle in the air at a particular speed. The speed, in meters per second, is specified by a parameter value so it can be different each time the pattern is flown.

world.my first method
world.my first method *No parameters*
No variables
// Jet.a2w
NavyJet.circle *speed* = 50
NavyJet.circle *speed* = 70
NavyJet.circle *speed* = 90

Figure 2.10

Calling the circle method with varying speeds

The circle method is shown in Figure 2.11. It accomplishes the circle pattern by calling the built-in move at speed method and simultaneously turning one complete revolution. Note the parameter, called speed, indicated next to the method name at the top. Instead of specifying the speed as a literal value when the move at speed method is called, we pass along the value of the circle method's speed parameter.

NavyJet.circle
NavyJet.circle [123] speed
No variables
Do together
NavyJet   move at speed   forward   *speed* = speed meters per second   *duration* = 4 seconds   more...
NavyJet   turn   left   1 revolution   *duration* = 4 seconds   *style* = abruptly   more...

Figure 2.11

The circle method in Jet world

To add a parameter to a method, click the create new parameter button on the right side of the method editor. You're then asked to specify the name and type of the parameter. You can add as many parameters to a method as you'd like.

TRY THIS!

8. Modify the Frog world so that the hop method accepts a parameter that specifies the jumping distance.

9. Modify the Jet world so that the time it takes for the jet to complete one circle is determined by a calculation based on the speed, ensuring that the jet travels the same distance each time around.

10. Modify the Jet world so that the circle method accepts a second parameter specifying the time it takes for the jet to complete that circle.

11. Modify the Cheerleader world so that there is a single jump method with a parameter of type Pose that determines whether the cheerleader raises her right or left arm.

2.4   More to Explore

Let's look at a few more Alice environment features that make it easier to develop Alice animations. Remember that Appendices A and B are helpful resources.

Renaming Objects   In Alice, default object names are provided for you when an object is added to a world. Occasionally, you will find the need to rename an object. If you add several objects of the same type, the second (and any subsequent objects) will have a number appended to their name. To provide a different name, first click on the object's name in the object tree. Then double click on the object to select the object's current name. Type a new name, hit enter, and the object's name will be modified.

Objects as Data   We discussed several types of data used in Alice. In addition to numbers and Booleans, variables and parameters in Alice can also be objects (such as those in the animation) and properties (such as `Position`, `String`, or `Color`). When you create a new local variable, a parameter to a method, or a new object property, you can select these data types from the Object and Other menus.

Quad View   Having trouble setting your objects into the correct places in a world? Using quad view, you can place or move your objects in the world while observing their position through four different world views. To see quad view, click the `Add Objects` button and then click the quad view button above the view control buttons. Quad view shows the world from the top, right, front, and normal views, as shown in Figure 2.12.

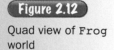

Figure 2.12

Quad view of `Frog` world

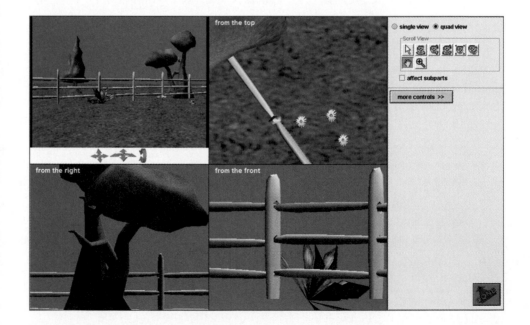

Duplicating Objects Occasionally, you will want to use two or more copies of an object in a world. Instead of creating each object from the appropriate class, then changing its characteristics, it's easier to use the `Copy Objects` button. Click on the `Add Objects` button and then click the `Copy Objects` button (the last button on the right under the single/quad view selector). While the `Copy Objects` button is depressed, any object in the world that you click on or drag will be duplicated. This is particularly helpful if you need several objects with similar characteristics.

Summary of Key Concepts

- We can add methods to objects to define additional behaviors for those objects.

- Defining appropriate methods in objects lets us organize our code and allows behaviors to be repeated easily.

- Object properties can be used by any method of the object, but a variable declared in a method can only be used in that method.

- Expressions let us calculate new values dynamically from the current value of variables.

- A function such as `random number` returns a value that can be used in the method that calls it.

- Writing methods so that they are based on the parameter values passed to them makes them more versatile and useful.

Exercises

EX 2.1 Name and describe the two methods that were added to the `cheerleader` object in `Cheerleader` world. How many times was each method called? From where were they called?

EX 2.2 Why do we organize our code into custom methods of particular objects?

EX 2.3 In `Frog` world, the `distance` variable was declared locally in the `hop` method. What does that imply?

EX 2.4 Write a statement that moves an object called `car` forward a distance equal to three times the value of the variable `total`.

EX 2.5 Write a statement that sets the value of a variable called `length` to one-fourth of the value currently stored in the variable `height`.

EX 2.6 Write a statement that sets the value of a variable called `side` to a random number in the range 10 to 50 (integers only).

EX 2.7 Write a statement that increments the current value of a variable `count` by one.

EX 2.8 Why is it often useful to design a method to accept one or more parameters?

EX 2.9 What is the minimum and maximum number of local variables and parameters a method can have?

EX 2.10 Compare and contrast a local variable and a parameter.

Programming Projects

PP 2.1 Create an Alice world in which a bird flies across the sky. Use an appropriate class from the **Animals** gallery to make the bird. Add a method called `flap` to the bird that causes both wings to move up and down in unison one full stroke while moving the bird forward a set distance.

PP 2.2 Create an Alice world that shows an astronaut bounding across the lunar landscape, then planting a flag. Create the astronaut using the `Astronaut` class in the **Space** gallery and the flag from the `Flagpole` class in the **Objects** gallery. Add a `bound` method to the astronaut that causes him to take an exaggerated step forward in the light gravity of the moon, and a `plant flag` method that shows him putting the flag in the lunar surface.

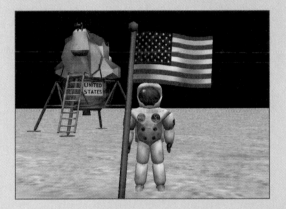

PP 2.3 Create an Alice world that shows a mummy stalking slowly with arms outstretched toward the pharaoh. When the mummy gets close, the pharaoh should gesture mystically, causing the mummy to fall backward. Create the mummy and pharaoh characters from classes in the **Egypt** gallery. Add methods called `step` and `fall` to the mummy and a `gesture` method to the pharaoh.

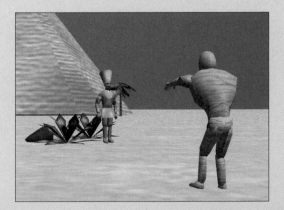

PP 2.4   Create an Alice world that shows a person rowing a rowboat across the water. Use an appropriate person from the **People** gallery and an object created from the Rowboat class in the **Vehicles** gallery. Add a method called row to the person that causes the person to make one stroke with both oars and consequently causes the boat to move forward a randomly determined distance.

PP 2.5   Using the FanDancer class from the **Japan** gallery, create an Alice world that shows a woman performing a fan dance. The dance should show the dancer moving right and left, with appropriate arm and head movements. Use separate custom methods to define elements of the dance.

PP 2.6   Create an Alice world that shows a classic Wild West shootout between a sheriff and an outlaw in the street. Use the Sheriff class and the Cowboy class from the **Old West** gallery to make the combatants. Create a draw method for each, using a parameter to control the speed of the draw. Also create a result method for each, in which one falls down and the other raises his hands in victory.

PP 2.7   Create an Alice world in which three beetles are seen scurrying around the ground. Create a beetle from the Beetle class in the **Animals > Bugs** gallery. Add a method called scurry that causes the beetle to turn in a random direction and then move forward a random distance. Duplicate that beetle object twice and call the scurry method of all three objects several times from my first method.

PP 2.8   Create an Alice world that shows a search and rescue operation in which a helicopter flies in a pattern above the ocean, occasionally stopping to hover for a while as if looking for something. Eventually the helicopter swoops in to save a person who was adrift. Create a hover method for the helicopter that accepts the number of seconds it should hover as a parameter. Create a search method and a rescue method to handle those aspects of the operation.

PP 2.9 Create an Alice world that shows a tennis player taking a few practice swings. Use an appropriate person from the **People** gallery and the `TennisRacket` class in the **Sports** gallery to make a tennis player. Create `forehand` and `backhand` methods for the player with appropriate movements.

PP 2.10 Create an Alice world that shows a Tyrannosaurus Rex dinosaur closing in on and attacking an unsuspecting Triceratops. The dinosaurs can be created from appropriate classes in the **Animals > Dinosaurs** gallery. Add a `step` method to the T-Rex that causes it to take one step forward, and an `attack` method that causes it to lean forward and bite. Add an `eat` method to the Triceratops that causes it to munch on a nearby plant (unaware that it is his last meal).

CHAPTER 3

Decisions and Loops

CHAPTER OBJECTIVES

In this chapter you will:

- Make decisions in your programs using an `If/Else` statement.
- Base decisions on conditions that use equality and relational operators as well as Boolean functions.
- Use logical operators to create complex conditions.
- Nest `If/Else` statements and loops.
- Execute a set of statements repeatedly using `While` and `Loop` statements.
- Use a loop control variable to tailor loop processing.

In Chapter 1 we introduced the `Do together` and `Do in order` statements to control whether animation steps happen simultaneously or in a particular order. In this chapter we explore some other control statements that allow us to make basic decisions and to execute statements repetitively. These types of controls are fundamental to programming in general and will allow us to make more interesting animations in Alice.

3.1 Making Decisions

We often encounter the need to make decisions in our programs. Should the boat turn to the right or left? Should the girl wave or move away? We often want to control what happens next based on the current circumstances or on some computed likelihood.

> ▶ Statements that control the flow of a program are based on Boolean conditions that are either true or false.

Control statements allow us to control the flow of our program's logic. Control statements make decisions based on the result of a *condition*. The condition produces a Boolean (true or false) result, which determines which statements are executed next.

The If/Else Statement

The basic control statement that allows us to make a decision in Alice is the If/Else statement. When you add an If/Else statement to a method by dragging it from the list below the method editor, it takes the form shown in Figure 3.1.

Figure 3.1

The default structure of an If/Else statement

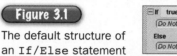

This default structure of an If/Else statement contains three important components that need to be filled in to make it useful. The first is the condition used to make the decision. When you add the statement initially, you choose to make the condition simply true or false (in Figure 3.1 it shows true). But this is simply a placeholder for our condition. We replace that section with an expression that makes the decision we desire.

> ▶ An If/Else statement determines which of two sets of statements are executed.

When executed, an If/Else statement first checks the value of the condition. If the result is true, the statements between the If and Else portions (shown as the first *Do Nothing* section) are executed. If the condition is false, the statements after the Else portion (shown as the second *Do Nothing* section) are executed. Therefore, one or both of the *Do Nothing* sections should be filled in with the appropriate code for the situation.

The logic of an If/Else statement is shown in Figure 3.2. Note that an If/Else statement ensures that one set of statements or the other is executed, but not both. After making the decision and executing the appropriate statements, processing continues with the statement following the If/Else statement.

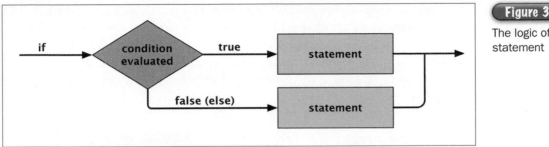

Figure 3.2

The logic of an `If/Else` statement

Let's look at an example. In the `Intersection` world, shown in Figure 3.3, a boy riding a bike comes to an intersection in the road. At that point, he will decide to either turn right or continue going straight. The road is composed of several objects made using the `Road` class from the **City** gallery. The boy on the bike is a composite object made from the `BikeKid` class in the **People** gallery.

Figure 3.3

The `Intersection` world

The code for `my first method` of the `Intersection` world is shown in Figure 3.4. In it, the `bikeKid` object first moves forward two meters toward the intersection. Then the `choosePath` method of the `bikeKid` object is called to determine whether to make the turn or keep moving straight ahead. Finally, the bike moves forward another five meters in whichever direction it is now facing.

Figure 3.4

`my first method` for the `Intersection` world

We wrote the `choosePath` method, shown in Figure 3.5, as part of the `bikeKid` object. It contains an `If/Else` statement to control whether the bike turns or not. Suppose we want a 30% chance that the bike will turn right and a 70% chance it will continue straight. The `choose true` condition of the `If/Else` statement returns a true or false result determined randomly. In this case, we set the condition to return true 30% of the time.

Figure 3.5

The `choosePath` method of `bikeKid`

The `choose true` condition is a function provided by the `world` object, and therefore is available in any animation you create. To make use of it, simply drag the `choose true` function from the function details panel (when the `world` object is selected) to the condition of the `If/Else` statement and pick the percentage desired.

> ▶ When appropriate, the `Else` portion of an `If/Else` statement can be left empty.

In this example, if the condition is true, the `turn` method of the `bikeKid` object is called, turning it to the right 90 degrees (one-quarter of a revolution). If the condition is false, the `Else` portion of the `If/Else` statement is executed, doing nothing and therefore leaving the bike pointing in its original direction. In either case, when the `choosePath` method completes, `my first method` resumes, and the `bikeKid` object moves forward five meters in whichever direction it is now pointing.

TRY THIS!

1. Modify `Intersection` world so that the bike turns 65% of the time.

2. Modify `Intersection` world so that the animation of the bike turn is smoother, moving forward and turning right at the same time.

Let's now explore an example that makes use of the `Else` portion of an `If/Else` statement. In the world called `Intersection2`, our `bikeKid` encounters a different type of intersection. This time, he is forced to turn either to the right or the left (assuming we don't want him to ride on the surrounding grass). The initial view of this world is shown in Figure 3.6.

Figure 3.6

The `Intersection2` world

We use the same logic for my `first method` in this example as we did in the first `Intersection` world. That is, we move the `bikeKid` toward the intersection, call the `choosePath` method, and then move it forward again.

This time, however, the `choosePath` method turns the bike either to the right or the left. In this scenario there is no option to keep moving straight ahead. This new version of the `choosePath` method is shown in Figure 3.7.

Figure 3.7

Using the `Else` portion of an `If/Else` statement

In this version, the option of turning right or left is given an equal 50/50 chance. If the randomly computed value is less than or equal to 50, the bike is turned to the right. Otherwise, in the `Else` portion of the `If/Else` statement, the bike is turned to the left. If the bike turns left, the `bikeKid` object also plays a bicycle bell sound after the turn is made. You can put as many statements in either section of the `If/Else` statement as needed. These statements are executed sequentially (in order) by default.

TRY THIS!

3. Modify the `Intersection2` world so that the bicycle's left turn and the bell ringing occur simultaneously.

4. Modify `Intersection2` so that the `bikeKid` object plays the bicycle bell sound no matter which way it turns. Play the sound after the turn is completed.

5. Modify `Intersection2` so that the bell sound is played while the turn is being made, no matter which way the bike turns.

Note that the calculation of the random chance to turn is done differently in this latest example. We created a new local variable called `turningChance`, which is assigned a random value between 1 and 100 (inclusive). The condition of the `If/Else` statement then checks to see if that value is less than or equal to 50 using the ≤ operator. This is one of six *equality and relational operators* you can use to compare numeric data in Alice. Table 3.1 summarizes these operators, which are provided as functions of the `world` object.

Table 3.1

The equality and relational operators

Operator	Example	Result
`==`	`a == b`	True if a is equal to b and false otherwise.
`!=`	`a != b`	True if a is not equal to b and false otherwise.
`<`	`a < b`	True if a is less than b and false otherwise.
`<=`	`a <= b`	True if a is less than or equal to b and false otherwise.
`>`	`a > b`	True if a is greater than b and false otherwise.
`>=`	`a >= b`	True if a is greater than or equal to b and false otherwise.

> ▶ The equality and relational operators produce Boolean results and are often used in conditions.

Think about the two versions of the `choosePath` method we've seen. One uses the `choose true` function, which returns a Boolean result, in the condition of the `If/Else` statement. The other uses the `random number` function to determine a numeric value, which is then analyzed in the `If/Else` condition using a Boolean relational operator. These are two different ways to accomplish the same goal. Both `Intersection` and `Intersection2` can be written using either technique. In some situations, though, it's important to be able to compare numeric values using the equality and relational operators.

6. Modify the original `Intersection` world so that it uses a local variable to store the percentage chance for turning.

7. Modify the `Intersection2` world so that the bike turns left 75% of the time and right 25% of the time.

8. Modify `Intersection2` so that the condition in the `If/Else` statement of the `choosePath` method uses a less than operator (<) while keeping the same turning likelihood.

9. Modify `Intersection2` so that the `choosePath` method uses a Boolean local variable instead of the `turningChance` integer variable. Assign a true or false value to the Boolean variable and modify the `If/Else` condition accordingly.

Nested `If/Else` Statements

So far, the statements we've put inside an `If/Else` statement have been straight-forward—moving an object or playing a sound. But a statement inside an `If/Else` statement could itself be an `If/Else` statement. This is known as a *nested if statement*.

Let's look at one more variation on our intersection example to see the usefulness of nested if statements. In the world called `Intersection3`, the `bikeKid` comes upon a four-way intersection, as shown in Figure 3.8. In this situation, he can choose to turn left, continue straight, or turn right. There are now three options. As before, after making his decision he'll move forward five meters along his chosen path.

> ▶ An `If/Else` statement can be part of either section of another `If/Else` statement, which lets us make an intricate series of decisions.

Figure 3.8

The `Intersection3` world

The choosePath method for Intersection3 is shown in Figure 3.9. Note that the Else portion of the first If/Else statement contains another If/Else statement. The logic of this method is set up so that bikeKid has a 30% chance of turning right, a 35% chance of turning left, and a 35% chance of continuing straight ahead.

Figure 3.9

Using a nested
If/Else statement

The first condition will return true 30% of the time. If it does, the bike is turned right, the entire Else portion is skipped, and the method concludes. If that condition returns false, however, its Else portion is performed, which immediately executes another If/Else statement. The condition of that If/Else returns true 50% of the time. If true, the bike turns left and the bicycle bell sound is played. If false, no turn is made (the bike keeps its straight ahead direction), and a "whoo hoo" sound is played.

Think about how those probabilities play out. There's a 70% chance the bike will not turn right, in which case, half the time (35%) it will turn left and half the time (35%) it will continue straight.

An If/Else statement represents a decision between two options. If there are three or more options (that is, more than one decision to make), then nested if statements are often a good solution.

TRY THIS!

10. Modify the Intersection3 world so that, if the bike continues straight ahead, it spins around a full revolution while making the "whoo hoo" sound.

11. Modify Intersection3 so that the bike turns right 20% of the time, turns left 40% of the time, and continues straight 40% of the time.

12. Modify Intersection3 so that there is a 60% chance that the bicycle bell sound will play if the bike turns left (otherwise it remains silent). Similarly, give only a 45% chance that the "whoo hoo" sound is played if the bike continues straight. Do not modify the chances of turning.

3.2 Repetition

As the name implies, *repetition statements* allow the programmer to repeat one or more statements a number of times. Repetition statements are also called *loops*. The two primary repetition statements in Alice are the `While` statement and the `Loop` statement, which we will now explore.

The `While` Statement

A `While` statement is based on a Boolean condition, just like an `If/Else` statement. A `While` loop repeatedly executes the statements it contains (called the *body* of the loop) as long as its condition is true.

> ▶ A `While` loop executes its statements repeatedly until its condition becomes false.

When you add a `While` statement to a method by dragging it up from the control statement list, it appears as shown in Figure 3.10. Like the `If/Else` statement, you choose an initial value of true or false for the condition, which you can then replace if desired. The `While` statement initially contains no statements. The *Do Nothing* portion should be replaced with whatever statements you wish to repeat.

Figure 3.10

The default form of a `While` statement

When a `While` loop executes, first the condition is evaluated. If the condition is true, the statements in the `While` loop are executed. Then the condition is evaluated a second time. If the condition is still true, the body of the loop is executed again. This process continues until the condition becomes false, at which point processing continues with the statement following the `While` loop. This logic is depicted in Figure 3.11.

Figure 3.11

The logic of a `While` statement

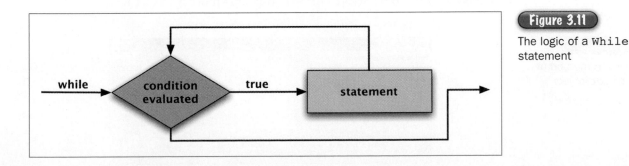

Take a moment to compare and contrast an `If/Else` statement and a `While` loop. The condition of an `If/Else` statement is used to decide between two options, and is evaluated only once. The condition of a `While` loop, on the other hand, is used to decide if its statements should be executed yet again, and may be evaluated many times.

 An infinite loop is a loop whose condition never becomes false.

If the condition of a `While` loop never becomes false, the loop will never end. This is referred to as an *infinite loop*. In most situations, programmers seek to avoid creating infinite loops.

In the world called `Shark`, shown in Figure 3.12, a shark continually circles a sailboat on the ocean. (If you look closely, the sailor in the boat is not happy about this situation.) Only the shark's dorsal fin protrudes above the ocean surface.

Figure 3.12

The `Shark` world

The shark object, which we've renamed `Bruce` in this world, is made from the `Shark` class in the **Animals** gallery. The boat is made from the `Sailboat` class in the **Vehicles** gallery. The sailor is made from the `Student1` class in the **People** gallery.

The `Shark` world's `my first method` simply calls the `swim` method of the shark, so we don't bother to show that here. The shark object does not have a `swim` method built in, so we wrote our own. It is shown in Figure 3.13.

Figure 3.13

The `swim` method of the `Bruce` object

The swim method is made up of an infinite While loop that contains the statements that cause Bruce to swim in a circle. Because the loop condition is always true, Bruce will continue to swim until the world stops executing. After all, in the real world sharks can't stop swimming!

In the body of the loop, the shark's move method and turn method are executed simultaneously, both taking eight seconds to complete. By turning a full revolution and moving forward at the same time, Bruce swims in a circle. The circumference of the circle is eight meters. So each time through the loop (that is, each loop *iteration*), the shark makes one complete circle around the boat.

TRY THIS!

13. Add a second shark to Shark world. Position the second shark opposite Bruce, swimming in the same direction and in approximately the same circle.

14. Modify Shark so that a Pterodactyl from the **Animals** gallery glides around the boat's mast, moving twice as fast as Bruce and in the opposite direction.

Let's make the Shark world more interesting. In Shark2, we modify the shark's behavior so that on every third lap around the boat, there's a 75% chance that Bruce will rise to the surface. Figure 3.14 shows an image of the shark on the surface of the water as he progresses around the back of the boat.

Figure 3.14

The Shark2 world, showing the shark while surfacing

The shark's `swim` method for the `Shark2` world is shown in Figure 3.15. In it we've introduced two variables—one to compute a random number to determine if the shark will surface and the other to count the number of laps the shark makes around the boat.

Figure 3.15

The `swim` method in `Shark2`

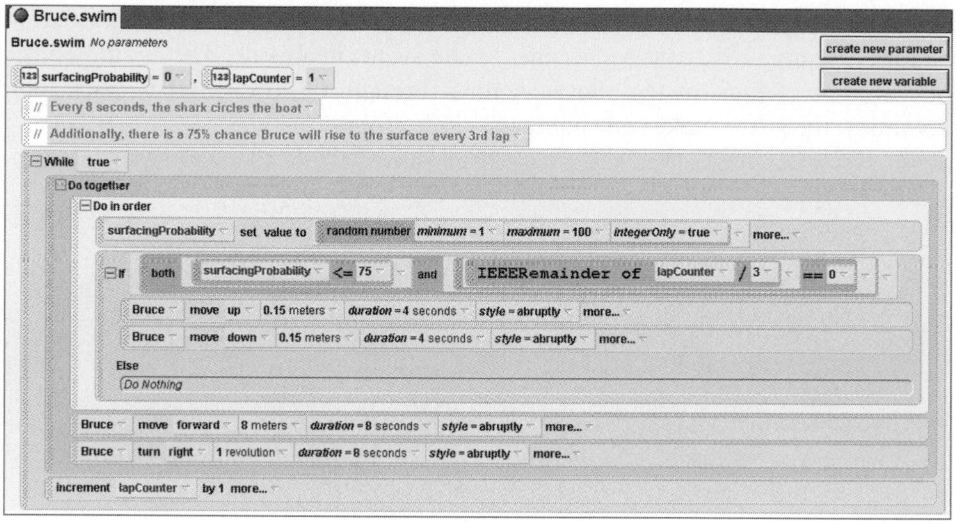

During each iteration of the loop, an `If/Else` statement is used to determine if the shark should rise to the surface. The `If/Else` condition takes into account two factors—the shark will only rise if the randomly computed probability is less than or equal to *75 and* if the value of `lapCounter` is a multiple of three (every third lap).

We use the `IEEERemainder` function, available in the world's function list, to determine if the value of `lapCounter` is a multiple of 3. The `IEEERemainder` function returns the remainder after one number is divided by another. Every third time around the boat, the remainder produced when `lapCounter` is divided by three will be zero.

If the conditions are right, we make the shark rise to the surface by moving him up .15 meters, then back down the same amount. This movement is done while the shark continues to circle the boat.

The condition used in the `If/Else` statement is an expression that combines two separate conditions into one. The `both a and b` condition is a *logical operator* that returns true only if both a and b are true. In this situation, a is the probability check and b is the lap counter check.

> ▶ Logical operators allow us to construct complex conditions for decisions and loops.

Alice supports three logical operators that we can use in Boolean conditions. The operators are listed and described in Table 3.2. Like the equality and relational operators, you can access the logical operators in the function list of the `world` object.

Operator	Description
`not a`	True if a is false, and false if a is true.
`both a and b`	True if a and b are both true, and false otherwise.
`either a or b, or both`	True if a or b or both are true, and false otherwise.

Table 3.2

The logical operators

TRY THIS!

15. Modify the `Shark2` world so that `Bruce` potentially rises to the surface every other lap.

16. Modify `Shark2` so that the percentage chance of the shark rising to the surface is stored in a variable, initialized to 75. Whenever the shark rises to the surface, decrease the chance he'll rise next time by 5 percent.

In both `Shark` and `Shark2`, we used an infinite loop to keep the shark moving until the animation was terminated. In most cases, however, you'll want to use a particular expression as the condition of a `while` loop. Consider the `Collision` world, shown in Figure 3.16. In it, two trucks are heading straight toward each other on a city street.

Figure 3.16

The `Collision` world

The trucks were created using the `CementTruck` and `DumpTruck` classes in the **Vehicles** gallery. The road, buildings, lampposts, and fire hydrant were created using various classes in the **City** gallery.

In the `Collision` world, a loop is used to move the two trucks toward each other until they collide. The `Collision` world's `my first method` is shown in Figure 3.17. In each iteration of the loop, both trucks are moved forward 0.25 meters, and the camera zooms in closer to the action.

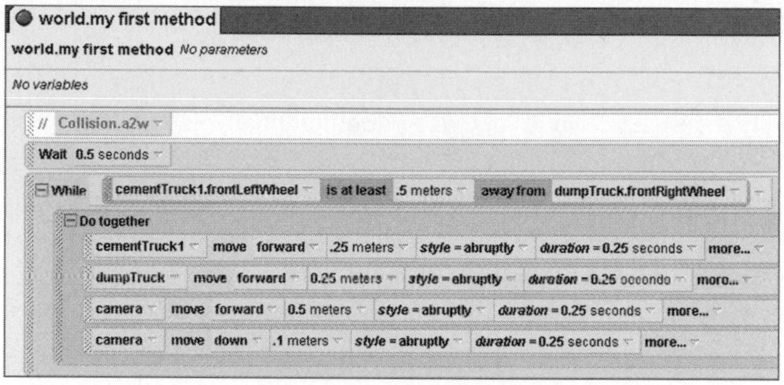

Figure 3.17

The `Collision` world's `my first method`

The condition of the loop in `Collision` is a call to a *proximity function* that returns true if the two trucks are at least half a meter away from each other. Actually, the function is called on a front wheel of one truck and compared to the front wheel of the other truck. When the trucks get too close, the condition becomes false and the loop terminates.

TRY THIS!

17. Modify `Collision` world so that when the trucks collide, a crashing sound is played and the cement truck's right front wheel breaks loose and continues to roll down the street.

18. Modify `Collision` so that the vehicles and camera move twice as fast.

The Loop Statement

A second type of repetition statement in Alice, the `Loop` statement, allows us to control the exact number of times a loop executes. In its simplest form, a loop will execute a specific number of times and then stop. When you drag a new `Loop` statement into a method, it prompts you for the number of times you want the loop to execute.

> ▶ A `Loop` statement executes the loop body a specific number of times.

In the `Dragon` world, for instance, we have a dragon on a castle's drawbridge. When the animation plays, the dragon extends his outer wings and then flaps them exactly five times. The `Dragon` world is shown in Figure 3.18.

Figure 3.18

The Dragon world

The dragon was created from the Dragon class and the castle from the Castle class, both found in the **Medieval** gallery.

The dragon's flap wings method, shown in Figure 3.19, contains the loop that causes the wings to repetitively flap up and down. Before that happens, though, the flap wings method calls the dragon's prepare to fly method, which positions the outer wings to an appropriate preset object pose.

dragon.flap wings
dragon.flap wings *No parameters*
No variables
// Extends the dragon's outer wings to prepare for flying
dragon.prepare to fly
Loop 5 times   times   show complicated version
Do together
// Flaps the left and right wings down
dragon.leftWingClose roll left 0.2 revolutions *duration* = 0.25 seconds more...
dragon.rightWingClose roll right 0.2 revolutions *duration* = 0.25 seconds more...
Do together
// Flaps the left and right wings up
dragon.leftWingClose roll right 0.2 revolutions *duration* = 0.25 seconds more...
dragon.rightWingClose roll left 0.2 revolutions *duration* = 0.25 seconds more...

Figure 3.19

The flap wings method

The body of the Loop statement contains two Do together statements, which move the left and right wings simultaneously. The first Do together rolls the wings 0.2 revolutions, producing a downward flap, and the second Do together statement reverses the roll, producing an upward flap.

TRY THIS!

19. Modify Dragon world so that the dragon moves its tail to the left and right while its wings are flapping.

20. Modify Dragon so that the dragon flies into the sky. During each downward stroke, move the dragon up 1 meter and forward 1 meter. During each upward stroke, move the dragon up and forward 0.5 meters. Change the initial camera view to be able to see the flight.

Behind the scenes, the Loop statement is actually constructed using a condition that tests the value of an integer variable, called the *loop control variable*, and terminates when it reaches a specified end value. The loop control variable, which is called index, is initialized to a starting value (commonly 0) and is incremented by one each time through the loop. The logic of a Loop statement is shown in Figure 3.20.

Figure 3.20

The logic of a Loop statement

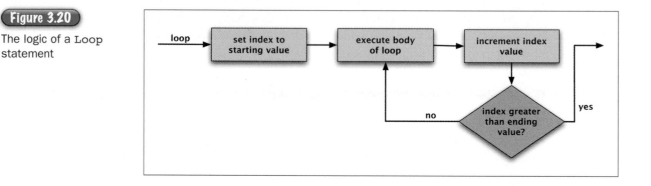

Once the loop is added to a method, you can modify the starting and ending values of the loop control variable by clicking on the button labeled show complicated version that appears next to the Loop statement. This version also allows you to modify the amount that the variable is incremented each time.

▶ The alternate version of the Loop statement provides explicit access to the loop control variable.

We use this version of the Loop statement in the SpeedingCar world, in which a car races through the desert toward a rest stop (which is so far away it initially can't be seen). The starting view of this world is shown in Figure 3.21. As the animation plays, the car accelerates, moving faster and faster, passing various other objects, until it finally comes to a stop at its destination. In this world, the camera's vehicle property is set to be the car object so that the view stays with the car as it moves.

Figure 3.21

The `SpeedingCar` world

The `car` object was created using the `Car` class from the **Vehicles** gallery. The trucks and signs that the car passes during the animation were created using various classes from the **Vehicles** and **Roads and Signs** galleries. The rest stop (the car's destination) was created using the `Rest station` class from the **Buildings** gallery.

The `drive` method of the `car` object is shown in Figure 3.22. In it, a `Loop` statement controls the forward movement and the acceleration of the car. Each time through the loop, the car travels for half a second at a certain speed. Plus, in each iteration the speed is increased. Therefore, each time through the loop the car travels faster and covers more distance.

Figure 3.22

The car's `drive` method

The loop control variable, which is called `index`, runs from 1 to 20, incrementing by 1 each time the loop executes. That is, the first time through the loop, `index` has a value of 1. The second time through the loop, `index` has a value of 2. This continues until the upper limit of 20 is reached.

We set up the call to the car's `move at speed` method so that speed at which the car travels is a function of the loop control variable. The first time through the loop, the car moves at speed `index * 3`, or 3 meters per second. The second time through the loop, the speed is 6 meters per second. And so on. By building the loop in this fashion, the car accelerates by a factor of 3 every half second.

TRY THIS!

21. Modify the SpeedingCar world so that it calculates the total distance the car travels during its trip to the rest stop. Print the result when the car comes to a stop.

22. Modify SpeedingCar so that it displays the distance the car has traveled while it is moving. Continuously display the result on a 3D text object that stays visible in the upper portion of the display window.

Nested Repetition Statements

▶ When loops are nested, the inner loop executes all of its iterations for each iteration of the outer loop.

Repetition statements can be nested, just as If/Else statements can. That is, the body of a loop can contain another loop. When loops are nested, each iteration of the outer loop causes the inner loop to execute completely.

In the Safe world, shown in Figure 3.23, we have placed a safe on a table in a room. We used the Safe class from the **Objects** gallery to make the safe, but its dial is not detailed enough for our purposes. So we replaced that dial with one created from the Dial class of the **Controls** gallery. The new dial has clear tick marks along the dial edge, which works better for this animation. To "attach" the dial to the safe, we set the dial object's vehicle property to be the door. That way, when the safe's door opens, the dial moves with it.

Figure 3.23

The Safe world

The Safe world's my first method is shown in Figure 3.24. After an initial pause, the camera is moved to a pre-defined dummy position named close up of safe to provide a better view of the dial. Next, we call two methods that we added to the safe object. First the turn dial method is executed, which causes the dial to spin back and forth. Then the open door method is called, revealing the contents of the safe.

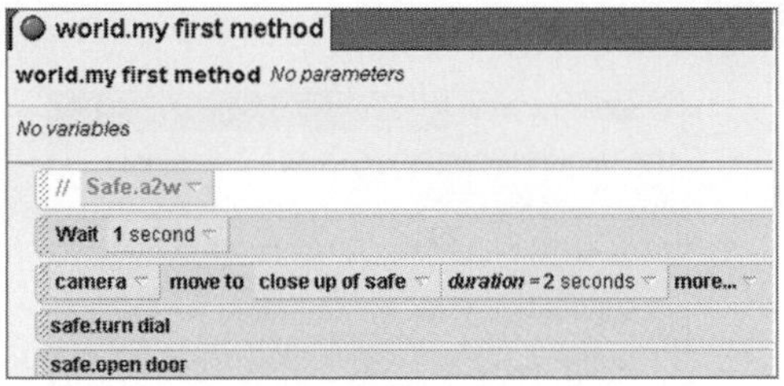

Figure 3.24

The Safe world's my first method

The turn dial method uses nested loops to control the dial movement. The outer loop controls how many times the dial is turned and whether it's turning right or left. The inner loop controls how far (how many ticks) the dial is moved during that particular turn. Each time this animation is run, the dial turns three times (left, then right, then left), and moves a different amount of ticks on each turn. The turn dial method is shown in Figure 3.25.

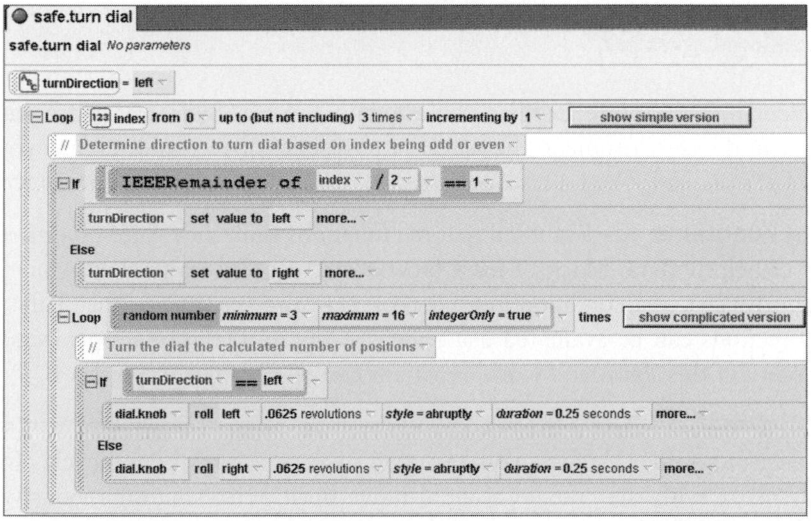

Figure 3.25

The turn dial method

The outer loop iterates exactly three times, and the value of its loop control variable is used to determine which way the dial turns in each iteration. If the loop control variable is an odd number, a variable called turnDirection is set to the value "left." Otherwise, turnDirection is set to "right." We use the IEEERemainder function to determine if the loop control variable is odd or even. This technique is similar to one we used in the Shark2 world earlier in this chapter.

Once the direction of the turn is established, the inner loop is used to rotate the dial a certain amount. The loop is constructed to randomly calculate a number between 3 and 16 (inclusive), and then rotate the dial that number of tick marks.

Each iteration of the loop moves the dial one tick mark in the proper direction by rolling the dial one-sixteenth of a revolution (or 0.0625).

The safe's open door method is shown in Figure 3.26. In it, after a brief pause, the handle of the door is rotated and the door is swung open.

Figure 3.26

The safe's open door method

safe.open door
safe.open door *No parameters*
No variables
Wait 0.25 seconds ▽
safe.door.handle ▽	roll left ▽	0.25 revolutions ▽	more... ▽
safe.door ▽	turn left ▽	0.25 revolutions ▽	more... ▽

TRY THIS!

23. Modify Safe world so that the dial first moves right, then left, then right again.

24. Modify Safe world so that a tick sound is played as the dial is rotated.

3.3 More to Explore

Remember that the more familiar you are with the capabilities of a programming language and its environment, the richer and more effective you can make your programs. Let's take a look at a few more features you should explore on your own.

Built-In Functions Keep in mind that the functions built into Alice objects return a variety of helpful data. Many of these functions return Boolean values which can be used directly as a test condition in a Loop or If/Else statement. The results of numeric functions can be evaluated using the equality and relational operators. A full listing of all of the object and world functions can be found in Appendix B.

Vehicle Property The vehicle property of an object allows you to "attach" one object to another. Assume you have two objects, a boy and a bicycle. To make the boy move with the bike, you could move both objects simultaneously. However, if you set the boy's vehicle property to the bike, the boy moves with the bike whenever and wherever the bike moves. Using the vehicle property is often the best choice when you need to move objects in unison.

3D Text The primary way to add textual information to an Alice world is to use a three-dimensional text object. You can create a 3D text object, such as the one in Figure 3.27, using the last tool in the set of local galleries. The tool allows you to specify the text, font, and other properties. Once created and added to the world, the text object's properties can be modified as you would any other object's properties. In particular, you can change the displayed text by setting the text property. 3D text is very useful for displaying game scores, timers, and other on-screen information.

Figure 3.27

A 3D text object

Importing Sounds Effective use of sound effects and songs can enhance an Alice world. Objects in an Alice world can play both .mp3 and .wav files. A few basic sound effects are available by default, but you may want to import your own sound clip into an object via the properties panel. Once imported, an object can play a sound by calling the `play sound` method and specifying the desired audio clip.

Summary of Key Concepts

- Statements that control the flow of a program are based on Boolean conditions that are either true or false.

- An `If/Else` statement determines which of two sets of statements are executed.

- When appropriate, the `Else` portion of an `If/Else` statement can be left empty.

- The equality and relational operators produce Boolean results and are often used in conditions.

- An `If/Else` statement can be part of either section of another `If/Else` statement, which lets us make an intricate series of decisions.

- A `While` loop executes its statements repeatedly until its condition becomes false.

- An infinite loop is a loop whose condition never becomes false.

- Logical operators allow us to construct complex conditions for decisions and loops.

- A `Loop` statement executes the loop body a specific number of times.

- The alternate version of the `Loop` statement provides explicit access to the loop control variable.

- When loops are nested, the inner loop executes all of its iterations for each iteration of the outer loop.

Exercises

EX 3.1 Write an `If/Else` statement that causes an object called `coach` to point at an object called `player` if the value of the variable `score` is less than 20.

EX 3.2 Write an `If/Else` statement that causes an object called `dancer` to spin in place two revolutions if the current day of the week is Tuesday. *Hint:* Use the `day of week` world function (see Appendix B).

EX 3.3 Write an `If/Else` statement that turns an object called `boat` one-eighth revolution to the right if the value of the variable `switch` is even and to the left if the value of `switch` is odd. *Hint:* A number is even if it is evenly divisible by two.

EX 3.4 Write an `If/Else` statement that causes an object called `zamboni` to turn around if the value of `passes` is between 50 and 100.

EX 3.5 Write an `If/Else` statement that increments the value of `count1` if the value of `total` is evenly divisible by four or five and increments the value of `count2` otherwise.

EX 3.6 Write a `While` statement that causes an object called `skydiver` to move down 1 meter as long as it is above an object called `target`. *Hint:* Use the `is above` proximity function (see Appendix B).

EX 3.7 Write a `While` statement that reduces the value of the variable `speed` by half as long as the distance between `car1` and `car2` is less than five meters. *Hint:* Use the `distance behind` world function (see Appendix B).

EX 3.8 Write a `While` statement that updates the value of a variable called `seconds` and displays it in a 3D text object called `countdown`. Start `seconds` at 10 and loop until it reaches 0.

EX 3.9 Write a `Loop` statement that causes an object called `skater` to spin in place 10 times.

EX 3.10 Write a `Loop` statement that uses a loop control variable, called `num`, ranging from 1 to 5. On each iteration of the loop, move an object called `plane` forward and down `num` meters.

Programming Projects

PP 3.1 Create an Alice world that shows the double-wheeled `FerrisWheel` from the **Amusement Park** gallery in action. Rotate the main axle continuously counter-clockwise, once every 10 seconds, until the world is terminated. For every full rotation of the main axle, rotate both of the individual wheels four times clockwise.

PP 3.2 Create an Alice world in which a `Biplane` from the **Vehicles** gallery flies in from the right side of the viewing area, makes seven consecutive vertical loops as it moves across the sky, then flies off to the left. Its propeller should be turning the entire time.

PP 3.3 Create an Alice world in which four different characters, made from various classes in the **People** gallery, perform 20 jumping jacks in unison. Give one of the characters (being a little more out of shape than the others) a 30% chance that he will choose to replace a jumping jack with an easier stretch.

PP 3.4 Create an Alice world in which an ice skater skates on a frozen lake in a figure-eight pattern repeatedly until the world terminates. Use the `IceSkater` class from the **People** gallery and the `FrozenLake` class from the **Environments** gallery. Have the skater glide on her right foot on the top half of the "8" and on her left foot on the bottom half of the "8." Add a 50% chance that the skater may pause to do a pirouette in the center of the figure-eight pattern.

PP 3.5 Create an Alice world in which two frogs race toward a finish line. Use a loop in which both frogs hop forward once in each iteration. Determine the distance of each hop randomly. End the animation when one of the frogs crosses the finish line. The `Frog` class is in the **Animals** gallery.

PP 3.6 Create an Alice world in which a ball rolls off a table, bounces on the ground, and eventually comes to rest. Use the `ToyBall1` class from the **Sports** gallery to create the ball. Use a loop to control the bounces, decreasing the height of the rebound by half every time. Move the ball away from the table slightly on each bounce. Continue the bounces until the rebound height decreases to an insignificant amount.

PP 3.7 Create an Alice world in which a horse is relaxing in a field. Use the `Horse` class in the **Animals** gallery. Define five different basic actions for the horse (sway its tail, dip its head, whinny, etc.). Use a loop to constantly keep the horse active, randomly choosing the next action. Add pauses of random duration between actions as well.

PP 3.8 Create a wind-up turtle using the `WindupKey` class from the **Objects** gallery and the `Turtle` class from the **Animals** gallery. Create an Alice world in which the turtle walks forward while the key on its back turns. For each full rotation of the key, the turtle should take two steps (right front and left rear feet first, then left front and right rear feet). Use the control variable of a loop to determine how many seconds it takes for the key to fully rotate one time—one second the first iteration, two seconds the second, three the third, and so on. This will create the impression that the toy is winding down. Stop the turtle's movement after 10 key rotations.

PP 3.9 The *drinking bird* is a toy that's been around since the 1940s. It mimics the motion of a bird bobbing up and down and eventually dipping its bill into a water glass. Thermodynamically powered, it repeats this motion over and over. Create an Alice world that uses the DrinkParrot class from the **Objects** gallery to demonstrate the motions of this classic toy. Use the Mug class in the **Kitchen** gallery for the target beverage.

PP 3.10 Create an Alice world in which a blimp floats through the air in a figure-eight pattern. Underneath, three ships on the open ocean move in various patterns and at various speeds. Whenever the blimp is above one of the ships (according to the is above function), it attempts to drop a crate of supplies onto the ship (it may miss). The blimp and ships can be created from various classes in the **Vehicles** gallery, and the crate can be made from the Crate class in the **Objects** gallery. Only one crate object needs to be created, letting it "ride" in the blimp. After dropping it onto a boat, turn the crate invisible and move it back to the blimp to be ready for the next drop. Allow the animation to continue until the world is terminated.

CHAPTER 4

Events

CHAPTER OBJECTIVES

In this chapter you will:

- ▶ Explore the different types of events that can be processed in an Alice world.
- ▶ Distinguish between events that fire once and those that fire repeatedly.
- ▶ Examine the difference between loop processing and event processing.
- ▶ Create events that respond immediately to input from the keyboard and mouse.
- ▶ Use events to monitor conditions and changes in the values of variables.

In Chapter 3 you saw how conditional and loop statements give us greater control over objects, allowing us to specify the circumstances under which objects behave in particular ways. In this chapter, we explore another mechanism for controlling the processing in a program, *events*. We can set up a program to handle several kinds of events whenever they occur. One of the biggest benefits of event processing is the ability to create interactive worlds that respond to user input from the mouse and keyboard.

4.1 Introduction to Event Processing

Most modern software applications use a graphical user interface (GUI) made up of one or more windows that often contain input components such as buttons, text fields, lists, and menus. The GUI lets the user use both the mouse and keyboard to interact with a program. Every time the user clicks the mouse button or presses a keyboard key, an *event* is generated (or fired). The program responds to each event appropriately, which is called *event processing* or *event handling*.

> ▶ Events are generated under various circumstances, such as when the user presses a mouse button or keyboard key.

The mouse is actually a source of multiple types of events. Simply moving the mouse is an event to which we can respond. Dragging the mouse (moving the mouse while holding down a button) is another type of mouse event. The clicking of a mouse button and the releasing of a mouse button can be treated as two separate events. Similarly, we can distinguish between a keyboard key being pressed and a key being released if desired.

Not all events are generated due to user action. An event could be generated when the value of a variable changes, for instance. As the name implies, the When the world starts event occurs when the world first launches. This is the only event we've made use of so far, and have probably already begun to take it for granted.

> ▶ We can set up a program to respond to some events and ignore others.

Of course, just because we can respond to an event, doesn't mean we choose to. In many situations, we don't care about many of the events that can occur. As the designers of a program, we decide which events to process and which to ignore.

Alice worlds can process 13 different types of events. These events can be broken down into four categories, as shown in Table 4.1.

We define how events are handled in a particular world in the Events editor of the Alice environment. Whenever you create a new world, one event handler is created by default. It causes my first method to execute when the world first begins running (see Figure 4.1). Until now, this default event is the only one our programs have processed. If we didn't process this event, or some other, an Alice world would do nothing. We can add other events using the create new event button. Once an event is added to the Events editor, it can be set up to execute any statement by dragging the appropriate statement or method call into the event handler.

Figure 4.1

The default event in Alice

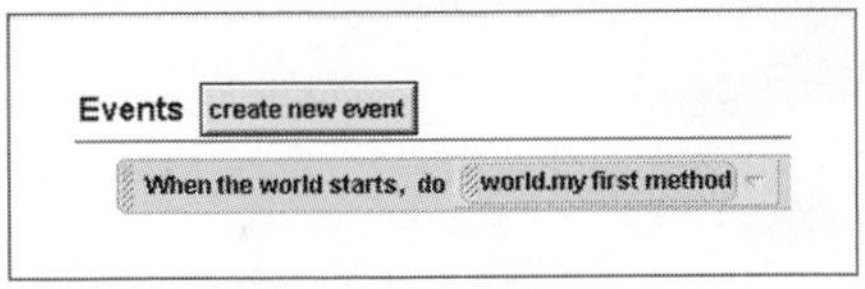

World Events	
When the world starts	This event occurs once when the world first begins running (playing).
While the world is running	This event is processed repeatedly as long as the world is running.
Keyboard Events	
When a key is typed	This event occurs when the user presses and releases a keyboard key.
While a key is pressed	This event is processed repeatedly while the user holds down a keyboard key.
Let the arrow keys move an object	This event allows the user to change the position of an object by pressing the arrow keys on the keyboard.
Mouse Events	
When the mouse is clicked on something	This event is generated when the user clicks and releases a mouse button on an object.
While the mouse is pressed on something	This event is processed repeatedly as long as the user holds down a mouse button on an object.
Let the mouse move the camera	This event allows the user to change the position of the camera by dragging the mouse.
Let the mouse orient the camera	This event allows the user to change the orientation of the camera (the direction in which it is pointing) by dragging the mouse.
Let the mouse move objects	This event allows the user to change the position of one or more objects by dragging the mouse.
Condition Events	
When a variable changes	This event occurs when the value of a specified variable changes.
While something is true	This event is processed repeatedly as long as a specified condition produces a true result.
When something becomes true	This event occurs when a specified condition first produces a true result and repeatedly thereafter until the world terminates.

Table 4.1

A summary of Alice events

World Events

World events are a class of events that are generated based on situations that occur in a running Alice world. In Alice, there are two types of world events. The first, `When the world starts`, has been used in all examples we've explored so far to "kick things off." By default, this event handler calls `my first method`, but it could be modified to call something else, or it doesn't have to be used at all.

The `When the world starts` event is generated only once, when the world first launches. If the world is stopped and restarted, the statement associated with this event is executed again. However, if the world is paused and then resumed, this event is not generated and processing simply continues where it left off.

The second type of world event is `While the world is running`. To add this event to the Events editor, right click on a `When the world starts` event and select `change to` from the menu that appears (see Figure 4.2). The `While the world is running` event, among others, is not listed in the menu you see when you push the `create new event` button—to get one you must change a `When the world starts` event.

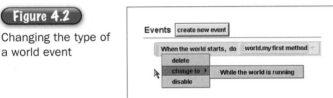

Figure 4.2

Changing the type of a world event

The basic form of the `While the world is running` event is shown in Figure 4.3. Note that it has three sections. In addition to the main repetitious processing, this event can be configured to execute an initial statement when the world starts and a final statement when the world stops. A separate statement can be dragged into each of the three sections. The statements in the `Begin` and `End` sections, if present, are executed only once at the appropriate times. The statement in the `During` section is executed repeatedly as long as the world is playing.

> ▶ Some events in Alice have `Begin`, `During`, **and** `End` sections to tailor the way the event is handled.

Figure 4.3

The basic form of a `While the world is running` event

The `Windmill` world, shown in Figure 4.4, shows a windmill on a hill. The windmill is created from the `Windmill` class in the **Buildings** gallery. When the animation is played, the windmill's blades turn continuously until the world is terminated.

Figure 4.4

The `Windmill` world

Figure 4.5 shows the event processing of the `Windmill` world. In the `During` section of the `While the world is running` event, the windmill's blades are rotated to the right one revolution. This call to the `windmill` object's `roll` method is repeated as long as the world is running. Since there is no need for them in this example, the `Begin` and `End` sections are left empty.

Events | create new event

While the world is running
  Begin: <None>
  During: Windmill.Blades — roll right — 1 revolution — *style* = abruptly — *duration* = 2 seconds — more...
  End: <None>

Figure 4.5

Event processing in `Windmill` world

Note that instead of using an event, we could have used an infinite (`While true`) loop, as we saw in Chapter 3, to make the windmill blades move continuously. But there is a big difference. If we use a loop, our program's processing gets stuck in that loop and no other actions can take place. By using events, we can keep the windmill blades rotating continuously while other actions are processed at the same time.

> ▶ Processing events is often a better solution than a loop-based alternative.

TRY THIS!

1. Modify `Windmill` so that there is a pause of 0.5 seconds before the windmill blades start turning.

2. Modify `Windmill` so that three planes fly by, one at a time, while the windmill blades are turning. Have the planes' movement managed by a method called `flyPlanes` in the `world` object.

4.3 Keyboard Events

▶ Keyboard events can recognize the use of any standard keyboard key, including the arrow keys, the enter key, and the space bar.

Keyboard events provide the ability for Alice worlds to respond to user-initiated keyboard presses. There are three types of keyboard-related events available in Alice, `When a key is typed`, `While a key is pressed`, and `Let the arrow keys move an object`. The last event specifically manages the use of the arrow keys, but the first two events can react to the depression of any of the standard keyboard keys:

- digits: 0 to 9

- letters: a to z

- arrow keys: up, down, right, and left

- special: the space bar or enter key

Let's look at an example called `Rockette` in which a single dancer waits to perform some leg kicks for us. The initial view of this world is shown in Figure 4.6. The rockette is made from the `Rockette` class of the **People** gallery. When this world is played, the rockette object (renamed `Lisa`) waits for user input. When the "r" key is typed, `Lisa` kicks her right leg and turns her head to the right.

Figure 4.6

The `Rockette` world

The leg and head movement of the rockette are defined in the `kick` method of the `Lisa` object. The method accepts a string parameter, "left" or "right," that will designate which leg to kick. The partially completed method, shown in Figure 4.7, processes the right leg kick. Processing the left leg kick is left as an exercise.

Figure 4.7

The `kick` method of the `Lisa` rockette

The `kick` method first checks the parameter `leg` to verify that its value is equal to the value "right." If so, her right thigh is turned 0.4 revolutions and her head is turned to the right 0.25 revolutions. Both of these actions take are set to take only 0.3 seconds to complete. After a brief pause, the leg and head are returned to their original positions.

To respond to user input, the `Rockette` world processes a `When a key is typed` event. When the keyboard's "r" key is typed, the `kick` method is called with the parameter value "right."

TRY THIS!

3. Modify `Rockette` so that the dancer's left leg kicks, with the corresponding head turn, when the "l" key is typed.

4. Modify `Rockette` so that the dancer performs a left knee raise when the "h" key is pressed and a right knee raise when the "g" key is pressed.

The second keyboard-based event is `While a key is pressed`. This event triggers an action as long as the user is holding down a particular keyboard key. Note the difference between these two keyboard event types. The `When a key is typed` event executes its statement once when the user types (presses and releases) a key. The `While a key is pressed` event executes its statement repeatedly for as long as the user presses (holds down) a keyboard key.

> ▶ Some events fire once when the initiating action occurs; other events fire repeatedly as long as the action is occurring.

To get a `While a key is pressed` event, you change a `When a key is typed` event using the drop-down menu that appears when you right click the event.

This process is shown in Figure 4.8. This is similar to the process of creating a `While the world is running` event, discussed in the previous section.

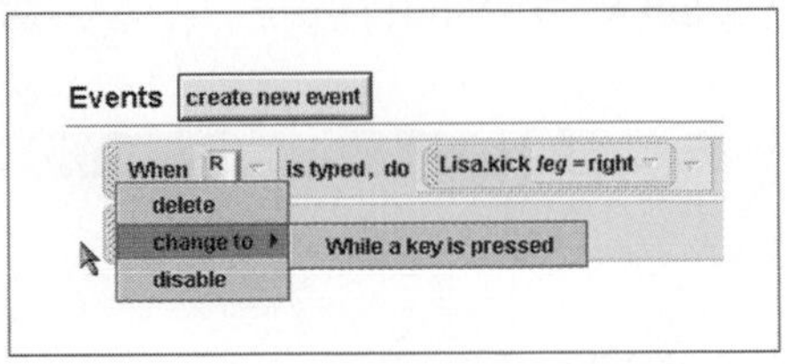

Figure 4.8

Creating a `While a key is pressed` event

Also similar to the `While the world is running` event, the `While a key is pressed` event has `Begin`, `During`, and `End` sections. The basic form is shown in Figure 4.9. The statements corresponding to the `Begin` and `End` sections execute once, when the key is first pressed and when it is finally released, respectively.

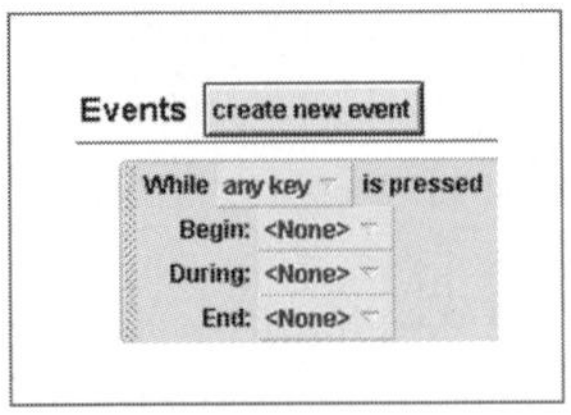

Figure 4.9

The basic form of a `While a key is pressed` event

The final keyboard-based event is `Let the arrow keys move an object`. Any Alice object can be linked to this event, allowing the user to move the selected object within the world using the four arrow keys on the keyboard.

When you first add the event to the event editor, the `Let the arrow keys move an object` event defaults to moving the camera, as shown in Figure 4.10. To manage a different object, drag the object's tile to the event.

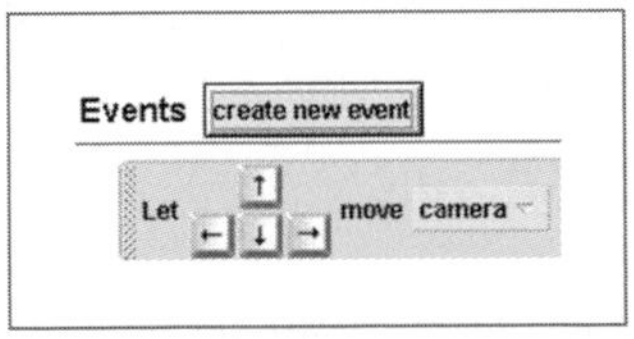

Figure 4.10

The basic form of the `Let the arrow keys move an object` event

TRY THIS!

5. Modify the `Rockette` world so that the dancer repeatedly kicks her left leg and then her right leg for as long as the user holds down the "b" key.

6. Modify the `Rockette` world so that the user can move the dancer around the room using the arrow keys.

 **Mouse Events**

Mouse events allow the user to use the mouse to interact with a running Alice world. There are five types of mouse events in Alice:

- `When the mouse is clicked on something`

- `While the mouse is pressed on something`

- `Let the mouse move the camera`

- `Let the mouse orient the camera`

- `Let the mouse move objects`

The first two events might remind you of the `When a key is typed` and `While a key is pressed` events from the previous section. They have similar behaviors. The `When the mouse is clicked on something` event occurs once when the mouse button is pressed and released on an object. The `While the mouse is pressed on something` occurs repeatedly for as long as the mouse button is pressed and held down on an object.

Let's look at another example. The `Rocker` world (see Figure 4.11) contains a musician holding a bass guitar. The musician was created from the `Kelly` class in the **People** gallery and the guitar was created from the `Bass` class in the **Musical Instruments** gallery.

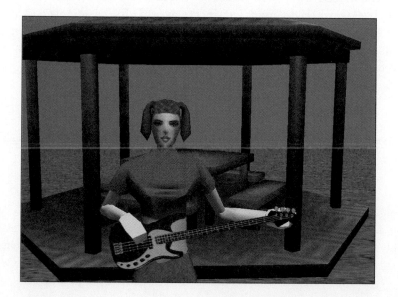

The `Rocker` world

We imported a bass guitar riff and associated it with the guitar. We use the When the mouse is clicked on something event, shown in Figure 4.12, to play the sound clip when the user clicks the mouse on the guitar.

Figure 4.12

Event handling in
Rocker world

Note that the sound is played only when the user clicks on the guitar. Clicking the mouse on the musician or anywhere else in the world produces no effect.

TRY THIS!

7. Modify Rockette world so that the dancer spins around when the mouse is clicked on her.

8. Modify Rocker world so that the musician's head leans back and forth while the mouse button is pressed on the musician.

9. Add a musician playing a saxophone to Rocker world. Play a saxophone riff (provided in the world) when the user clicks on the musician or the sax.

Two other mouse events allow the user to manipulate the camera with the mouse. The Let the mouse move the camera event allows the user to move the camera forward, backward, right, and left in the world. Its basic form is shown in Figure 4.13. There are no options or parameters for this event. Similarly, the Let the mouse orient the camera event can be used to rotate the camera. Both of these events can be active at the same time.

Figure 4.13

The basic form of the
Let the mouse move
the camera event

The mouse events that manipulate the camera are particularly useful while you are building a world. By allowing the mouse to move and orient the camera, even temporarily, you can easily inspect various objects and examine them from different angles.

TRY THIS!

10. Modify the Rocker world so that the mouse can be used to move the camera around the world.

11. Modify the Windmill world to allow the user to both move and orient the camera with the mouse.

The final mouse event to explore is `Let the mouse move objects` (see Figure 4.14). The object managed by this event is actually a list of objects; multiple objects can be moved at the same time. Managing lists of objects is discussed further in the next chapter.

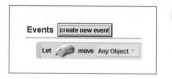

Figure 4.14

The basic form of the `Let the mouse move objects` event

Condition Events

Many of the events we have discussed so far occur because of some type of user action. There are three other events that are triggered by the logic you set up in your program: `While something is true`, `When something becomes true`, and `When a variable changes`. Each of these events is based on the status of a variable or expression.

The first two events, `While something is true` and `When something becomes true`, are triggered when an expression produces a true result.

The `Concert` world example, shown in Figure 4.15, uses the `While something is true` event to control the sound from a rock concert. The `Concert` world is comprised of two sets of speakers and three push buttons on a simple table. The speakers were created from the `Speakers` class in the **Musical Instruments** gallery and the buttons were created from the `Button` class in the **Controls** gallery.

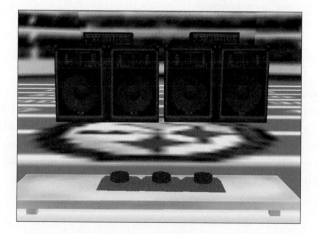

Figure 4.15

The `Concert` world

We named the three button objects left button, middle button, and right button. We added a Boolean property to each button named depressed which is false when the button is in the raised position, and true when the button is in the depressed position. Each button also contains a method called depressButton, which animates the downward motion of the button when it is pressed, and a method called raiseButton, which animates its upward motion. Finally, a button's playMusic method is used to control the playing of a specific sound clip.

In its current state, only the left button has the proper events set up for it. When the user clicks the mouse on the left button, either the depressButton or raiseButton method is called, depending on the current state of the button. In addition to animating the movement of the button in response to the user's action, the methods also toggle the value of the depressed variable for the button.

Finally, we used the While something is true event to monitor the state of the left button object. Whenever the button's depressed value is true, the button will play its assigned musical track repeatedly. The event processing for this world is shown in Figure 4.16. The While something is true event contains Begin, During, and End sections for fine-grained control.

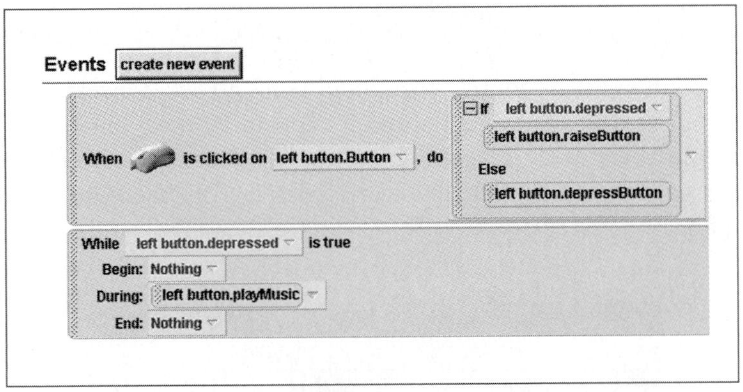

Figure 4.16

Event processing in the Concert world

The When something becomes true event can be used to identify the first time a condition becomes true. Once true, the event will perform the specified action, and that action will remain in effect (or running) until the world stops. Note the subtle difference between While something is true, which stops when its condition becomes false, and When something becomes true, which, once started, does not stop until the world terminates.

TRY THIS!

12. Modify Concert world so that the middle and right buttons play their musical tracks (which have already been imported for each button) when depressed.

13. Modify Concert world to play the stadium's crowdSound when all three buttons are depressed.

14. Using a Boolean variable to monitor its state, modify the Windmill world so that when the mouse is clicked on the windmill, the windmill stops turning, and when clicked again, it begins turning again.

The final condition event, When a variable changes, is used to monitor a particular variable for any changes to its value. This event is not limited to monitoring variables of the Boolean type; other types of values such as numbers, colors, and character strings can also be monitored.

In the Cow world, shown in Figure 4.17, we use the When a variable changes event to monitor a Boolean variable named mooTime. The mooTime variable is false when the world starts; it is set to true 10 seconds after the world starts playing. Once the mooTime variable changes to a true value, the When a variable changes event triggers the cow's moo. The event processing for Cow world is shown in Figure 4.18.

Figure 4.17

The Cow world

Figure 4.18

Event processing in Cow world

> Events [create new event]
>
> When the world starts, do | world.my first method
>
> When world.mooTime changes, do | cow | play sound cow.moo (0:01.567) | more...

The time counter shown in the bottom left corner is a 3D text object that initially displays the text "0.0". As the seconds are counted, this text object, named `time sign`, is updated.

The main loop for this world resides in `my first method`, shown in Figure 4.19. Once each second, the cow's tail swishes twice, the text object is updated, and the time counter (`secondsSinceStart`) is updated.

Figure 4.19

The Cow world's my first method

> ● world.my first method
>
> **world.my first method** *No parameters*
>
> *No variables*
>
> // Mooing Cow.a2w
>
> Wait 0.5 seconds
>
> □ While | world.secondsSinceStart < 11
>
> □ Do together
>
> cow.tailSwish *times* = 2 *speed* = 2
>
> time sign set text to | world.secondsSinceStart as a string | more...
>
> increment world.secondsSinceStart by 1 more...
>
> Wait 1 second
>
> world.mooTime set value to true more...
>
> □ Do together
>
> cow.headTurn
>
> cow.openJaw

TRY THIS!

15. Modify the Cow world so that the updates to the 3D text object (`time sign`) occur through a `When a variable changes` event.

4.6 More to Explore

Before we conclude this chapter, let's add a few more Alice environment and language details to our arsenal.

Object Groups If you add a large number of objects to a world, the object tree may become cluttered. To help manage the objects, you can organize them into groups. If you right click in the object tree area and create a group, a folder will appear into which you can drag other objects. This feature is only for organizing the object tree. Objects in groups cannot be manipulated as a single entity. For instance, you cannot call the same method on all members of a group in one statement. To do that, you need to add objects to a list or array, as you will see in Chapter 5.

Dummy Objects   It's often helpful to create a set of predefined locations in a world to coordinate the movement of objects in an animation. Predefined locations are particularly useful when you want to reset the camera's view at various points in the animation. To do so, you add a *dummy object* at the desired location, then move the camera (or other object) to the dummy object when appropriate. A dummy object is invisible and is used simply as a reference. To capture a position, move the camera in the world as needed, and press the `drop dummy at camera` button (see Appendix A), which will add a dummy object to the object tree.

Input Dialogs   The functions provided for the `world` object include three that allow you to ask the user for input while a world is playing. The functions allow you to ask the user for a number, a yes or no answer, or a string. Each of the functions can be customized so that the resulting pop-up dialog window prompts the user for the appropriate input, as shown in Figure 4.20.

Figure 4.20

An Alice input dialog box

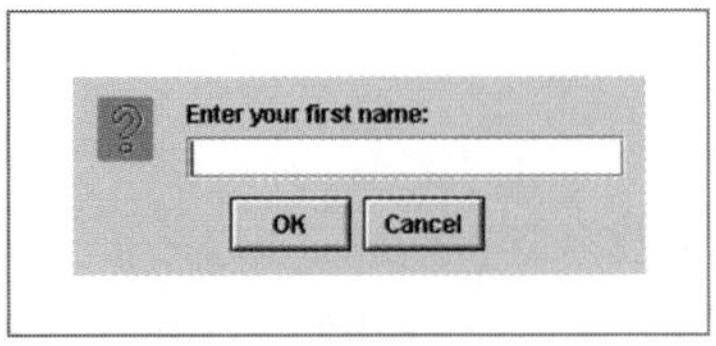

Enter your first name:

OK   Cancel

Print   The statement list under the method editor includes a `print` statement that allows you to send text output to the screen while your world is running. This output appears at the bottom of the window that opens as the world is running. It is particularly helpful when you are debugging the logic of an Alice world and you need to verify the result of a computation or determine that a method is behaving as expected.

Summary of Key Concepts

- Events are generated under various circumstances, such as when the user presses a mouse button or keyboard key.

- We can set up a program to respond to some events and ignore others.

- Some events in Alice have `Begin`, `During`, and `End` sections to tailor the way the event is handled.

- Processing events is often a better solution than a loop-based alternative.

- Keyboard events can recognize the use of any standard keyboard key, including the arrow keys, the enter key, and the space bar.

- Some events fire once when the initiating action occurs; other events fire repeatedly as long as the action is occurring.

Exercises

EX 4.1 Does an Alice world always need to use a `When the world starts` event to invoke `my first method`? Explain.

EX 4.2 What happens when an event occurs that your program is not set up to handle?

EX 4.3 Explain the difference between performing an action (like spinning windmill blades) in an infinite loop versus using a `While the world is running` event.

EX 4.4 Give an example of the same type of event being used multiple times in the same world.

EX 4.5 Give an example of the same object being manipulated in different ways by different types of events.

EX 4.6 Name and describe three events that are not caused directly by the actions of the user.

EX 4.7 Explain the difference between the `When a key is typed` and `While a key is pressed` events.

EX 4.8 Why doesn't clicking on the musician in `Rocker` world cause the guitar riff to play? How could the event processing be modified so that the sound is played if either the musician or the bass is clicked?

EX 4.9 Explain the relationship between the two events used in `Concert` world.

EX 4.10 Explain the difference between the `While something is true` and `When something becomes true` events.

PP 4.1 Create an Alice world in which several amusement park rides (ferris wheel, carousel) are moving constantly while the world is running.

PP 4.2 Create an Alice world showing two frogs prepared to jump. When the user clicks one of the frogs using the mouse, that frog should jump a random distance forward.

PP 4.3 Create an Alice world showing a kitchen environment with various appliances (refrigerator, oven, microwave, toaster) and other appropriate items created from classes in the **Kitchen** gallery. Allow the user to click on the appliances to open and close their doors and otherwise interact with the kitchen objects.

PP 4.4 Create an Alice world in which a lighthouse stands on the edge of some water. Add a light source to the lighthouse that constantly turns. Allow the user to click on the lighthouse with the mouse to turn off the light and to turn it back on again. Use the `Lighthouse` class from the **Beach** gallery and the `DirectionalLight` class from the **Lights** gallery.

PP 4.5 Create an Alice world in which a helicopter hovers, blades constantly turning. Allow the user to (1) move the helicopter up and down using the up and down arrow keys, (2) turn the helicopter to the right or left using the right and left arrow keys, and (3) move forward using the space bar.

PP 4.6 Create an Alice world in which the user can move a tank forward and backward using the up and down arrow keys, and turn right and left using the right and left arrow keys. Allow the "l" and "r" keys to rotate the tank turret left and right, respectively. Use the Tank class in the **Vehicles** gallery.

PP 4.7 Create an Alice world in which a motorboat is controlled using three arrow keys: the up arrow moves the boat forward and the right and left arrows turn the boat. Set up a series of obstacles and gates and track the time it takes the boat to reach a finish line.

PP 4.8 Create an Alice world in which the right and left arrow keys are used to move a net (made from the `HockeyGoal` class from the **Sports** gallery) right and left around the perimeter of a circle. Keep the camera behind the net as it moves. Have a ball randomly shoot out from the center of the circle in random directions and with random time delays. The goal is to move the net around the circle to catch the ball. Keep score.

PP 4.9 Create a ring catching game using a torus and cone created from the **Shapes** gallery. The ring should fall from the sky while the user moves the cone along the ground with the mouse. The user's objective is to catch the ring with the cone. Following each attempt, reset the ring's position. Stop when the user has caught 10 rings.

PP 4.10 Modify Programming Project 3.10, in which a blimp drops cargo onto ships cruising below, so that it uses events to monitor the relationship between the blimp and the ships.

CHAPTER 5

Lists and Arrays

CHAPTER OBJECTIVES

In this chapter you will:

▶ Store and manage objects in linear data structures called lists and arrays.

▶ Compare and contrast lists and arrays.

▶ Use the `For all together` and `For all in order` statements.

▶ Change the contents of lists dynamically using built-in list methods.

▶ Randomly choose an object in a list or array.

Using the techniques we've explored so far, it would be difficult to manage a herd of cattle or a large group of people. In this, our last chapter that specifically focuses on Alice, we explore concepts and programming elements that will let us develop animations that contain large groups of objects. Specifically, we explore the use of data structures called lists and arrays that help us store, organize, and manage groups of objects.

5.1 Managing Multiple Objects

The variables we've used so far to create Alice worlds refer to a single value or object. If we wanted to use three frogs in an animation, each was accessed by its own name (such as `frog`, `frog2`, and `frog3`). This approach is acceptable only when the number of objects is relatively low. What if we wanted to create a swarm of bees or have a long series of cars moving down a street? Having a separate name (variable) for every object quickly becomes unfeasible.

We want our programming solutions to *scale* as the size of the problem grows. That is, we want to express solutions in a way that is largely independent of the number of objects involved. That implies being able to manage a group of objects as a collection.

 A data structure holds and manages a group of objects using one variable name.

A *data structure* is a programming element that holds and manages several objects. A data structure is itself an object that we can access by name. We can then use special statements or build a loop to perform an operation on each object in the structure. And when we need to, a data structure provides a way to access the individual elements from the collection.

Alice supports two basic kinds of data structures: lists and arrays. Both are *linear* data structures, which means they conceptually keep objects in a particular order. Sometimes we can take advantage of this organization; sometimes the linear aspect is irrelevant.

Figure 5.1 shows a data structure managing several penguin objects. Conceptually, this structure could be either a list or an array. The name of the data structure is `colony`, and that refers to the entire collection. The numeric value shown above each object in the collection is called an *index*, which gives us a way to refer to a particular object in the group. Note that the indexes start at 0. There are 10 penguins in this data structure, indexed from 0 to 9.

Figure 5.1

A colony of penguins managed by a data structure

Lists and arrays have many of the same characteristics, and in some situations it really wouldn't matter which one you use. There are some key differences though. Lists are unbounded in terms of size—they grow and shrink as needed, whereas arrays are created with a fixed size. So in general, if the situation requires that the number of elements in the structure change over time, a list may be the best choice. However, arrays are generally more efficient internally, so if the elements in the structure are basically fixed, an array may be the way to go. We'll discuss these issues further as we explore each data structure in more detail.

> ▶ The elements stored in lists and arrays can be accessed using a numeric index, which starts at 0.

 ## Lists

The SchoolOfFish world, shown in Figure 5.2 contains ten objects created from the Fish class in the **Animals** gallery. The animation shows the fish darting around in unison, staying together in formation.

Figure 5.2

The SchoolOfFish world

To accomplish the uniform movement of all fish we could use a Do together statement with ten essentially identical instructions telling each fish to move. But even with only ten fish that would be a tedious solution. Now imagine if there were 20 fish, or 100!

Instead, we create a *list* of Fish objects, add the ten fish to the list, then use the For all together statement to have all the fish in the list move in unison. The For all together statement allows you to apply an operation to every object in a list simultaneously. The SchoolOfFish world's my first method is shown in Figure 5.3.

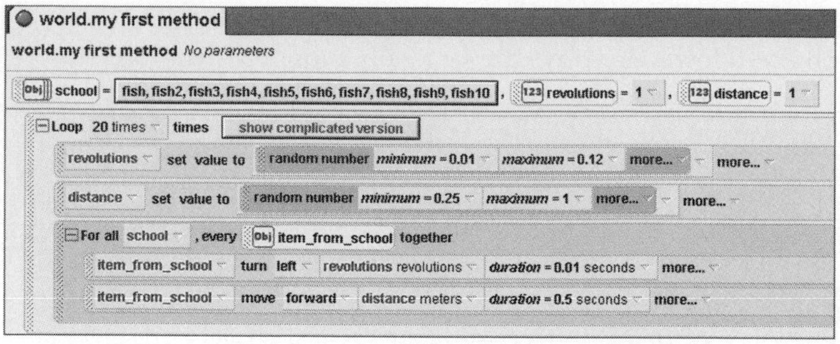

Figure 5.3

Processing in the
SchoolOfFish world

Note that in the For all together statement, "together" refers to applying an operation to all objects in the list. The statements in the For all together statement are executed sequentially (unless you use a regular Do together statement). In this example, the fish all turn in unison, and then they all move forward in unison.

You create a list variable using the create new variable button, just as you would any other. But when you check the make a List box, you're able to add multiple items to the list. See Figure 5.4.

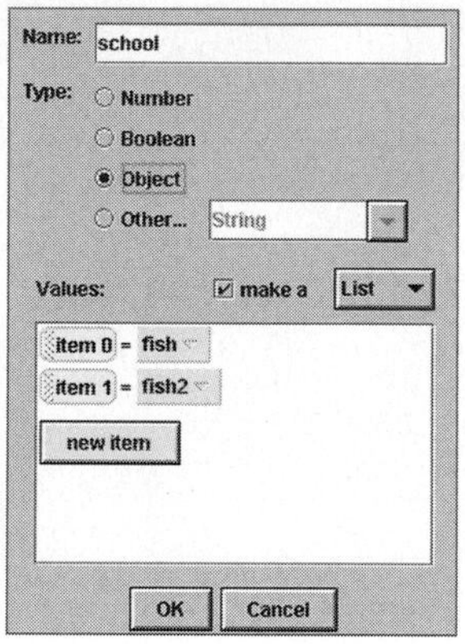

Figure 5.4

Creating a list of objects

TRY THIS!

1. Modify the SchoolOfFish world so that there is an even chance that the school will turn left or right on each iteration.

2. Modify SchoolOfFish to add a second school of fish using a different fish class.

Note that in this example the order of the fish in the list is irrelevant. We're simply capitalizing on the grouping aspect of the data structure to get them to behave as we desire.

In addition to the For all together statement, the For all in order statement can be applied to lists as well. As the name implies, the For all in order method applies an operation to every object in the list one at a time, in the order they exist in the list. That would allow you, for instance, to have a line of Rockette dancers each kick one at a time down the line.

List Methods

In addition to the two statements that can be applied to lists (`For all together` and `For all in order`), list objects have several built-in methods that can be useful as well. When you drag a list variable into a statement in the method editor, you're given the opportunity to use them, as shown in Figure 5.5.

set value ▸
insert \<item\> at beginning of world.my first method.school ▸
insert \<item\> at end of world.my first method.school ▸
insert \<item\> at position \<index\> of world.my first method.school ▸
remove item from beginning of world.my first method.school
remove item from end of world.my first method.school
remove item from position \<index\> of world.my first method.school ▸
remove all items from world.my first method.school
item responses ▸

Figure 5.5

List methods

The list methods give you the ability to insert an item at the beginning or end of a list, or at a particular index value. When inserting at position i, all items at indexes i or greater are shifted up to make room for the new item. Remember that the first item in a list has an index of 0. So if a list contains the elements

    A B C D E F

and element X is inserted at index 3, the list becomes

    A B C X D E F

Element X is now at index 3, and elements D, E, and F have been shifted to indexes 4, 5, and 6, respectively.

> ▶ When performing list operations, list elements are shifted to make room for new items or to close the gap after a removal.

The list methods also give you the ability to remove an item from the beginning or end of a list, or from a particular index value. When deleting the item at index i, all items at indexes greater than i are shifted down to "close the gap." The final list method allows you to remove all items from a list.

There are also a variety of list functions that return a value of one kind or another. When a list variable is dragged into a location where a value can be used, another pop up menu appears as shown in Figure 5.6.

first item from list
last item from list
random item from list
ith item from list ▸
is list empty
list contains ▸
size of list
first index of ▸
last index of ▸

Figure 5.6

List functions

The methods and functions that can be used with lists are also described in detail in Appendix B.

TRY THIS!

3. Modify the SchoolOfFish world so that a shark is inserted in the front of the school list and begins to swim with the school.

4. Modify the SchoolOfFish world so that in every iteration there is a 30% chance that a random fish will be removed from the school list and therefore no longer follow the others.

5.3 Arrays

As we mentioned earlier in this chapter, an array is similar to a list in many ways. They are both linear data structures and use a numeric index to access individual elements in the collection. An array is created the same way a list is. When you create a new variable, a drop-down menu lets you choose to create a list or an array. An array, however, has a fixed size after it has been created; a list can grow and shrink as needed.

The For all together and For all in order statements cannot be applied to arrays. Nor can the list methods discussed in the previous section.

> ▶ An array is generally more efficient than a list, but it has a fixed size.

So why use an array given the capacity limitations? First of all, many programming languages don't have built-in list structures—arrays may be the only choice. When both are available, an array is usually more efficient in terms of how much memory it takes up and how fast it can access its individual elements. This efficiency issue has to do with how arrays and lists are managed internally.

For this discussion, we will simply say that a good rule of thumb is to use an array when you need to access individual elements by their index values and when there is no need to change the elements stored in the array. In other cases, a list is probably a better choice.

Let's look at an example that uses an array. The WackAMole world is shown in Figure 5.7. You've likely seen this kind of game at carnivals or arcades, where a "mole" pops out of one of holes and the player tries to bop it with a mallet before it drops down into the hole again. When one mole drops down, another pops up at random.

Figure 5.7

The WackAMole world

The WackAmoleBooth class in the **Amusement Park** gallery contains a single mole object as a component piece. It also contains a bopper object. Both the mole and bopper are available as separate classes as well. In this example, we used the component version, deleting the bopper and duplicating the mole several times.

Our example simply shows the moles popping up and down. When the animation is played, one mole pops up and remains up for a randomly determined amount of time. When it drops down, another mole simultaneously pops up.

The WackAMole world's my first method is shown in Figure 5.8. We duplicated the mole object seven times, creating a total of eight, and placed the moles in the front eight holes of the booth. We also added them to an array so that they could be easily accessed by an index number. Keep in mind that array indexes start at 0.

Figure 5.8

The processing in WackAMole world

Two integer variables, index and previous, are used to keep track of the next mole to raise and mole to drop down. After raising the initial mole, an endless loop continually waits a randomly determined amount of time, randomly chooses the next mole to raise, then simultaneously drops the current one and lifts the next.

The array structure is key to this processing. First, it gives us a single variable through which the instructions to move a mole up and down can be issued. Secondly, the index values of the array give us a convenient way to randomly choose the next mole and keep track of the current one.

TRY THIS!

5. Add four more moles to the WackAMole world to fill the remaining row of holes in the booth and participate in the popping fun.

6. Modify WackAMole world so that the user can mouse click on a mole when it's raised to "wack" it. Keep track of the score.

5.4 More to Explore

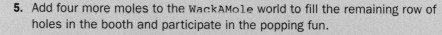

Let's conclude this last Alice chapter with a few more tips about using the Alice environment.

Saving Objects Sometime you put a lot of effort into developing the behaviors of a particular object and would like to use it or something similar in another animation. Instead of recreating the object from scratch, you'd be better off saving the object in one world and bringing it into the next. To save your object as a file, right click on it in the world view or in the object tree and choose the save object option. In another world, you can import the object using the import option on the File menu.

Opacity The opacity property of an object determines how much the user can see through it, as if it were a ghost. A value of 1.0 makes an object fully opaque (light does not pass through it), while a value of 0.0 makes an object fully invisible. One way to use this property is to make an object fade away by decreasing the opacity value slowly over time in a loop. Similarly, you could make an object fade in by increasing the value.

Textures A texture map is an image that is "wrapped" tightly around an object to give its surface a new look. In Alice you can import any graphic file (.gif, .jpeg, .bmp, or .tif) to use as a texture map in the properties panel of a particular object. Once uploaded, you can set the skin texture property of an object to the uploaded texture map image.

Summary of Key Concepts

- A data structure holds and manages a group of objects using one variable name.

- The elements stored in lists and arrays can be accessed using a numeric index, which starts at 0.

- When performing list operations, list elements are shifted to make room for new items or to close the gap after a removal.

- An array is generally more efficient than a list, but it has a fixed size.

Exercises

EX 5.1 Other than those discussed in this chapter, describe an Alice world that would be difficult to accomplish without using a data structure. Explain.

EX 5.2 What do we mean when we say we want our programming solutions to scale as the problem size grows?

EX 5.3 Compare and contrast the `For all together` and `For all in order` statements.

EX 5.4 Given the list below, what are the index values of M, G, R, and D?

    M T E G N R A Y D

EX 5.5 Given the list below, what would the list look like after inserting X at index 2? What are the index values of W and G after the insertion is performed?

    L W B Q K G P

EX 5.6 Given the list below, what would the list look like after removing the element at index 4? What are the index values of Z and B after the removal is performed?

    Z E V M K B S C U A G

EX 5.7 A list is a linear structure, but the fish in `SchoolOfFish` world are not arranged in a line. Explain.

EX 5.8 When is it appropriate to use an array instead of a list?

EX 5.9 What is the highest index of an array that can hold 55 elements?

EX 5.10 How would you create an array of numbers in Alice?

Programming Projects

PP 5.1   Create an Alice world in which a group of ballerinas dance in unison, making appropriate poses and turns.

PP 5.2   Create an Alice world in which a line of Rockettes performs various kicks and turns in unison. Also include some moves that are executed in sequence down the line.

PP 5.3   In 1978 a disco group called the Village People had a hit song called "Y.M.C.A.", which became a cult classic. Create an Alice world in which four characters perform the "Y.M.C.A." dance in unison, making the basic letter shapes using their arms.

PP 5.4   Create an Alice world that simulates people waiting in line at a bank teller window. Randomly determine the amount of time it takes to serve each customer. When a customer leaves, each person in line should move forward one space. Display the wait time for each customer when the customer is finally served.

PP 5.5 Create an Alice world in which a group of 12 soldiers march in three rows of four soldiers each. After marching forward a certain distance, have the soldiers halt and salute. Use the `ToySoldier` class from the **People** gallery.

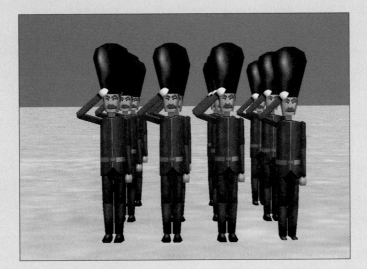

PP 5.6 Create an Alice world in which an entire squad of cheerleaders performs various cheerleading moves in unison. Include some actions that each cheerleader in the squad performs solo, one after the other. You may want to base your cheerleader object on the one in the `Cheerleader` world example from Chapter 2.

PP 5.7 Programming Project 4.9 proposed a basic ring catching game that used a torus and a cone made from classes in the **Shapes** gallery. Using an array of torus objects, extend this idea so that multiple rings can fall at the same time at different speeds. Increase the quantity of the rings as the game progresses. Keep track of the number of rings caught and missed.

PP 5.8 Create an Alice world that presents a game in which anvils fall from the sky. The user's goal is to use the mouse to click on each anvil before it reaches the ground. Use an array of objects created from the `Anvil` class in the **Objects** gallery. For each anvil, randomly determine its location and falling speed. Keep track of the number of anvils caught and missed.

PP 5.9 Create an Alice world that plays a game in which a tank shoots at planes that are crossing in the distance. Use the `Tank` class in the **Vehicles** gallery. Allow the user to rotate the turret right and left and change the angle of the barrel up or down using the arrow keys. Use the space bar to "fire" a ball. Store various types of planes in an array to use as the targets, moving them across the sky at various heights and distances. Keep track of the number of hits.

PP 5.10 Create an Alice world that plays a memory game (sometimes called Simon) in which four buttons are presented to the user. The buttons light up in a particular sequence that the user has to match by clicking the same sequence of buttons with the mouse. Have each button "light up" by changing its color briefly both when the sequence is played and when the user presses the button. The length of the sequence increases by one each time. Play continues until the user makes a mistake or does not press the correct button within a short period of time. Use the `Button` class in the **Controls** gallery to make the button set.

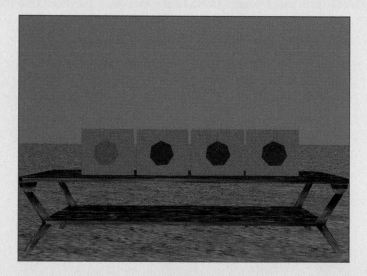

Transition to Java

CHAPTER OBJECTIVES

In this chapter you will:

▶ Compare the concepts you saw in Alice to their counterparts in Java.

▶ Learn about program development environments for Java.

▶ Access the Java API support library and its online documentation.

▶ Explore several Java program examples.

▶ Practice using various Java statements.

▶ Explore the basics of the ThunkIt program example.

With this chapter, we turn our focus away from Alice and begin to embrace Java. The beautiful thing about this transition is that many of the concepts you learned while using Alice also apply in Java. This chapter introduces the Java programming language and several issues related to Java programming. It also introduces the ThunkIt program, a puzzle game that we will use as an example throughout the rest of this book.

6.1 Comparing Alice and Java

In the previous chapters of this book, our focus was creating worlds in Alice. We saw how Alice animations are made up of objects, which are created from classes. An object has methods, which we call to get the object to behave in specific ways. An object also has properties, which we set and change as needed. All of these concepts apply to Java programs as well.

Before we dive into the details of some Java examples, let's begin by comparing Alice and Java. A general comparison of Alice and Java is provided in Table 6.1. This comparison is simply an overview—we'll explore these issues further as needed.

Table 6.1

A comparison of Alice and Java

Alice	Java
Used to create animations.	Used for many purposes.
One drag-and-drop development environment.	Many development environments; most are text oriented.
Programs (worlds) can be executed (played) immediately.	Programs must be compiled before they can be executed.
Environment prevents syntax and usage errors.	Compiler reports syntax and usage errors.
All objects are created before the world is played.	Objects are created dynamically as needed during program execution.
Objects are set up through direct manipulation in the environment.	Objects are set up using constructors.
New methods and properties are added to objects (not classes).	Methods and properties are defined in classes.
Only predefined classes can be used.	Predefined classes are available but the programmer can create any other classes needed.
Classes are organized into galleries.	Classes are organized into packages and imported as needed.
No clear use of inheritance.	Inheritance is used to derive new classes.
Strongly typed.	Strongly typed.
Has various predefined data types.	Has eight primitive data types plus unlimited object types (classes).
Assignment, equality, relational, and logical operators.	Similar functionality although some operators are different.
Text output using the `print` statement.	Text output using calls to the `print` or `println` methods.

Control statements for decisions and repetition.	Similar control statements.
Has statements for concurrency (such as `Do together`).	Achieves concurrency via threads.
One type of comment.	Three types of comments.
Processing begins with `my first method`.	Processing begins with the `main` method.

Alice is a wonderful environment for creating animations and for teaching the basics of object-oriented programming. Unfortunately, that dedicated purpose is also limiting. To create other types of programs, we need a more versatile language. As we mentioned in Chapter 1, Java is a *general-purpose programming language*, which can be used to create just about any kind of program. Using Alice as our springboard, we'll now enter a programming world with virtually no limits.

Program Development

The Alice environment, with its method editor, object tree, and other features, is an *integrated development environment* (IDE). It's really the only development environment you can use to create Alice animations. By contrast, there are many development environments that you can use to create and test Java programs, including jGRASP, DrJava, Eclipse, and NetBeans. These environments all have their own set of tools to manage the classes and objects you create. Your instructor may direct you to use a particular development environment. We don't assume the use of any particular one in this book, though there are several IDEs provided on the book's CD for your use.

> ▶ You can use one of several development environments to create Java programs.

Most Java development environments have you create and edit a method by typing the program statements. This is in contrast to the Alice environment, where you drag statements and objects around and select values from drop-down menus. Both approaches have advantages and disadvantages. Text-based editing is more flexible, but it allows you to make more mistakes. The drag-and-drop approach eliminates some potential problems, but can be annoying as you become more experienced.

To get a Java program up and running, the classes involved must be translated into an executable form. A programmer writes classes in Java *source code*, which a tool called the *compiler* translates into Java *bytecode*. It's actually the bytecode that gets interpreted and executed when the program is run. This compilation step was hidden in Alice.

> ▶ Java code gets translated into bytecode before it is executed.

The compiler also looks for problems with your program and will issue error messages accordingly. If any errors are detected during compilation, the bytecode version of the program is not created. *Compile-time errors* are issued if your program breaks the language's *syntax* rules, such as forgetting a semicolon where one is needed, or if you use an object in an inappropriate way, such as calling a method that doesn't exist. The drag-and-drop nature of the Alice method editor avoids compile-time problems by filling in the code details automatically and only allowing you to use appropriate program elements.

> ▶ A program may have syntax errors, which the compiler will catch, and logic errors, which it will not.

Of course, getting a program to execute doesn't mean it's free of errors. In both Alice and Java, we have to deal with *logical errors*, which occur if a program produces incorrect results or otherwise behaves in an unintended manner. Some logical errors cause a program to terminate abnormally.

Figure 6.1 shows a very basic view of the program development process with the compilation step thrown into the mix. After editing your program, you attempt to compile it. If compile-time errors occur, you modify the program as needed to eliminate them. If the program compiles correctly, you run the program, evaluate the results, and then fix any logical errors.

Figure 6.1

Basic program development with a compilation step

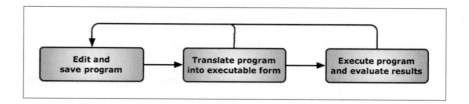

Classes and Objects

In Alice, you create an object by clicking on its class in the gallery and adding it to the world (or dragging it into the world). In Java, you create an object by executing a programming statement, as shown in Figure 6.2.

Figure 6.2

Creating an object in Java

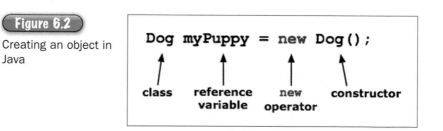

> ▶ A constructor is used to set up a newly created object.

This statement creates a new object called myPuppy from the Dog class. More precisely, it creates a new Dog object using the new operator, sets up the object using a special method called a *constructor*, and assigns the new object to the myPuppy variable. A constructor has the same name as the class from which the object is created, and it often takes parameters that define the initial value of certain properties.

Being able to create an object dynamically in a program is a great advantage. If we want a swarm of bees in an Alice world, we have to create all of the bee objects separately. In Java, a program statement that creates an object can be put in a loop so that multiple objects can be created in the blink of an eye. Furthermore, we can wait until we need an object to create it—we don't have to create every possible object that we might want in a program beforehand.

In Alice, new methods and properties can be added to a particular object that we have already added to the world. Other objects, even those created from the same class, cannot use the new method (though we can duplicate the object after it was added). In Java, all methods and properties are defined to be part of a class, and any object created from that class can make use of them.

Alice has a set of predefined classes from which we can create objects and it is essentially impossible to create new classes. Java has an extensive library of predefined classes as well. Plus, in Java, we can create our own classes as needed.

Alice classes are organized into galleries. Similarly, Java classes are organized into *packages*. When you want to use a class, you *import* it so that it can be referenced appropriately. The library of predefined classes is often referred to as the *Java API*, which stands for application programming interface. The Java API is made up of hundreds of classes organized into dozens of packages. An extensive online reference to the Java API is available, as shown in Figure 6.3. This is a valuable reference that you should bookmark and get comfortable using.

> ▶ The Java API is a library of classes that we can use in any Java program.

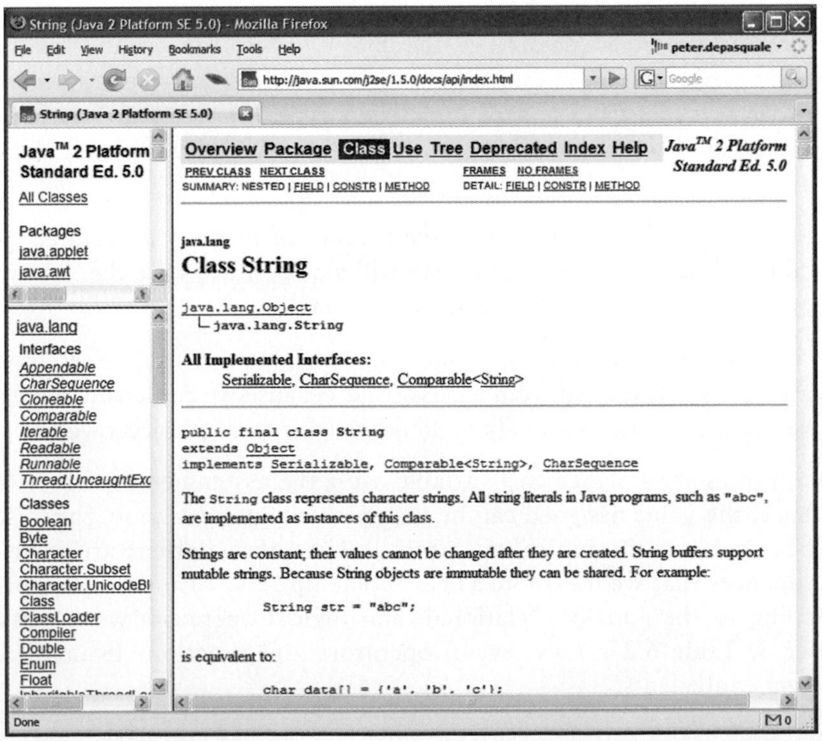

Figure 6.3

The Java API online reference

There's one more important idea to get onto the table at this point. In an object-oriented language such as Java, a class can be created from another class using *inheritance*. That is, a *child class* can be derived from an existing *parent class*, automatically inheriting the methods and properties of the parent. The child class can then distinguish itself from its parent by adding other methods and properties as appropriate.

For example, a class called `Car` could serve as the parent of a class called `Porsche`. Establishing this relationship automatically makes all methods and properties of the `Car` class part of the `Porsche` class as well. We can then add methods and properties that distinguish a Porsche from other cars.

A limited form of inheritance occurs in Alice behind the scenes when modified objects are duplicated, but that situation is so convoluted that we didn't even broach the subject when discussing Alice. Inheritance in Java is much more straightforward. We'll see the basic concept of inheritance come up in various examples, and we explore it fully in Chapter 9.

Data and Operators

Both Alice and Java are *strongly typed* languages. As with Alice, that means that each variable must be *declared* before being used, establishing the particular type of data that it will hold. Any use of a variable must be consistent with its type. Therefore, the Java compiler will issue an error message if, for instance, you attempt to assign an integer value to a variable that's been declared to refer to a `Dog` object.

In addition to the object data types, the data types we can use in Alice include `Number`, `String`, and `Boolean`. Java has eight primitive data types: four types of integers (`byte`, `short`, `int`, and `long`), two types of floating point numbers (`float` and `double`), a character data type (`char`), and a Boolean data type (`boolean`).

The numeric primitive types differ in the amount of memory space used to hold their values, which is rarely an issue. We will almost always use the `int` type for integers and the `double` type for floating point values.

The primitive data types in Java are built into the language itself. Everything else in Java is an object, created from a class. And because we can create any type of class we need, there are essentially no limits to the types of objects we can create.

In Java, values are assigned to a variable using the assignment operator (=). As with Alice, the value assigned can be the result of an *expression*. Java uses the same basic set of mathematical operators as Alice, though there are some interesting nuances that we'll explore as they come up. Java also has operators corresponding to the equality, relational, and logical operators we discussed in Chapter 3. Table 6.2 shows several operators and functions from Alice and their Java equivalents.

	Alice	Java
Assignment	`set value`	`=`
Basic Arithmetic	+, −, *, /	+, −, *, /
Remainder	`IEEERemainder`	`%`
Equality	==, !=	==, !=
Relational	<, <=, >, >=	<, <=, >, >=
Logical NOT	`not a`	`!a`
Logical AND	`both a and b`	`a && b`
Logical OR	`either a or b, or both`	`a || b`

Table 6.2

Some operators in Alice and Java

Statements

The Java assignment statement uses the = operator. For example:

```
total = total + 25;
```

The `print` statement in Alice is a quick way to get text or numeric output, which is especially useful for debugging. In Java, similar output is produced using the `print` and `println` (pronounced "print line") methods, which are called through the `System.out` object. For example:

```
System.out.println("The result is: " + total);
```

This statement concatenates the current value of `total` to the string and prints it. The `println` method causes the output to move to the next line after printing, whereas the `print` method does not.

Java has similar control statements to Alice. They include an *if-else statement* for making decisions, and various statements that perform repetition. We'll see these in use as they come up.

```
if (height > 69)
   height = height / 2;
else
   System.out.println("Current height: " + height);
```

The `else` portion of an `if` statement can be omitted in Java if it is not needed. This is similar to the idea of a *Do Nothing* section in Alice. If more than one statement should be executed in either part, the statements must be enclosed in braces.

Java does not have a statement similar to the `Do together` statement in Alice, which directs a group of statements to be executed at the same time. This kind of *concurrency* is accomplished in Java using *threads*, which are created using specific classes. Threads are discussed in Chapter 9.

When a world first starts up in Alice, the method called my first method in the world object is executed. This is the default starting point of every world, which drives the rest of the animation. Similarly, when a Java program executes, the main method is executed first, which drives all other program activity. We define the main method as part of any class we choose to be the driver of our program.

6.2 Java Classes and Objects

Let's explore a Java program that simply displays three colored circles in a window. A screen shot of the DrawCircles program is shown in Figure 6.4.

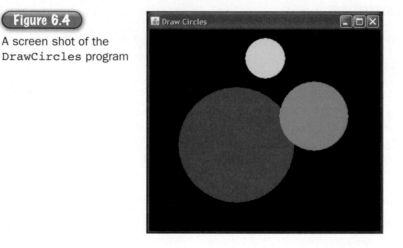

Figure 6.4

A screen shot of the DrawCircles program

In this example, each circle is an object. The window *frame* is another object. And the circles are drawn on an object called a *panel* that sits inside the frame.

Each of these objects has properties and methods. Each circle, for example, has properties that define its color, size, and location on the screen. A circle also has methods for drawing it in the window. The window frame has a method that lets us control what happens when the "close" button on the frame is pressed. The panel has methods that allow us to set its background color and its size.

Listing 6.1 shows the DrawCircles class, which contains the main method of the program. In Java, an entire class is defined in one file, including all of its properties and methods. In this case, the DrawCircles class has no properties and only one method.

Listing 6.1

```
//**************************************************************************
//   DrawCircles.java        Programming with Alice and Java
//
//   Demonstrates the use of a frame containing a panel on which shapes can
//   be drawn.
//**************************************************************************

import javax.swing.JFrame;

public class DrawCircles
{
   //-------------------------------------------------------------------------
   //   Creates and displays the application frame, which contains the drawing
   //   panel.
   //-------------------------------------------------------------------------
   public static void main(String[] args)
   {
      CirclePanel panel = new CirclePanel();

      JFrame frame = new JFrame("Draw Circles");

      frame.getContentPane().add(panel);
      frame.setDefaultCloseOperation(JFrame.EXIT_ON_CLOSE);
      frame.pack();
      frame.setVisible(true);
   }
}
```

As with Alice, comments (shown in green type) are included to document the purpose of the classes and methods, but otherwise have no effect on the program. Words in blue type are *reserved words* in the Java programming language.

The class definition begins with the line

```
public class DrawCircles
```

which is called the *class header*. The class includes everything between its opening brace ({) right after the header and closing brace (}) on the last line.

The main method is defined in a similar manner, starting with the *method header*

```
public static void main(String[] args)
```

and including everything within its braces. We'll explain the purpose of the reserved words public and static a bit later, as well as the method parameters. For now you simply need to know that a Java program needs to have a main method defined this way. When the program is executed, this method is executed first and drives everything else. That is, the DrawCircles class is the program *driver*.

Note that indentation is used to show containment—methods within classes and statements within methods. Although the computer doesn't care about indentation, it is important for human readability.

The `main` method first creates the panel on which the circles will be drawn. It then creates the frame used to display the panel, adds the panel to the frame, and calls a few other frame methods to set the stage properly. Note that both the panel and the frame objects are created, or *instantiated*, using the `new` operator. The panel is defined by the `CirclePanel` class, which we'll examine in detail shortly.

The frame is defined by the `JFrame` class, which is part of the Java API (the class library). Unlike the `CirclePanel` class, we did not write the `JFrame` class ourselves, we simply use it. The `import` statement above the class header informs the compiler that we will be using the `JFrame` class, which is part of the `javax.swing` package. The constructor of the `JFrame` class accepts a string parameter that is displayed in the frame's title bar.

The methods called on the frame object perform some important preparation steps. First, the panel is added to the frame—or, technically, to the *content pane* of the frame. A panel cannot be displayed by itself—it must be added to a window such as a frame. Then, the `setDefaultCloseOperation` method determines what will happen when the user presses the red X button in the corner of the frame. In this case we simply opted to terminate the program (exit), using a constant from the `JFrame` class. The `pack` method sizes the frame so that it fits tightly around its contents, in this case the panel. Finally, the `setVisible` method makes the frame appear on the monitor screen.

Now let's turn our attention to the `CirclePanel` class, shown in Listing 6.2. It extends the `JPanel` class, which means it inherits all the characteristics of a `JPanel` object. Because a `JPanel` object can be added to a frame, we were allowed to add our `CirclePanel` object to the frame in the `main` method. We discuss inheritance in more detail in Chapter 9.

Listing 6.2

```
//***********************************************************************
//  CirclePanel.java          Programming with Alice and Java
//
//  Represents the drawing panel in the DrawCircles program.
//***********************************************************************

import java.awt.*;
import javax.swing.JPanel;

public class CirclePanel extends JPanel
{
   private Circle circle1, circle2, circle3;
```

Listing 6.2 (continued)

```java
//--------------------------------------------------------------
//  Creates three Circle objects and sets panel characteristics.
//--------------------------------------------------------------
public CirclePanel()
{
    circle1 = new Circle(150, 200, 100, Color.red);
    circle2 = new Circle(200, 50, 35, Color.yellow);
    circle3 = new Circle(285, 150, 60, Color.green);

    setBackground(Color.black);
    setPreferredSize(new Dimension(400, 350));
}


//--------------------------------------------------------------
// Draws three circles on the panel.
//--------------------------------------------------------------
public void paintComponent(Graphics gc)
{
    super.paintComponent(gc);

    circle1.drawFilled(gc);
    circle2.drawFilled(gc);
    circle3.drawFilled(gc);
}
}
```

The CirclePanel class contains three Circle objects as properties (or instance data). The variables that refer to the objects are called circle1, circle2, and circle3. These variables are declared inside the class, but not in any method. That way, every method in the class can access them.

The CirclePanel contains two methods. More precisely, it contains a constructor called CirclePanel (same name as the class) and a method called paintComponent. The CirclePanel constructor was called when the panel was created in the main method. It creates the three circle objects using the new operator and sets some characteristics of the panel.

The paintComponent method is called whenever the panel needs to be rendered on the screen. The call to super.paintComponent makes sure the background of the panel is painted. Then the drawFilled method of each circle is called to draw the circles.

Note the use of the reserved words public and private throughout this class. These are *visibility modifiers*, which determine the scope of the things they modify. Classes and their methods are often declared public so that other classes can make use of them. Instance data is often private, so that other objects cannot reach in and

▶ Encapsulation is the concept that each object should manage its own data and prevent explicit external modifications.

modify them. This is the basis of the object-oriented concept of *encapsulation*—every object manages its own data. Alice had no real restrictions in this regard.

The Circle class is shown in Listing 6.3. It contains instance data that represents the circle's radius, color, and the (*x*, *y*) coordinate of the circle's center point. These values are set in the Circle constructor, which was called when each Circle object was created in the CirclePanel constructor.

Listing 6.3

```
//*************************************************************************
//  Circle.java        Programming with Alice and Java
//
//  Represents a circle with a particular size, color, and location. The
//  circle can be drawn filled or unfilled.
//*************************************************************************

import java.awt.*;

public class Circle
{
   private int radius;
   private Color color;
   private int x, y; // the circle's center point

   //-------------------------------------------------------------------
   //  Sets up the circle with the specified location, size, and color.
   //-------------------------------------------------------------------
   public Circle(int xCenter, int yCenter, int size, Color circleColor)
   {
      x = xCenter;
      y = yCenter;
      radius = size;
      color = circleColor;
   }

   //-------------------------------------------------------------------
   // Draws the circle, filled, in the specified graphics context.
   //-------------------------------------------------------------------
   public void drawFilled(Graphics gc)
   {
      gc.setColor(color);
      gc.fillOval(x − radius, y − radius, radius * 2, radius * 2);
   }

   //-------------------------------------------------------------------
   // Draws the circle, unfilled (outline only), in the specified graphics
```

Listing 6.3 (continued)

```
    // context.
    //----------------------------------------------------------
    public void drawUnfilled(Graphics gc)
    {
        gc.setColor(color);
        gc.drawOval(x − radius, y − radius, radius * 2, radius * 2);
    }
}
```

The `Circle` class has two methods for drawing the circle, one filled and one unfilled (creating just an outline where you can see the background underneath). In this example, only filled circles are drawn. A class will often have methods that a program does not use.

The coordinate system in Java has the origin in the upper left corner, as shown in Figure 6.5. Curved shapes are drawn using a *bounding rectangle*, as shown in Figure 6.6. The parameters to both the `fillOval` and `drawOval` methods are the *x* and *y* coordinates of the upper left corner, the oval's width, and the oval's height. Because we are drawing a circle, the width and height are the same.

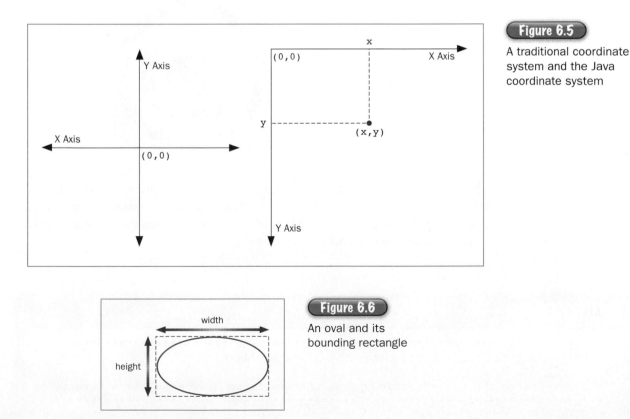

Figure 6.5

A traditional coordinate system and the Java coordinate system

Figure 6.6

An oval and its bounding rectangle

The Graphics class is defined in the java.awt package. It contains various methods to draw shapes. Each drawing surface (such as a panel) has its own *graphics context*, which is why we abbreviate the Graphics variable gc.

TRY THIS!

1. Modify the DrawCircles program so that it draws the green circle unfilled.

2. Change the color, size, and location of all three circles in the DrawCircles program.

3. Create and draw a fourth circle in the DrawCircles program.

6.3 Java Statements

Let's now examine several other examples of Java programs in order to explore various statements. A screen shot of the Bullseye program is shown in Figure 6.7. It draws concentric circles of alternating colors, with a red circle in the center, to depict a target.

Figure 6.7

A screen shot of the Bullseye program

The Bullseye class, which contains the main method, is shown in Listing 6.4. It is virtually identical to the driver class of the DrawCircles program in that it creates and sets up the program frame. Many of our Java programs that have a graphical component will have a similar main method.

Listing 6.4

```
//************************************************************************
//   Bullseye.java          Programming with Alice and Java
//
//   Demonstrates the use of various Java statements to draw a bullseye target.
//************************************************************************
```

Listing 6.4 (continued)

```java
import javax.swing.JFrame;

public class Bullseye
{
    //-----------------------------------------------------------------
    // Creates and displays the program frame.
    //-----------------------------------------------------------------
    public static void main(String[] args)
    {
        JFrame frame = new JFrame("Bullseye");
        frame.getContentPane().add(new BullseyePanel());
        frame.setDefaultCloseOperation(JFrame.EXIT_ON_CLOSE);
        frame.pack();
        frame.setVisible(true);
    }
}
```

Like the CirclePanel class, the BullseyePanel (see Listing 6.5) is derived from the JPanel class, which is why we can add it to the frame to be displayed. The BullseyePanel constructor sets the background and size of the panel. The paint-Component method uses a for loop to draw the concentric rings from the outside in. Note that in this example we are not using the Circle class—we simply draw the shape when needed.

Listing 6.5

```java
//************************************************************************
//  BullseyePanel.java         Programming with Alice and Java
//
//  Represents the panel on which the bullseye target is drawn.
//************************************************************************

import javax.swing.JPanel;
import java.awt.*;

public class BullseyePanel extends JPanel
{
    private final int MAX_WIDTH = 300, NUM_RINGS = 5, RING_WIDTH = 25;
```

Listing 6.5 (continued)

```java
//---------------------------------------------------------------
// Sets the panel characteristics.
//---------------------------------------------------------------
public BullseyePanel()
{
   setBackground(Color.cyan);
   setPreferredSize(new Dimension(300, 300));
}

//---------------------------------------------------------------
// Draws the bullseye target.
//---------------------------------------------------------------
public void paintComponent(Graphics gc)
{
   super.paintComponent(gc);

   int x = 0, y = 0, diameter = MAX_WIDTH;

   gc.setColor(Color.white);

   for (int count = 0; count < NUM_RINGS; count++)
   {
      if (gc.getColor() == Color.black) // alternate colors
         gc.setColor(Color.white);
      else
         gc.setColor(Color.black);

      gc.fillOval(x, y, diameter, diameter);

      diameter = diameter − (2 * RING_WIDTH);
      x = x + RING_WIDTH;
      y = y + RING_WIDTH;
   }

   // Draw the red bullseye in the center
   gc.setColor(Color.red);
   gc.fillOval(x, y, diameter, diameter);
   }
}
```

The for loop is similar to the complete version of the one used in Alice. The header of the for loop declares the variable count and initializes it to 0. After each iteration, the value of count is incremented. The loop continues until the value of count becomes equal to the value of the constant NUM_RINGS.

In each iteration of the loop, the current color of the graphics context is obtained. If it's black, the drawing color is set to white; if it's white, it's set to black. After drawing the circle, the diameter and location of the next circle is set. After the loop finishes, the red bullseye in the center is drawn.

TRY THIS!

4. Modify the `Bullseye` program so that the largest ring is white and the others alternate accordingly.

5. Modify the `Bullseye` program so that there are approximately twice as many rings that are each half as thin.

Now let's examine a Java program that does not have a graphical component. All input and output will occur in a text window. The `CoinFlip` program flips a virtual coin a certain number of times, keeping track of how many heads and tails result. A sample run of the `CoinFlip` program is shown in Figure 6.8.

```
How many flips (1-1000)? 5000
Not in range. How many flips (1-1000)? 1001
Not in range. How many flips (1-1000)? 0
Not in range. How many flips (1-1000)? 500

Total number of flips: 500
Heads: 258    Tails: 242
```

Figure 6.8

A sample run of the `CoinFlip` program

The `CoinFlip` class, containing the `main` method of the program, is shown in Listing 6.6. It makes use of the `Scanner` class to read input from the keyboard. A `System.out.print` statement is used to ask the user how many flips should be performed, specifying a range of 1 to 1000 for the response. The call to `scan.nextInt` causes the program to pause and wait for the user to enter a response. When the user presses Enter, the program stores the number of flips and continues executing.

Listing 6.6

```
//********************************************************************
//  CoinFlip.java        Programming with Alice and Java
//
//  Demonstrates the use of various Java statements.
//********************************************************************

import java.util.Scanner;

public class CoinFlip
{
   //-----------------------------------------------------------------
   //  Flips a coin several times, counting the number of heads and tails
```

Listing 6.6 (continued)

```java
//   that result.
//---------------------------------------------------------------------------
public static void main(String[] args)
{
    Scanner scan = new Scanner(System.in);
    System.out.print("How many flips (1-1000)? ");
    int flips = scan.nextInt();
    while (flips < 1 || flips > 1000)
    {
        System.out.print("Not in range. How many flips (1-1000)? ");
        flips = scan.nextInt();
    }

    Coin myCoin = new Coin();
    int heads = 0, tails = 0;

    for (int count=1; count <= flips; count++)
    {
        myCoin.flip();
        if (myCoin.isHeads())
            heads = heads + 1;
        else
            tails = tails + 1;
    }

    System.out.println();
    System.out.println("Total number of flips: " + flips);
    System.out.println("Heads: " + heads + "  Tails: " + tails);
}
}
```

The while loop then performs *input validation*. If the number of flips entered is in the proper range, the body of the while loop is never executed and processing continues. However, if the value is out of range, the user is prompted again and the value of flips is read again. Then the while loop evaluates the new input value. Processing stays locked in that loop until the user enters a value in the requested range.

Once we have a good input value, an object of type Coin is created. Then, using a for loop, the coin is flipped as many times as was specified. After each flip, one of two counters is updated to reflect the number of heads and tails that occur. After the loop concludes, the results are printed.

The Coin class is shown in Listing 6.7. It represents a single coin that can be flipped. The instance data of the coin stores the current face value as an integer, where 0 means heads and 1 means tails. The flip method calls the random method of the Math class to generate a random number between 0 and 1. That number is multiplied by 2 and converted (cast) into an integer, producing a random result of 0 or 1.

Listing 6.7

```java
//*****************************************************************************
//  Coin.java          Programming with Alice and Java
//
//   Represents a coin with two sides that can be flipped.
//*****************************************************************************

public class Coin
{
   private final int HEADS = 0, TAILS = 1;

   private int face; // current face showing on the coin

   //---------------------------------------------------------------------
   //  Sets up the coin by flipping it initially.
   //---------------------------------------------------------------------
   public Coin()
   {
      flip();
   }

   //---------------------------------------------------------------------
   // Flips the coin by randomly choosing a face value.
   //---------------------------------------------------------------------
   public void flip()
   {
      face = (int) (Math.random() * 2);
   }

   //---------------------------------------------------------------------
   // Returns true if the current face of the coin is heads.
   //---------------------------------------------------------------------
   public boolean isHeads()
   {
      return (face == HEADS);
   }
   //---------------------------------------------------------------------
   // Returns the current face of the coin as a string.
   //---------------------------------------------------------------------
   public String toString()
   {
      String faceName = "Heads";

      if (face != HEADS)
         faceName = "Tails";

      return faceName;
   }
}
```

▶ The toString method is called automatically when an object is printed.

The constructor calls flip initially to give the coin an initial random face value. The isHeads method returns a boolean result that is true if the face of the coin is currently heads (if not, it must be tails). Finally, the toString method is used to return a character string that represents the object. In this case, the toString method returns simply "Heads" or "Tails."

The toString method gets called automatically when an object is passed to a print or println method to be printed. In this example, the toString method is never called, but it's usually a good idea to define a toString method for most objects.

TRY THIS!

6. Modify the CoinFlip program so that it allows up to 10,000 flips.

7. Modify the CoinFlip program so that the Coin class uses an isTails method instead of isHeads.

6.4 Introduction to ThunkIt

We mentioned in Chapter 1 that, once we transitioned to Java, we would not only look at smaller programs, but also examine a large program called ThunkIt. Although there is much about the ThunkIt code you won't understand at this point, it's helpful to read code as well as write it. And you might be surprised, even with only one chapter's exposure to Java, how much of the basic processing you'll follow.

ThunkIt is a game. So, if you haven't already, the first step is to play it. A screen shot is shown in Figure 6.9. Get to know how it works and what its capabilities are from a user's perspective. The first thing you'll notice is that there are objects all over the place. During game play, the student character (an object) collects school supplies and moves blocks and barrels (more objects). Think a bit more and you'll come up with lots of other objects in the game, such as user interface buttons and various screens. Each play level is represented as an object. The grid in which the game is played is an object. The list of inventory items the student collects is an object.

Figure 6.9

A ThunkIt game level

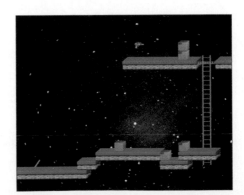

After playing the game, dive into the code. See how the various classes are organized into packages based on the role they play. Find the `main` method in the ThunkIt class and notice how similar it is to the graphics programs we explored in this chapter. Open up various class files at random and peruse the code. Notice the many statements that you can follow the logic of.

Note that the comment style used in the ThunkIt code is different from the style we've used in smaller programs. ThunkIt uses the javadoc commenting style. Javadoc is a tool that converts the javadoc comments in a program's classes and methods into web-based documentation for the program or system. This is the technique that was used to create the online documentation for the Java API. Javadoc comments are not particularly helpful for small programs, so in those cases we'll continue to stick with the alternate style.

As we continue to explore Java in subsequent chapters, we will also delve into specific details of the ThunkIt code.

TRY THIS!

8. Recompile the ThunkIt game, just to go through the process with a large program.

6.5 More to Explore

Java API Take some time to get comfortable navigating and reading the Java API documentation online. Although there will be many aspects of it that will not be clear at this point, the sooner you learn to use that resource the better off you'll be. Look up classes that we've mentioned in this chapter, such as `String`, and read about some of the many methods it provides.

Graphics Methods In this chapter we explored a few of the methods provided by the `Graphics` class for drawing shapes. You'll want to read about the other methods it has for drawing rectangles, arcs, etc.

Additional Operators Java has a wealth of operators, some of which simply provide convenient ways to accomplish the same computations that you could do another way. For example, the `+=` operator combines the process of adding something to a variable and assigning the result back into that variable. If you explore these additional capabilities of the language, you'll give yourself more options when it comes to writing code.

Summary of Key Concepts

- You can use one of several development environments to create Java programs.

- Java code gets translated into bytecode before it is executed.

- A program may have syntax errors, which the compiler will catch, and logic errors, which it will not.

- A constructor is used to set up a newly created object.

- The Java API is a library of classes that we can use in any Java program.

- Encapsulation is the concept that each object should manage its own data and prevent explicit external modifications.

- The toString method is called automatically when an object is printed.

Exercises

EX 6.1 Write a while loop that verifies that the user has entered a positive integer value.

EX 6.2 Write a for loop that computes the sum of the numbers from 20 to 60, inclusive.

EX 6.3 Write a for loop that prints the odd numbers from 1 to 99, inclusive.

EX 6.4 Write a code fragment that reads 10 integer values from the user and then prints the highest value entered.

EX 6.5 Write a method called powersOfTwo that prints the first 10 powers of 2 (starting with 2). The method takes no parameters and doesn't return anything.

EX 6.6 Write a method called larger that accepts two floating point parameters (of type double) and returns true if the first parameter is greater than the second, and false otherwise.

EX 6.7 Write a method called sumRange that accepts two integer parameters representing a range. Issue an error message and return zero if the second parameter is less than the first. Otherwise, the method should return the sum of the integers in the range, inclusive.

EX 6.8 What are the names and types of the instance data in the PlayManager class from ThunkIt?

EX 6.9 How many methods are in the `Cell` class from ThunkIt? How many of those methods return a value?

EX 6.10 Print a copy of the `LevelManager` class from ThunkIt and highlight all of the conditionals and loops in it.

Programming Projects

PP 6.1 Using the `Circle` class from this chapter, create a Java program that draws 100 circles of random size, color, and location. Ensure that in each case the entire circle appears in the visible area of the panel.

PP 6.2 Using the `Coin` class from this chapter, create a Java program that flips two coins until one of them comes up heads three times in a row.

PP 6.3 Create a Java program that displays 20 horizontal, evenly spaced parallel lines of random length.

PP 6.4 Create a program that draws 10,000 points in random locations within the visible area. Make the points on the left half of the panel appear in red and the points on the right half of the panel appear in green. Draw each point by drawing a line segment that is only one pixel in length.

PP 6.5 Create a program that draws a simple picket fence with vertical, equally spaced slats backed by two horizontal support boards. Show a simple house in the background behind the fence.

PP 6.6 Create a class called `Star` that represents a five-pointed star of a particular size and color. Then write a program that creates and draws four stars of various sizes at different locations.

PP 6.7 Create a class called `Account` that represents a basic bank account, keeping track of the account balance and providing methods to process deposits and withdrawals. Print an error message if an attempt is made to withdraw more than the current balance. Include a `toString` method that summarizes the state of the account. Create a driver program that creates two `Account` objects and processes various transactions.

PP 6.8 Create a class called `Die` that represents a single six-sided die (as in the singular of dice). Then write a program that creates and rolls two `Die` objects 500 times, and counts how many times snake eyes (both dice showing 1) comes up.

PP 6.9 Create a graphic version of the `Die` class from Programming Project 6.8 that shows the current face of the die with pips. Then write a program that creates and "rolls" two dice, displaying the final results graphically.

PP 6.10 Create a class called `QuiltSquare` that graphically represents one square of a quilt, using a geometric pattern of your choice. Then create a `Quilt` class that displays itself by rendering multiple `QuiltSquare` objects in a series of rows.

Events

CHAPTER OBJECTIVES

In this chapter you will:

▶ Explore the core elements of event processing in Java.

▶ Learn about the different types of events in Java.

▶ Explore various components used in a graphical user interface.

▶ Use listener objects to process Java events.

▶ See how inner classes can be used to effectively create listeners.

▶ Discuss various event processing situations in ThunkIt.

In Chapter 4 we saw how events and event handling could be added to Alice worlds so that user interactions could drive the objects' behavior. In Java, the concept is similar. In fact, it is the cornerstone of how programs with a graphical user interface are set up to react to various user actions. This chapter explains the way events are processed in Java and explores several of the most useful types of events.

7.1 Event Processing in Java

As we saw in Alice, an event represents some occurrence in which we may be interested. In Java, event processing is the technique by which a graphical user interface (GUI) is created. Often, events correspond to user actions, such as pressing a mouse button or typing a key on the keyboard.

A GUI *component* is an object that represents a screen element such as a button, text field, slider, or menu. Frames and panels are components, but they are also *containers* that can hold other components (as a frame holds a panel).

Most GUI components generate events that represent a user action related to that component. For example, a button component will generate an event to indicate that the button has been pushed. A program that is oriented around a GUI, responding to events from the user, is called *event-driven*.

In Java, a *listener* is an object that "waits" for an event to occur and responds when it does. Specifically, when an event occurs, a GUI component creates an event object and passes it to the appropriate method in the listener, which responds accordingly. An important part of designing a GUI-based program is establishing the relationship between the listener and the component that will generate the event. This relationship is shown in Figure 7.1.

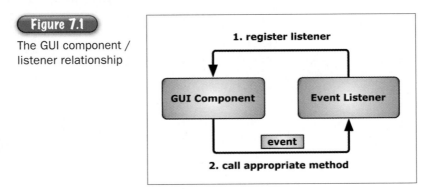

Figure 7.1

The GUI component / listener relationship

> ▶ A GUI is made up of components, events that represent user actions, and listeners that respond to those events.

For the most part, we will use components and events that are predefined by classes in the Java class library. We will tailor the behavior of the components, but their basic roles have been established already. We will, however, write our own listener classes to perform whatever actions we desire when events occur.

So, to create a Java program that uses a GUI, we must:

- create and set up the necessary components,

- implement listener classes that define what happens when particular events occur, and

- establish the relationship between the listeners and the components that generate the events of interest.

In some respects, once you have a basic understanding of event-driven programming, the rest is just detail. There are many types of components you can use that produce many types of events that you may want to acknowledge. But they all work in the same basic way. They all have the same core relationships to onc another.

Java components and other GUI-related classes are defined primarily in two packages: `java.awt` and `javax.swing`. (Note the `x` in `javax.swing`.) The *Abstract Windowing Toolkit* (AWT) was the original Java GUI package. It still contains many important classes that we will use. The *Swing* package was added later and provides components that are more versatile than those in the AWT package. Both packages are needed for GUI development, but we will use Swing components whenever there is an option.

In Alice there was no notion of the protection of methods or properties in an object. Events in Alice could therefore access any property in any object. In Java, we must be aware of the fact that data is usually declared `private` and thus inaccessible from outside the class in which it resides.

Buttons and Action Events

Let's look at a simple example that contains all of the basic GUI elements. A screen shot of the `PushCounter` program is shown in Figure 7.2. It presents the user with a single push button, labeled "Push Me!" Each time the button is pushed, a counter is updated and displayed.

Figure 7.2

A screen shot of the `PushCounter` program

Listing 7.1 shows the `PushCounter` class, containing the driver of the program. Similar to examples we explored in Chapter 6, the `main` method creates and sets up the program frame to display the primary panel.

Listing 7.1

```
//********************************************************************
//  PushCounter.java          Programming with Alice and Java
//
//  Demonstrates a graphical user interface and an event listener.
//********************************************************************
```

Listing 7.1 (continued)

```java
import javax.swing.JFrame;
public class PushCounter
{
   // ---------------------------------------------------------------
   // Creates and displays the main program frame.
   // ---------------------------------------------------------------
   public static void main(String[] args)
   {
      JFrame frame = new JFrame("Push Counter");

      PushCounterPanel panel = new PushCounterPanel();

      frame.getContentPane().add(panel);
      frame.setDefaultCloseOperation(JFrame.EXIT_ON_CLOSE);
      frame.pack();
      frame.setVisible(true);
   }
}
```

The panel in the PushCounter program is represented by the PushCounterPanel class, shown in Listing 7.2. The panel contains two GUI components, a button and a label. A component has to be added to the panel using the add method. Note that this is different from simply using a panel as a drawing surface, as we did in Chapter 6.

Listing 7.2

```java
//*************************************************************************
//  PushCounterPanel.java        Programming with Alice and Java
//
//  Represents the main panel for the PushCounter program, containing a
//  button and a label displaying how many times the button was pushed.
//*************************************************************************
import java.awt.*;
import javax.swing.*;
import java.awt.event.*;
public class PushCounterPanel extends JPanel
{
   private int count;
   private JLabel label;
   private JButton push;
   // ---------------------------------------------------------------
   // Sets up the interface on the panel.
   // ---------------------------------------------------------------
   public PushCounterPanel()
   {
```

Listing 7.2 (continued)

```
        count = 0;

        label = new JLabel("Pushes:" + count);
        push = new JButton("Push Me!");

        ButtonListener listener = new ButtonListener(this);
        push.addActionListener(listener);

        add(push);
        add(label);

        setBackground(Color.cyan);
        setPreferredSize(new Dimension(350, 60));
    }
    // ---------------------------------------------------------------------
    // Increments the counter and updates the label accordingly.
    // ---------------------------------------------------------------------
    public void incrementCount()
    {
        count++;
        label.setText("Pushes: " + count);
    }
}
```

A *label* is a GUI component created from the JLabel class, and can be used to display a line of text or an image. In this example, the label is used to display the number of times the button has been pushed. Labels are useful for displaying information or for labeling other components in the GUI. However, labels are not interactive. That is, the user does not interact with a label directly. The component that makes the PushCounter program interactive is the button that the user pushes with the mouse.

A push button is a component that allows the user to initiate an action with a press of the mouse. There are other types of button components that we explore in later examples. The JButton class represents a push button. A call to the JButton constructor takes a String parameter that specifies the text shown on the button.

A JButton generates an action event when it is pushed. There are several types of events defined in the Java standard class library, and we explore some of them throughout this chapter. Different components generate different types of events.

The only event of interest in this program occurs when the button is pushed. To respond to the event, we need a listener object for that event, so we must write a class that represents the listener. In this case, we need an action event listener.

In the PushCounter program, the ButtonListener class (shown in Listing 7.3) represents the action listener. An action listener is created by implementing the ActionListener interface; therefore we include the implements clause in the

ButtonListener class header. Recall that this means that the ButtonListener class must implement all methods listed in the ActionListener interface. In this case, the only method in the ActionListener interface is the actionPerformed method.

Listing 7.3

```java
//***********************************************************************
//  ButtonListener.java        Programming with Alice and Java
//
//  Represents the push button listener for the PushCounter program.
//***********************************************************************

import java.awt.event.*;

public class ButtonListener implements ActionListener
{
   private PushCounterPanel panel;

   // ---------------------------------------------------------------------
   // Stores the panel in order to update the counter.
   // ---------------------------------------------------------------------
   public ButtonListener(PushCounterPanel pushPanel)
   {
      panel = pushPanel;
   }

   // ---------------------------------------------------------------------
   // Updates the counter and label when the button is pushed.
   // ---------------------------------------------------------------------
   public void actionPerformed(ActionEvent event)
   {
      panel.incrementCount();
   }
}
```

The component that generates the action event (in this case the button) calls the actionPerformed method when the event occurs, passing in an ActionEvent object that represents the event. Sometimes we will use this event object, and other times it is sufficient to know that the event occurred. In this example, we have no need to interact with the event object. When the event occurs, the listener calls the incrementCount method of the panel to increment the count and update the text of the label.

> ▶ A listener can be created by implementing an appropriate listener interface.

To set up the relationship between the listener and the component that will generate the event, we add the listener to the button component by calling the appropriate method. After creating the listener object in the PushCounterPanel constructor, we call the addActionListener method to add it to the button. That call formally establishes the fact that the button will call the `actionPerformed` method of the listener whenever the button is pushed.

Review this example carefully, noting how it accomplishes the three key steps to creating an interactive GUI-based program. It creates and sets up the GUI components, creates the appropriate listener for the event of interest, and sets up the relationship between the listener and the component that will generate the event.

TRY THIS!

1. Modify the `PushCounter` program to add another button and listener that decrements the counter and updates the text field accordingly.

2. Add a button and corresponding listener to the `PushCounter` program to zero the counter.

3. Modify the `PushCounter` program to add another button and listener that will modify the label's text prefix (from "Pushes: " to "Button Clicks: ").

Action Listeners in ThunkIt

As you might expect, action events are a big part of how buttons are handled in ThunkIt. Many of the panels in ThunkIt contain buttons that allow the user to select what to do next. For instance, we have buttons on our main menu screen that are used to select different game-related functionality (level selection, reading about the game story, displaying the about window, etc.). Buttons and button listeners are also used to navigate forward and backward in the Instructions and Story screens.

Examine the various listeners in the ThunkIt `Controller` class to see how buttons are processed on many of the panels. Most are used for navigation purposes, and result in a new panel being displayed.

 **Event Types**

Like Alice, Java supports a variety of event types. We have already discussed the most popular type, the `ActionEvent`, used to handle actions such as button pushes. A summary of Java events is shown in Table 7.1. This list is not exhaustive, and we will not explore all the events. In upcoming examples, we'll focus on events that are used more frequently than others.

Table 7.1

A summary of Java events

Event	What It Indicates	Listener Interface(s)
`ActionEvent`	A button was pushed, enter was pressed in a text field, or a menu item was selected.	`ActionListener`
`ChangeEvent`	An object's state changed in some way.	`ChangeListener`
`ComponentEvent`	A component was hidden, moved, resized, or shown.	`ComponentListener`
`ContainerEvent`	A component was added or removed from a container.	`ContainerListener`
`FocusEvent`	A component gained or lost the keyboard focus.	`FocusListener`
`ItemEvent`	The state of a selectable item (check box, menu, scroll pane) changed.	`ItemListener`
`KeyEvent`	A keyboard key was pressed.	`KeyListener`
`MouseEvent`	The mouse interacted with a component (mouse button push, rollover, drag).	`MouseListener` `MouseMotionListener`

`WindowEvent`	The application window was opened, closed, iconified, maximized, minimized, etc.	`WindowFocusListener`
		`WindowListener`
		`WindowStateListener`

In the previous example we saw the use of a push button. Now let's look at an example that uses a few other components, including some other kinds of buttons. Figure 7.3 shows the Snowman program, which gives the user the ability to tailor a drawing of a snowman using various controls.

Figure 7.3

A screen shot of the Snowman program

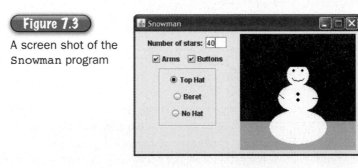

The controls include a *text box* into which the user can type the number of stars that will be drawn in the sky. They also include a *check box* that determines whether the snowman is drawn with arms or not. Another check box determines whether the snowman has buttons or not. Finally, the controls contain a set of *radio buttons* that determine which type of hat, if any, the snowman is wearing.

Any time a change is made to any of these controls, the picture is redrawn accordingly. The stars are drawn in random locations and change every time the picture is redrawn.

The Snowman class contains the main method of the program that sets up the program frame. It is like similar driver classes we've seen in several previous examples and we won't bother showing it here. The program frame displays an object created from the SnowmanPanel class, shown in Listing 7.4.

Listing 7.4

```java
//********************************************************************
//   SnowmanPanel.java           Programming with Alice and Java
//
//   Represents the main panel for the Snowman program. Uses inner classes
//   for the listeners.
//********************************************************************

import java.awt.*;
import javax.swing.*;
import java.awt.event.*;

public class SnowmanPanel extends JPanel
{
   private JCheckBox armsCheckBox, buttonsCheckBox;
   private JTextField starsField;
   private JRadioButton topHat, beret, noHat;
   private SnowmanDrawPanel drawPanel;

   //----------------------------------------------------------------
   // Sets up the interface of the control panel.
   //----------------------------------------------------------------
   public SnowmanPanel()
   {
      drawPanel = new SnowmanDrawPanel();

      JLabel starsLabel = new JLabel("Number of stars:");
      starsField = new JTextField(3);
      starsField.setText(Integer.toString(drawPanel.DEFAULT_STARS));
      starsField.addActionListener(new StarsListener());

      armsCheckBox = new JCheckBox("Arms");
      buttonsCheckBox = new JCheckBox("Buttons");
      CheckBoxListener checkBoxListener = new CheckBoxListener();
      armsCheckBox.addItemListener(checkBoxListener);
      buttonsCheckBox.addItemListener(checkBoxListener);

      topHat = new JRadioButton("Top Hat", true);
      beret = new JRadioButton("Beret", false);
```

Listing 7.4 (continued)

```java
      noHat = new JRadioButton("No Hat", false);
      RadioButtonListener radioButtonListener = new RadioButtonListener();
      topHat.addActionListener(radioButtonListener);
      beret.addActionListener(radioButtonListener);
      noHat.addActionListener(radioButtonListener);
      ButtonGroup hatGroup = new ButtonGroup();
      hatGroup.add(topHat);
      hatGroup.add(beret);
      hatGroup.add(noHat);
      JPanel hatPanel = new JPanel();
      hatPanel.setPreferredSize(new Dimension(100, 100));
      hatPanel.setBorder(BorderFactory.createEtchedBorder());
      hatPanel.add(topHat);
      hatPanel.add(beret);
      hatPanel.add(noHat);

      JPanel controlPanel = new JPanel();
      controlPanel.add(starsLabel);
      controlPanel.add(starsField);
      controlPanel.add(armsCheckBox);
      controlPanel.add(buttonsCheckBox);
      controlPanel.add(hatPanel);
      controlPanel.setPreferredSize(new Dimension(170, 200));

      add(controlPanel);
      add(drawPanel);
   }

   //*****************************************************************************
   // The listener for the text field that determines the number of stars.
   //*****************************************************************************
   private class StarsListener implements ActionListener
   {
      public void actionPerformed(ActionEvent event)
      {
         drawPanel.setNumStars(Integer.parseInt(starsField.getText()));
         drawPanel.repaint();
      }
   }

   //*****************************************************************************
   // The listener for both check boxes that determine whether the arms and
   // buttons are drawn.
   //*****************************************************************************
   private class CheckBoxListener implements ItemListener
   {
      public void itemStateChanged(ItemEvent event)
      {
         drawPanel.setArms(armsCheckBox.isSelected());
         drawPanel.setButtons(buttonsCheckBox.isSelected());
```

Listing 7.4 (continued)

```
            drawPanel.repaint();
        }
    }

    //***************************************************************************
    // The listener for the radio buttons that determine the hat style.
    //***************************************************************************
    private class RadioButtonListener implements ActionListener
    {
        public void actionPerformed(ActionEvent event)
        {
            Object source = event.getSource();

            if (source == topHat)
                drawPanel.setHat("top hat");
            else
                if (source == beret)
                    drawPanel.setHat("beret");
                else
                    drawPanel.setHat("no hat");
            drawPanel.repaint();
        }
    }
}
```

One key difference between the PushCounter example and the Snowman program is how listeners are created. Instead of using a separate public class for each listener, the SnowmanPanel class contains private classes that define the listeners. A class can contain other classes, called *inner classes*, just as it contains various instance data and methods. By nesting one class within another, only the outer class can make use of the inner class. This is particularly helpful when creating listener classes, which often need access to GUI components—it eliminates the need to set up special communication between the panel and the listener.

> ▶ Listeners are often defined as inner classes because of the intimate relationship between the listener and the GUI components.

The starsField object is created from the JTextField class. A text field allows the user to enter input in a one-line text field in the GUI. When the user presses the return (or enter) key while the cursor is in a text field, the component generates an action event. Note that the StarsListener inner class implements the ActionListener interface. The listener object is added to the text field in the constructor. In this example, when the user presses return, the text in the field is obtained, converted to a number, and the setNumStars method is called in the drawing panel. Then the drawing panel is repainted.

A check box is a button that can be toggled on or off using the mouse, indicating that a particular condition is set or unset. Although you may have a group of check boxes indicating a set of options, each check box operates independently. In this example, we use two check boxes, one to indicate whether the snowman's arms are drawn and one to indicate whether the snowman's buttons are drawn. Both can be checked, both can be unchecked, one can be checked while the other is not, and vice versa.

The `JCheckBox` class represents a check box. In this example, one listener, created from the `CheckBoxListener` inner class, is used to respond to a change in either button. When a check box status is changed, an *item event* is generated. Thus the `CheckBoxListener` class implements the `ItemListener` interface and its only method, called `itemStateChanged`. In this example, when either button is changed, the status of each is reported to the drawing panel using calls to the `setArms` and `setButtons` methods. Then the drawing panel is repainted.

> ▶ Radio buttons operate as a group, providing a set of mutually exclusive options.

A radio button is used with other radio buttons to provide a set of mutually exclusive options. Unlike a check box, a radio button is not particularly useful by itself. It has meaning only when it is used with one or more other radio buttons. Only one option out of the group is valid. At any point in time, one and only one button of the group of radio buttons is selected (on). When a radio button from the group is pushed, the other button in the group that is currently on is automatically toggled off.

A radio button is represented by the `JRadioButton` class. To define a set of radio buttons that work together, they are added to an object created from the `ButtonGroup` class. That way, one program can have multiple sets of radio buttons that work in different groups.

In this example, one listener is created and added to all three radio buttons. The `RadioButtonListener` class implements the `ActionListener` interface because a radio button, when selected, generates an action event. The `actionPerformed` method in the `RadioButtonListener` class first gets the source of the event. It then calls the `setHat` method of the drawing panel, passing in a string that represents the appropriate type of hat depending on which button was pressed. Then the drawing panel is repainted.

Note that for display purposes, the set of radio buttons are added to a separate `JPanel` object called `hatPanel`. This panel is given a border so that the three buttons are grouped visually to indicate that they work together.

The drawing panel is represented by the `SnowmanDrawPanel` class, shown in Listing 7.5. It provides the surface on which the snowman is drawn and includes various methods for setting the characteristics of the drawing. In the `paintComponent` method, the drawing is done relative to constants that represent the midpoint of the snowman horizontally and the top of the snowman's hat vertically. In this way, the entire snowman can be moved by changing a single value.

Listing 7.5

```java
//***************************************************************************
//   SnowmanDrawPanel.java        Programming with Alice and Java
//
//   Represents the drawing panel for the Snowman program.
//***************************************************************************
import java.awt.*;
import javax.swing.*;
import java.awt.event.*;
import java.util.Random;

public class SnowmanDrawPanel extends JPanel
{
   public final int DEFAULT_STARS = 40;

   private int numStars;
   private boolean arms, buttons;
   private String hat;
   private Random rand;

   //--------------------------------------------------------------------
   // Sets up the default status of the drawing panel.
   //--------------------------------------------------------------------
   public SnowmanDrawPanel()
   {
      numStars = DEFAULT_STARS;
      arms = false;
      buttons = false;
      hat = "top hat";

      rand = new Random();

      setBackground(Color.blue);
      setPreferredSize(new Dimension(200, 200));
   }

   //--------------------------------------------------------------------
   // Paints the snowman on this panel.
   //--------------------------------------------------------------------
   public void paintComponent(Graphics gc)
   {
      super.paintComponent(gc);

      final int MID = 100, TOP = 50;

      gc.setColor(Color.cyan);
      gc.fillRect(0, 150, 200, 50); // ground

      gc.setColor(Color.white);
      for (int count=1; count <= numStars; count++)
         gc.fillOval(rand.nextInt(190), rand.nextInt(140), 1, 1); // stars

      gc.fillOval(MID-20, TOP, 40, 40);        // head
      gc.fillOval(MID-35, TOP+35, 70, 50);     // upper torso
      gc.fillOval(MID-50, TOP+80, 100, 60);    // lower torso
```

Listing 7.5 (continued)

```
      gc.setColor(Color.black);
      gc.fillOval(MID-10, TOP+10, 5, 5);          // left eye
      gc.fillOval(MID+5, TOP+10, 5, 5);           // right eye
      gc.drawArc(MID-10, TOP+20, 20, 10, 190, 160);       // smile

      if (arms)
      {
         gc.drawLine(MID-25, TOP+60, MID-50, TOP+40);     // left arm
         gc.drawLine(MID+25, TOP+60, MID+55, TOP+60);     // right arm
      }

      if (buttons)
      {
         gc.fillOval(MID-3, TOP+50, 6, 6);        // button
         gc.fillOval(MID-3, TOP+60, 6, 6);        // button
      }

      if (hat.equals("top hat"))
      {
         gc.drawLine(MID-20, TOP+5, MID+20, TOP+5);       // brim of hat
         gc.fillRect(MID-15, TOP-20, 30, 25);             // top of hat
      }
      else
         if (hat.equals("beret"))
         {
            gc.setColor(Color.red);
            gc.fillOval(MID-15, TOP-3, 30, 10);
         }
   }

   //-----------------------------------------------------------------
   // Sets the value that determines if the arms are drawn.
   //-----------------------------------------------------------------
   public void setArms(boolean status)
   {
      arms = status;
   }

   //-----------------------------------------------------------------
   // Sets the value that determines if the buttons are drawn.
   //-----------------------------------------------------------------
   public void setButtons(boolean status)
   {
      buttons = status;
   }

   //-----------------------------------------------------------------
   // Sets the value that determines the number of stars that are drawn.
   //-----------------------------------------------------------------
   public void setNumStars(int count)
   {
      numStars = count;
   }
```

Listing 7.5 (continued)

```
//-----------------------------------------------------------------------
// Sets the value that determines the style of hat, if any, that is drawn.
//-----------------------------------------------------------------------
public void setHat(String currentHat)
{
    hat = currentHat;
}
}
```

TRY THIS!

4. Modify the Snowman program to add a text field that accepts the snowman's name. Display the name on the base of the snowman.

5. Modify the Snowman program so that a check box determines whether the snowman is smiling or frowning.

6. Modify the Snowman program to add another radio button that corresponds to another hat style option.

7.3 Mouse Events

As the name implies, a mouse event is generated when the mouse interacts with a GUI component. A mouse event is usually generated by the component that the mouse cursor is currently over. Components can generate mouse events that indicate that:

- a mouse button was pressed.

- a mouse button was released.

- a mouse button was clicked (pressed and released at the same location).

- the mouse cursor entered (moved over) a component.

- the mouse cursor exited (moved off) a component.

- the mouse was moved.

- the mouse was dragged (moved while a mouse button was pressed).

The methods used to respond to all of these events are listed in two listener interfaces. The MouseListener interface contains methods for the first five events listed above. The MouseMotionListener interface contains methods for the mouse moved and mouse dragged events.

▶ Java mouse events are separated into two categories with two listener interfaces.

Let's look at an example that uses various mouse events. The `SpaceshipFlight` program draws a spaceship on a panel, as shown in Figure 7.4. The spaceship moves around the panel, following the motion of the mouse. When the mouse button is pressed, the spaceship fires a laser beam. When the mouse button is released, the laser beam stops firing.

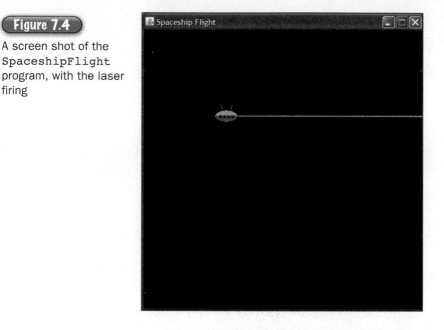

Figure 7.4

A screen shot of the `SpaceshipFlight` program, with the laser firing

The `SpaceshipFlight` class, which is not shown here, contains the `main` method that creates the program frame, similar to many previous examples. The spaceship is drawn on an object of the `SpaceshipPanel` class, shown in Listing 7.6. As we did with the `Snowman` program, the `SpaceshipPanel` class contains the listener it needs as an inner class.

Listing 7.6

```
//***********************************************************************
//   SpaceshipPanel.java        Programming with Alice and Java
//
//   Represents the panel on which the spaceship is drawn. Generates mouse
//   events that control the flight and behavior.
//***********************************************************************

import java.awt.*;
import javax.swing.*;
import java.awt.event.*;
```

Listing 7.6 (continued)

```java
public class SpaceshipPanel extends JPanel
{
   private Spaceship ship;

   //-----------------------------------------------------------------
   // Sets up the panel. Uses one listener for mouse and mouse motion events.
   //-----------------------------------------------------------------
   public SpaceshipPanel()
   {
      ship = new Spaceship();

      SpaceshipListener monitor = new SpaceshipListener();
      addMouseMotionListener(monitor);
      addMouseListener(monitor);

      setCursor(Cursor.getPredefinedCursor(Cursor.CROSSHAIR_CURSOR));
      setBackground(Color.black);
      setPreferredSize(new Dimension(480, 480));
   }

   //-----------------------------------------------------------------
   // Draws the spaceship.
   //-----------------------------------------------------------------
   public void paintComponent(Graphics gc)
   {
      super.paintComponent(gc);
      ship.draw(gc, getWidth());
   }

   //*****************************************************************
   // The listener for all mouse events.
   //*****************************************************************
   private class SpaceshipListener implements MouseListener, MouseMotionListener
   {
      //-----------------------------------------------------------------
      // Changes the ship's location as the mouse moves.
      //-----------------------------------------------------------------
      public void mouseMoved(MouseEvent event)
      {
         ship.setLocation(event.getX(), event.getY());
         repaint();
      }

      //-----------------------------------------------------------------
      // Changes the ship's location as the mouse is dragged.
      //-----------------------------------------------------------------
      public void mouseDragged(MouseEvent event)
      {
         ship.setLocation(event.getX(), event.getY());
         repaint();
      }
```

Listing 7.6 (continued)

```
//-----------------------------------------------------------------
// Puts the ship in "shooting" mode when the mouse button is pressed.
//-----------------------------------------------------------------
public void mousePressed(MouseEvent event)
{
   ship.setShooting(true);
   repaint();
}


//-----------------------------------------------------------------
// Stops the ship from shooting when the mouse button is released.
//-----------------------------------------------------------------
public void mouseReleased(MouseEvent event)
{
   ship.setShooting(false);
   repaint();
}


//-----------------------------------------------------------------
// Empty definitions for unused events.
//-----------------------------------------------------------------
public void mouseClicked(MouseEvent event) {}
public void mouseEntered(MouseEvent event) {}
public void mouseExited(MouseEvent event) {}
   }
}
```

> ▶ A listener may have to provide empty method definitions for unused events to satisfy the interface.

In this example, we have only one listener that handles all mouse-based events. The `SpaceshipListener` inner class implements both the `MouseListener` and `MouseMotionListener` interfaces. Therefore, it must provide a definition for all methods in both interfaces. Since we are ignoring mouse clicked, mouse entered, and mouse exited events, the corresponding methods are given empty definitions at the bottom of the class.

A mouse moved event is fired repeatedly as the mouse cursor moves across a component. Each time it occurs, the `mouseMoved` method is called, which obtains the coordinates where the event occurred (that is, the location of the mouse cursor) and sets the position of the spaceship. Then the panel is repainted. Mouse moved events occur so often that this approach creates the illusion that the spaceship is moving across the screen.

Similarly, a mouse dragged event is fired repeatedly as the mouse is moved, but only when the mouse button is held down. The `mouseDragged` method is identical to the `mouseMoved` method. As the mouse is moved or dragged, the spaceship's position is updated and the panel is redrawn.

When the mouse button is pressed down, the `mousePressed` method is called which sets the "shooting status" of the ship to true. When the panel is repainted, the laser beam is drawn. When the mouse button is released, the `mouseReleased` method sets the shooting status to false.

The spaceship is represented by the `Spaceship` class, shown in Listing 7.7. The ship is drawn based on constants for its width and height to make it easy to change its size.

Listing 7.7

```java
//********************************************************************
//  Spaceship.java        Programming with Alice and Java
//
//  Represents a spaceship drawn in some graphics context. Maintains the
//  ship's location and whether or not the ship is shooting a laser beam.
//********************************************************************
import java.awt.*;

public class Spaceship
{
   private int x, y;
   private boolean shooting;
   private final int WIDTH = 40, HEIGHT = 20;

   //-----------------------------------------------------------------
   // Sets the ship's location.
   //-----------------------------------------------------------------
   public void setLocation(int xPos, int yPos)
   {
      x = xPos;
      y = yPos;
   }

   //-----------------------------------------------------------------
   // Sets the shooting mode of the ship.
   //-----------------------------------------------------------------
   public void setShooting(boolean value)
   {
      shooting = value;
   }

   //-----------------------------------------------------------------
   // Draws the ship in the specified graphics context.
   //-----------------------------------------------------------------
   public void draw(Graphics gc, int screenWidth)
   {
      int baseX = x - WIDTH;
      int baseY = y - HEIGHT/2;
```

Listing 7.7 (continued)

```
      // antennae
      gc.setColor(Color.green);
      gc.drawLine(baseX + 10, baseY − 10, baseX + WIDTH/2, y + HEIGHT/2);
      gc.drawLine(baseX + WIDTH/2, y + HEIGHT/2, x − 10, baseY − 10);

      // body
      gc.setColor(Color.orange);
      gc.fillArc(baseX, baseY, WIDTH, HEIGHT, 0, 180);
      gc.setColor(Color.magenta);
      gc.fillArc(baseX, baseY, WIDTH, HEIGHT, 0, -180);

      // windows
      gc.setColor(Color.blue);
      for (int i=0; i < 4; i++)
         gc.fillOval(baseX + (i+1) * 7, baseY + 8, 6, 6);

      // laser
      if (shooting)
      {
         gc.setColor(Color.yellow);
         gc.drawLine(x, y, screenWidth, y);
      }
   }
}
```

TRY THIS!

7. Modify the `SpaceshipFlight` program so that when the mouse button is clicked, an energy field surrounds the space ship until the mouse is clicked again.

8. Modify the `SpaceshipFlight` program so that when the ship flies above a certain vertical threshold its laser (if shooting) becomes blue.

9. Modify the `SpaceshipFlight` program so that it uses two separate listener classes, one for mouse events and one for mouse motion events.

Mouse Listeners in ThunkIt

ThunkIt uses mouse events and listeners in several key ways. For instance, the user can choose which level to play by double clicking on the level in the list. The double clicking action initiates game play on the selected level, just as pressing the Play Selected menu button does. The `LevelSelectionMouseListener` class, shown in Listing 7.8, handles the processing of the double click action.

Listing 7.8

```java
public class LevelSelectionMouseListener extends MouseAdapter
{
    /**
     * Handles mouse events on the level selection screen.
     *
     * @param    event    the mouse event
     */
    public void mouseClicked(MouseEvent event)
    {
        int levelNum = -1;
        boolean standard = true;

        // Deselect opposing list selections (if any)
        if (event.getSource() == levelMenu.getProvidedList())
        {
            levelMenu.clearCustomList();
            levelNum = levelMenu.getProvidedLevelNum();
        }
        else if (event.getSource() == levelMenu.getCustomList())
        {
            levelMenu.clearProvidedList();
            levelNum = levelMenu.getCustomLevelNum();
            standard = false;
        }

        // If the event is a double click, play the selected
        // level (note that we are dealing with 2 lists)
        if (event.getClickCount() == 2)    // double click
        {
            if (levelNum != -1)
            {
                changeContent(PLAY_PANEL, "startPlay");
                playMgr.initLevelForPlay(standard, levelNum);
                playPanel.startTimer();
            }
        }
    }
}
```

The LevelSelectionMouseListener is an inner class located in the Controller class. This class handles both level selection lists (the list of game levels that comes with ThunkIt and the list of user-generated custom levels, if any). Therefore, the listener determines the source of the event and unselects any previously selected levels from either list.

Keep in mind we must distinguish between a single click and a double click. The user could single click on a level, then press the Play Level button. That processing is handled by the button's listener. If the user double clicks, however, the `Level SelectionMouseListener` handles it in a similar manner.

7.4 Keyboard Events

As we saw in Alice, a *keyboard event* (also called a *key event*) occurs when a keyboard key is pressed. Key events allow a program to respond immediately as the user presses keys—there is no waiting for the enter key to be pressed as with a text field.

In Alice, we set up a separate event for every key to which we wanted to respond. There was also a separate event type that allowed you to move an object with the arrow keys. In Java, we set up a listener that responds when *any* key is pressed, then decide what to do based on the specific key pressed.

Figure 7.5 shows a screen shot of a program called `ImageFlicker` that displays an image in a frame. When the user presses the numeric keys 1, 2, or 3, an image corresponding to that number appears. When the space bar is pressed, one of those images is picked at random.

Figure 7.5

A screen shot of the `ImageFlicker` program

The `ImageFlicker` class, containing the `main` method, is shown in Listing 7.9. The panel on which the image is displayed is represented by the `ImageFlickerPanel` class, shown in Listing 7.10. The listener for key events, called `KeyboardListener`, is implemented as an inner class of the panel.

Listing 7.9

```
//********************************************************************
//   ImageFlicker.java       Programming with Alice and Java
//
//   Demonstrates the use of key events.
//********************************************************************

import javax.swing.*;

public class ImageFlicker
{
   //------------------------------------------------------------------
   // Creates and displays the main program frame.
   //------------------------------------------------------------------
   public static void main(String[] args)
   {
      JFrame frame = new JFrame("Image Flicker");

      frame.getContentPane().add(new ImageFlickerPanel());
      frame.setDefaultCloseOperation(JFrame.EXIT_ON_CLOSE);
      frame.pack();
      frame.setResizable(false);
      frame.setVisible(true);
   }
}
```

Listing 7.10

```
//********************************************************************
//   ImageFlickerPanel.java       Programming with Alice and Java
//
//   Represents the display panel for the ImageFlicker program.
//********************************************************************

import java.awt.*;
import java.util.*;
import javax.swing.*;
import java.awt.event.*;

public class ImageFlickerPanel extends JPanel
{
   private Image image1, image2, image3;
   private Image currentImage;
   private Random rand;

   //------------------------------------------------------------------
   // Loads the images and sets the panel characteristics.
   //------------------------------------------------------------------
```

Listing 7.10 (continued)

```java
public ImageFlickerPanel()
{
   addKeyListener(new KeyboardListener());

   image1 = (new ImageIcon("babyFace.jpg")).getImage();
   image2 = (new ImageIcon("closeUp.jpg")).getImage();
   image3 = (new ImageIcon("twoBoys.jpg")).getImage();
   currentImage = image1;

   rand = new Random();

   setBackground(Color.black);
   setPreferredSize(new Dimension(500, 375));
   setFocusable(true);
}

//--------------------------------------------------------------------------
// Draws the image on the panel.
//--------------------------------------------------------------------------
public void paintComponent(Graphics gc)
{
   super.paintComponent(gc);
   gc.drawImage(currentImage, 0, 0, null);
}

//**************************************************************************
// The listener for keyboard presses.
//**************************************************************************
private class KeyboardListener implements KeyListener
{
   //-----------------------------------------------------------------------
   // Switches the current image based on the key pressed.
   //-----------------------------------------------------------------------
   public void keyPressed(KeyEvent event)
   {
      switch (event.getKeyChar())
      {
         case '1':
            currentImage = image1;
            break;

         case '2':
            currentImage = image2;
            break;

         case '3':
            currentImage = image3;
            break;

         case ' ':
            switch (rand.nextInt(3))
```

Listing 7.10 (continued)

```
            {
                case 0:
                    currentImage = image1;
                    break;
                case 1:
                    currentImage = image2;
                    break;
                case 2:
                    currentImage = image3;
            }
        }
        repaint();
    }

    //-----------------------------------------------------------------
    // Empty definitions for unused events.
    //-----------------------------------------------------------------
    public void keyReleased(KeyEvent event) { }
    public void keyTyped(KeyEvent event) { }
    }
}
```

The `KeyListener` interface contains three methods: `keyPressed`, which is called as soon as a key is pressed down, `keyReleased`, which is called when a key is released, and `keyTyped`, which is called when a pressed key produces a character. The `keyTyped` event handles *key repetition*, the notion that when a key is held down, it's as if that key were being pressed repeatedly and quickly. In the `ImageFlicker` program, the `keyPressed` event is processed and the others are given empty definitions.

The `KeyEvent` object passed to the `keyPressed` method can be used to determine which key was pressed. In this example, the `getKeyChar` method is called to return the character of the pressed key. You can also call the `getKeyCode` method, which returns a code corresponding to the key. The code is helpful when looking to see if the key pressed was an arrow key, function key, the enter key, or any other key that doesn't have an obvious character representation.

In the `keyPressed` method of the `ImageFlicker` program, a `switch` statement is used to determine which key was pressed and to set the appropriate image. If the space bar is pressed, a random number is chosen and a nested `switch` statement is used to pick one of the three. When any other key is pressed, processing falls through the outer `switch` statement without having an effect.

The component that generates key events is the one that currently has the *keyboard focus*. Usually, the keyboard focus is held by the primary "active"

▶ To generate a keyboard event, a component must have the keyboard focus.

component. A component usually gets the keyboard focus when the user clicks on it with a mouse. The call to the setFocusable method in the panel constructor sets the keyboard focus to the panel.

TRY THIS!

10. Modify the ImageFlicker program so that it processes a fourth image using the "4" key, and include that image in the random choice that occurs when the space bar is pressed.

11. Modify the ImageFlicker program so that it handles the key released event instead of the key pressed event.

Keyboard Listeners in ThunkIt

ThunkIt uses keyboard listeners so the user can use the keyboard during game play to control the student character moving around the level, as well as to pause and restart the game. The PlayPanelListener class is responsible for responding to key events generated while a level is being played.

The key events processed by our listener fall into three distinct situations during game play:

- The escape key is pressed, which will pause the game and display the paused menu;

- The "r" key is pressed, which will restart the level immediately; or

- Any other key is pressed.

In the final situation, the keystroke is stored so that the student character can respond accordingly. This key event may be the result of the user pressing one of the arrow keys for character movement, or pressing a number key to choose to use an inventory item.

7.5 More to Explore

We've only begun to touch on the world of events in Java. To become truly versed in Java events, be sure to investigate them all. You now know the basic approach to handling events through listeners. You won't have any trouble adapting what you have learned to support other types of events in your GUI applications.

Change Events Change events occur when a component changes. Sliders are one type of GUI component which, when changed (slid), creates a change event object. What other GUI components that create change events can you find in the Java library?

Window Events Window events capture changes to the application window(s), such as minimize, maximize, close, iconify, and deiconify. Try creating a window listener class to respond to some of these events with the sample programs presented in this chapter.

Adapters Adapter classes are library classes that implement GUI listener interfaces that contain more than one method. The methods in adapter classes are empty, containing no statements. For example, the `MouseAdapter` class implements the `MouseListener` interface, providing empty definitions for all `MouseListener` methods. You can create a listener by extending an adapter class (using inheritance) instead of implementing the listener interface directly. By extending an adapter class, you don't have to provide empty definitions for unused events, because the adapter class has already done that for you. Inheritance is discussed further in the next chapter.

Summary of Key Concepts

- A GUI is made up of components, events that represent user actions, and listeners that respond to those events.

- A listener can be created by implementing an appropriate listener interface.

- Listeners are often defined as inner classes because of the intimate relationship between the listener and the GUI components.

- Radio buttons operate as a group, providing a set of mutually exclusive options.

- Java mouse events are separated into two categories with two listener interfaces.

- A listener may have to provide empty method definitions for unused events to satisfy the interface.

- To generate a keyboard event, a component must have the keyboard focus.

Exercises

EX 7.1 Use the Java API and other references to make a list of ten different GUI components.

EX 7.2 Using just the Java API, make a list of as many GUI listener interface classes as you can find.

EX 7.3 Explain the relationship between a listener and a component.

EX 7.4 Describe how you would use a mouse event object to see whether the left or right button on the mouse was clicked.

EX 7.5 Write a sample `keyListener` that verifies whether the user pressed the key sequence control-5 (that is, pressed and held the control key down while the number 5 key was pressed).

EX 7.6 What is a `HyperlinkListener`? Which component(s) or objects can have a `HyperlinkListener` registered to it?

EX 7.7 Define the purpose of an inner class. What do we gain by using them?

EX 7.8 What is a `MenuEvent`? Which components can create `MenuEvents`?

EX 7.9 What would happen if the `repaint` method calls were removed from the `mouseMoved` method in the `SpaceshipListener` class of the `SpaceshipFlight` program?

EX 7.10 What is the effect of removing the `setFocusable` method call in the `ImageFlickerPanel` constructor? Why does this result occur?

Programming Projects

PP 7.1 Design and implement an application that serves as a mouse odometer, continually displaying how far, in pixels, the mouse has moved (while in the program window). Display the current odometer value using a label. *Hint:* Compare the current position of the mouse to the last position and use a distance formula to determine how far the mouse has traveled.

PP 7.2 Design and implement an application that displays a button and a label. Every time the button is pushed, the label should display a random number between 1 and 100, inclusive.

PP 7.3 Design and implement a program whose background changes color depending on where the mouse pointer is located. If the mouse pointer is on the left half of the program window, display red; if it is on the right half, display green.

PP 7.4 Design and implement an application that draws a circle on a graphic panel by using a rubberbanding technique. The circle size is determined by a mouse drag. Use the original mouse click location as a fixed center point. *Hint:* Compute the distance between the mouse pointer and the center point to determine the current radius of the circle.

PP 7.5 Design an application that draws a traffic light and uses a key press to change the state of the light. Each time the space key is pressed, change the state of the light.

PP 7.6 Modify the design and implementation of Programming Project 7.5. Instead of a key press, use a mouse click to change the state of each light. Each of the three lights on the stoplight should be able to be controlled individually.

PP 7.7 Create an application that displays a text label, which is modified each time the user presses a key. That is, append each key to the label to create the effect that the user is typing the label.

PP 7.8 Design and implement an application that displays colored lines on a panel. Use mouse clicks to control the start and end of each line and use key presses to designate the desired color of the line.

PP 7.9 Design and implement an application that displays an animation of a car (side view) moving across the screen from left to right. Create a car class that represents the car.

PP 7.10 Design and implement an application that plays a game called Catch-the-Creature. Use an image to represent the creature. Have the creature appear at a random location for a random duration, then disappear and reappear somewhere else. The goal is to "catch" the creature by pressing the mouse button while the mouse pointer is on the creature image. Create a separate class to represent the creature, and include in it a method that determines whether the location of the mouse click corresponds to the current location of the creature. Display a count of the number of times the creature is caught.

Lists and Arrays

CHAPTER OBJECTIVES

In this chapter you will:

- ▶ Learn about collections and the Java Collections API.
- ▶ Define and use classes that handle generic types.
- ▶ Use the `ArrayList` class to manage data.
- ▶ Define and use Java arrays for data organization.
- ▶ Understand bounds checking with arrays.
- ▶ Explore the creation and use of multidimensional arrays.
- ▶ Discuss how lists and arrays are used in ThunkIt.

In Chapter 5 we saw that lists and arrays help us manage a large number of objects in Alice. Java has similar structures with precisely the same benefits. This chapter explores the creation and use of lists and arrays in Java. It also discusses how lists and arrays are used throughout the ThunkIt program.

8.1 Java Collections

As we saw when we were creating Alice worlds, we need help when dealing with a large number of objects. When writing a program that manages, for instance, a list of 100 names, it is not practical to declare a separate variable for each name. We've seen that lists and arrays solve this problem by letting us declare one variable that can hold multiple, individually accessible values.

A *collection* is an object that serves as a repository for other objects. It provides services to add, remove, and otherwise manage the elements it contains. The underlying *data structure* used to implement the collection is independent of the operations the collection provides.

> ▶ A list is just one of several types of collections available in the Java API.

The Java standard class library includes several classes that define collections. They are referred to as the Java Collections API. The classes in the Java Collections API define a variety of specific collections, which are implemented in various ways.

The collection we focus on in this chapter is a list. In particular, we will use the `ArrayList` class, which implies that its underlying implementation uses an array. We could also use the `LinkedList` class to manage a list of objects. The `ArrayList` and `LinkedList` classes are implemented in different ways, but from our perspective of using the list, the results are basically the same.

Generic Types

Before we explore lists in Java, we need to discuss a programming technique that is used to define Java collections. Java enables us to define a class based on a *generic type*. That is, we can define a class so that it stores, operates on, and manages objects whose type is not specified until the class is instantiated. Generic types are sometimes called *parameterized types*.

Suppose we wanted to define a class called `Group` that stores and manages a group of objects. We could define `Group` so that internally it stores references to the `Object` class. Then, any type of object could be stored in the group. In fact, multiple types of unrelated objects could be stored in the group. However, the extreme flexibility that comes from using `Object` references brings with it a loss of control.

A better approach is to define the `Group` class to store a generic type `T`. (We can use any identifier we want for the generic type; using `T` is a convention.) The header of the class contains a reference to the type in angle brackets. For example:

```
class Group <T>
{
    // Code that manage objects of type T
}
```

Then, when a `Group` is needed, it is instantiated with a specific class used in place of `T`. For example, if we wanted a group of `Product` objects, we could use the following declaration:

```
Group<Product> group1 = new Group<Product>;
```

The type of the `group1` variable is `Group<Product>`. In essence, for the `group1` object, the `Group` class replaces `T` with `Product`. Now suppose we wanted a `Group` in which to store `Friend` objects. We could make the following declaration:

```
Group<Friend> group2 = new Group<Friend>;
```

For `group2`, the `Group` class essentially replaces `T` with `Friend`. So, although the `group1` and `group2` objects are both `Group` objects, they have different types because the generic type is taken into account. One is a group of products, the other is a group of friends.

Using generics provides a safer implementation than using `Object` as the collection type, because we cannot use `group1` to store `Friend` objects, nor can we use `group2` to store `Product` objects. This approach ensures type compatibility among the objects in a particular collection.

> ▶ Generic classes ensure type compatibility among the objects stored by the collection.

A generic type such as `T` cannot be instantiated. It is merely a placeholder to allow us to define the class that will manage a specific type of object that is established when the class is instantiated. The collection classes in the Java Collections API are all implemented using generic types.

In some collections, it's desirable to store items that are `Comparable`, so that they can be kept in order relative to each other. That is, we may want to combine the concept of storing a generic type `T` with the restriction that `T` be a type that implements the `Comparable` interface. To do this for the `Group` class, we would declare it as follows:

```
class Group<T extends Comparable<T>>
{
    // Code that manage objects of type T
}
```

8.2 The ArrayList Class

The `ArrayList` class is part of the `java.util` package of the Java standard class library. It defines a list that dynamically grows and shrinks as needed. A data element can be inserted into or removed from any location (index) of an `ArrayList` object with a single method invocation.

> ▶ The capacity of an `ArrayList` object changes dynamically as needed.

Unless we specify otherwise, an `ArrayList` is not declared to store a particular type. That is, an `ArrayList` object stores a list of references to the `Object` class, which means that any type of object can be added to an `ArrayList`. Because an `ArrayList` stores references, a primitive type must be stored in an appropriate wrapper class in order to be stored in an `ArrayList`. Figure 8.1 lists several methods of the `ArrayList` class.

Figure 8.1

Some methods of the ArrayList class

```
ArrayList()
   Constructor: creates an initially empty list.

boolean add (Object obj)
   Inserts the specified object to the end of this list.

void add (int index, Object obj)
   Inserts the specified object into this list at the specified index.

void clear()
   Removes all elements from this list.

Object remove (int index)
   Removes the element at the specified index in this list and returns it.

Object get (int index)
   Returns the object at the specified index in this list without removing it.

int indexOf (Object obj)
   Returns the index of the first occurrence of the specified object.

boolean contains (Object obj)
   Returns true if this list contains the specified object.

boolean isEmpty()
   Returns true if this list contains no elements.

int size()
   Returns the number of elements in this list.
```

It's best to embrace the generic implementation of the `ArrayList` class and specify the type of element the list will hold. For example, the following declaration creates an `ArrayList` object called `reunion` that stores `Family` objects:

```
ArrayList<Family> reunion = new ArrayList<Family>();
```

The type of the `reunion` object is `ArrayList<Family>`. Given this declaration, the compiler will not allow an object to be added to `reunion` unless it is a `Family` object (or one of its descendants through inheritance).

Let's look at an example that uses an `ArrayList` object. A screen shot of the `Dots` program is shown in Figure 8.2. The program responds to mouse pressed events. Whenever the user clicks the mouse on the panel, a dot appears at that location and a counter is updated. The `Dots` class, which contains the program's `main` method, is shown in Listing 8.1.

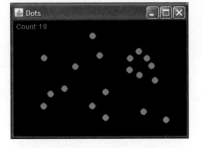

Figure 8.2

A screen shot of the
Dots program

Listing 8.1

```java
//********************************************************************************
//  Dots.java          Programming with Alice and Java
//
//  Demonstrates the use of an ArrayList.
//********************************************************************************

import javax.swing.JFrame;

public class Dots
{
   // ---------------------------------------------------------------------
   //  Creates and displays the program frame.
   // ---------------------------------------------------------------------
   public static void main(String[] args)
   {
      JFrame frame = new JFrame("Dots");
      frame.getContentPane().add(new DotsPanel());
      frame.setDefaultCloseOperation(JFrame.EXIT_ON_CLOSE);
      frame.pack();
      frame.setVisible(true);
   }
}
```

The `DotsPanel` class, shown in Listing 8.2, maintains an `ArrayList` of `Point` objects. Each point in the list corresponds to a location where the user clicked the mouse and, therefore, where a dot was drawn.

Listing 8.2

```java
//********************************************************************
//  DotsPanel.java           Programming with Alice and Java
//
//  Represents the primary drawing panel for the Dots program.
//********************************************************************

import java.util.ArrayList;
import javax.swing.JPanel;
import java.awt.*;
import java.awt.event.*;

public class DotsPanel extends JPanel
{
   private final int SIZE = 6; // radius of each dot

   private ArrayList<Point> pointList;

   // -----------------------------------------------------------------
   // Constructor: Sets up this panel to listen for mouse events.
   // -----------------------------------------------------------------
   public DotsPanel()
   {
      pointList = new ArrayList<Point>();

      addMouseListener(new DotsListener());

      setBackground(Color.black);
      setPreferredSize(new Dimension(300, 200));
   }

   // -----------------------------------------------------------------
   // Draws all of the dots stored in the list.
   // -----------------------------------------------------------------
   public void paintComponent(Graphics page)
   {
      super.paintComponent(page);

      page.setColor(Color.green);

      for (Point spot : pointList)
         page.fillOval((int)spot.getX()-SIZE, (int)spot.getY()-SIZE, SIZE*2,
            SIZE*2);

      page.drawString("Count: " + pointList.size(), 5, 15);
   }

   //********************************************************************
   // The listener for mouse events.
   //********************************************************************
   private class DotsListener extends MouseAdapter
```

Listing 8.2 (continued)

```
   {
      // -----------------------------------------------------------------
      // Adds the current point to the list of points and redraws the panel.
      // -----------------------------------------------------------------
      public void mousePressed (MouseEvent event)
      {
         pointList.add(event.getPoint());
         repaint();
      }
   }
}
```

The DotsListener inner class contains the mousePressed method that is invoked when the user clicks the mouse button. The location where the event occurred is obtained from the event object using the getPoint method. That point is added to the ArrayList and the panel is repainted.

In the paintComponent method, a for loop is used to iterate over the Point objects in the list, drawing each dot using the fillOval method. Without the list to keep track of all previous dot locations, they would be lost and only the current dot could be drawn. By using an ArrayList (instead of an array), there is no need to worry about filling up the list.

TRY THIS!

1. Modify the Dots program so that the first dot created is drawn in yellow, the newest dot is drawn in red, and all other dots are drawn in green.

2. Modify the Dots program so that, after 10 dots have been created, the oldest one disappears whenever a new one is created.

Lists in ThunkIt

ThunkIt relies heavily on lists and, specifically, the ArrayList class. It is convenient and easy to use, especially given the iterator version of the for loop that allows us to quickly process all items in a list.

At various points in the game, for example, we need a list of all non-empty cells in a level, a list of active elements, or a list of initial level data. The purpose of several methods in the program is to populate a list with particular objects and return it for processing.

As you continue to explore the ThunkIt code, note how dependent it's become on using the ArrayList class.

Java Arrays

As it was in Alice, an array in Java is a list of values. Each value is stored at a specific, numbered position in the array. The number corresponding to each position is called an *index* or *subscript*. Figure 8.3 shows an array of integers and the indexes that correspond to each position. The array is called `height`—it contains integers that represent several persons' heights in inches.

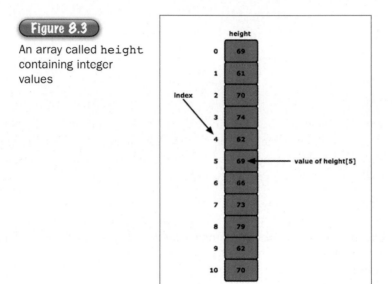

Figure 8.3

An array called `height` containing integer values

As in Alice, Java array indexes always begin at zero. Therefore the value stored at index 5 is actually the sixth value in the array. The array shown in Figure 8.3 has 11 values, indexed from 0 to 10.

> ▶ An array of size *N* is indexed from 0 to *N*−1.

To access a value in an array, we use the name of the array followed by the index in square brackets. For example, the following expression refers to the ninth value in the array `height`:

```
height[8]
```

According to Figure 8.3, `height[8]` (pronounced height-sub-eight) contains the value 79. Don't confuse the value of the index, in this case 8, with the value stored in the array at that index, in this case 79.

The expression `height[8]` refers to a single integer stored at a particular memory location. It can be used wherever an integer variable can be used. Therefore you can assign a value to it, use it in calculations, print its value, and so on. Furthermore, because array indexes are integers, you can use integer expressions to specify the index used to access an array. These concepts are demonstrated in the following lines of code:

```
height[2] = 72;
height[count] = feet * 12;
average = (height[0] + height[1] + height[2]) / 3;
System.out.println("Middle value: " + height[MAX/2]);
pick = height[rand.nextInt(11)];
```

Declaring and Using Arrays

Although array syntax is built into the language, arrays are objects just as an `ArrayList` is. To create an array, the reference to the array must be declared. The array can then be instantiated using the `new` operator, which allocates memory to store values. The following code represents the declaration for the array shown in Figure 8.3:

```
int[] height = new int[11];
```

The variable `height` is declared to be an array of integers whose type is written as `int[]`. All values stored in an array have the same type (or are at least compatible). For example, we can create an array that can hold integers or an array that can hold strings, but not an array that can hold both integers and strings. An array can be set up to hold any primitive type or any object (class) type. A value stored in an array is sometimes called an *array element*, and the type of values that an array holds is called the *element type* of the array.

> ▶ In Java, an array is an object and therefore must be instantiated.

Note that the type of the array variable (`int[]`) does not include the size of the array. The instantiation of `height`, using the `new` operator, reserves the memory space to store 11 integers indexed from 0 to 10. Once an array object is instantiated to be a certain size, the number of values it can hold cannot be changed. A reference variable such as `height`, declared to hold an array of integers, can refer to an array of any size. And like any other reference variable, the object (that is, the array) that `height` refers to can change over time.

Bounds Checking

Java performs automatic *bounds checking* whenever an array element is referenced, which ensures that the index is in range for the array being referenced. For example, suppose an array called `prices` is created with 25 elements. The valid indexes for the array are from 0 to 24. Whenever a reference is made to a particular element in the array (such as `prices[count]`), the value of the index is checked. If it is in the valid range of indexes for the array (0 to 24), the reference is carried out. If the index is not valid, an exception called `ArrayIndexOutOfBoundsException` is thrown.

> ▶ Bounds checking ensures that an index used to refer to an array element is in range.

In most cases, we'll want to perform our own bounds checking. That is, we'll want to be careful to remain within the bounds of the array when making references. (The alternative is to be prepared to handle the exception when it is thrown; exception handling is discussed in Chapter 10.)

Because array indexes begin at zero and go up to one less than the size of the array, it is easy to create *off-by-one errors* in a program. These are errors created by processing all but one element or by attempting to access one element too many.

One way to check for the bounds of an array is to use the `length` constant, which is an attribute of the array object that holds the size of the array. It is a public constant and therefore can be referenced directly. For example, after the array `prices` is created with 25 elements, the constant `prices.length` contains the value 25. Its value is set once when the array is first created and cannot be changed. The `length` constant, which is an integral part of each array, can be used when the array size is needed without having to create a separate constant. Remember that the length of the array is the number of elements it can hold; thus the maximum index of an array is `length-1`.

Let's look at an example. The `LetterCount` example, shown in Listing 8.3, determines how many of each letter, both upper- and lowercase, can be found in a particular string. A sample run of the program can be seen in Figure 8.4.

Listing 8.3

```java
//********************************************************************
//  LetterCount.java          Programming with Alice and Java
//
//  Demonstrates the use of arrays and the relationship between arrays and
//  strings.
//********************************************************************

import java.util.Scanner;

public class LetterCount
{
   //-----------------------------------------------------------------
   // Reads a sentence from the user and counts the number of uppercase and
   // lowercase letters contained in it.
   //-----------------------------------------------------------------
   public static void main(String[] args)
   {
      final int NUMCHARS = 26;

      Scanner scan = new Scanner(System.in);

      int[] upper = new int[NUMCHARS];
      int[] lower = new int[NUMCHARS];

      char current; // the current character being processed
      int other = 0; // counter for non-alphabetics
      System.out.println("Enter a sentence:");
      String line = scan.nextLine();

      // Count the number of each letter
      for (int ch=0; ch < line.length(); ch++)
      {
         current = line.charAt(ch);
         if (current >= 'A' && current <= 'Z')
            upper[current-'A']++;
```

Listing 8.3 (continued)

```java
        else
            if (current >= 'a' && current <= 'z')
                lower[current-'a']++;
            else
                other++;
    }

    // Print the results
    System.out.println();
    for (int letter=0; letter < upper.length; letter++)
    {
        System.out.print((char) (letter + 'A'));
        System.out.print(": " + upper[letter]);
        System.out.print("\t\t" + (char) (letter + 'a'));
        System.out.println(": " + lower[letter]);
    }

    System.out.println();
    System.out.println("Non-alphabetic characters: " + other);
    }
}
```

Figure 8.4

A sample run of the LetterCount program

```
Enter a sentence:
In Casablanca, Humphrey Bogart never says "Play it again, Sam".

A: 0            a: 10
B: 1            b: 1
C: 1            c: 1
D: 0            d: 0
E: 0            e: 3
F: 0            f: 0
G: 0            g: 2
H: 1            h: 1
I: 1            i: 2
J: 0            j: 0
K: 0            k: 0
L: 0            l: 2
M: 0            m: 2
N: 0            n: 4
O: 0            o: 1
P: 1            p: 1
Q: 0            q: 0
R: 0            r: 3
S: 1            s: 3
T: 0            t: 2
U: 0            u: 1
V: 0            v: 1
W: 0            w: 0
X: 0            x: 0
Y: 0            y: 3
Z: 0            z: 0

Non-alphabetic characters: 14
```

The array called upper is used to store the number of times each uppercase alphabetic letter is found in the string. The array called lower serves the same purpose for lowercase letters. Because there are 26 letters in the English alphabet, both the upper and lower arrays are declared with 26 elements. Each element contains an integer that is initially zero by default. These values serve as counters for each alphabetic character encountered in the input. The for loop scans through the string one character at a time. The appropriate counter in the appropriate array is incremented for each character found in the string.

Both of the counter arrays are indexed from 0 to 25. So we have to map each character to a counter. A logical way to do this is to use upper[0] to count the number of 'A' characters found, upper[1] to count the number of 'B' characters found, and so on. Likewise, lower[0] is used to count 'a' characters, lower[1] is used to count 'b' characters, and so on. A separate variable called other is used to count any non-alphabetic characters that are encountered.

To determine whether a character is an uppercase letter, we use the Boolean expression (current >= 'A' && current <= 'Z'). A similar expression is used for determining the lowercase letters. We could have used the static methods isUpperCase and isLowerCase in the Character class to make these determinations, but we didn't in this example to drive home the point that each character has a specific numeric value and order, based on the Unicode character set, that we can use in our programming.

We use the current character to calculate which index in the array to reference. We have to be careful when calculating an index to ensure that it remains within the bounds of the array and matches to the correct element. In the Unicode character set the uppercase and lowercase alphabetic letters are continuous and in order (see Appendix C). Therefore, taking the numeric value of an uppercase letter such as 'E' (which is 69) and subtracting the numeric value of the character 'A' (which is 65) yields 4, which is the correct index for the counter of the character 'E'. Note that nowhere in the program do we actually need to know the specific numeric values for each letter.

TRY THIS!

> 3. Modify the LetterCount program so that it no longer distinguishes between upper- and lowercase letters.
>
> 4. Modify the LetterCount program so that it continues to track both upper- and lowercase letters, but uses only one array to do so.
>
> 5. Modify the LetterCount program so that it also counts the digits 0–9 and reports the results.

Initializer Lists

You can use an *initializer list* to instantiate an array and provide the initial values for the elements of the array. This is essentially the same idea as initializing a variable of a primitive data type in its declaration, except that the initial value for an array contains multiple values.

The items in an initializer list are separated by commas and delimited by braces ({}). When an initializer list is used, the new operator is not used. The size of the array is determined by the number of items in the initializer list. For example, the following declaration instantiates the array scores as an array of eight integers, indexed from 0 to 7, with the initial values specified in the braces:

> ▶ An initializer list can be used to instantiate an array object instead of using the new operator.

```java
int[] scores = {87, 98, 69, 87, 65, 76, 99, 83};
```

An initializer list can be used only when an array is first declared.

The type of each value in an initializer list must match the type of the array elements. Let's look at another example:

```java
char[] vowels = {'A', 'E', 'I', 'O', 'U'};
```

In this case, the variable vowels is declared to be an array of five characters, and the initializer list contains character literals.

Figure 8.5 shows a screen shot of a program that uses arrays of integers, set up using initializer lists, to draw a rocket. The Rocket class, which contains the main method of the program, is virtually identical to others we've seen in previous examples, so we don't present it here.

Figure 8.5

A screen shot of the Rocket program

This program makes use of polygons and polylines to draw a rocket. A *polygon* is a multisided shape; it is defined in Java using a series of (x, y) points that indicate the vertices of the polygon. Arrays are often used to store the list of coordinates.

Polygons are drawn using methods of the Graphics class, much like the way rectangles and ovals are drawn. Like these other shapes, a polygon can be drawn filled or unfilled. The methods used to draw a polygon are called drawPolygon and fillPolygon. Both of these methods are overloaded. One version uses arrays of integers to define the polygon, and the other uses an object of the Polygon class to define the polygon.

In the version that uses arrays, the drawPolygon and fillPolygon methods take three parameters. The first is an array of integers representing the x coordinates of the points in the polygon, the second is an array of integers representing the corresponding *y* coordinates of those points, and the third is an integer that indicates how many points are used from each of the two arrays. Taken together, the first two parameters represent the (*x*, *y*) coordinates of the vertices of the polygons.

A polygon is always closed. A line segment is always drawn from the last point in the list to the first point in the list.

Similar to a polygon, a *polyline* contains a series of points connected by line segments. Polylines differ from polygons in that the first and last points are not automatically connected when it is drawn. Because a polyline is not closed, it cannot be filled. Therefore there is only one method, called drawPolyline, used to draw a polyline.

Listing 8.4 shows the RocketPanel class. The arrays called xRocket and yRocket define the points of the polygon that make up the main body of the rocket. The first point in the arrays is the upper tip of the rocket, and the points progress clockwise from there. The xWindow and yWindow arrays specify the points for the polygon that forms the window in the rocket. Both the rocket and the window are drawn as filled polygons.

Listing 8.4

```java
//********************************************************************
//   RocketPanel.java        Programming with Alice and Java
//
//   Represents the drawing panel for the Rocket program.
//********************************************************************

import javax.swing.JPanel;
import java.awt.*;

public class RocketPanel extends JPanel
{
   private int[] xRocket = {100, 120, 120, 130, 130, 70, 70, 80, 80};
   private int[] yRocket = {15, 40, 115, 125, 150, 150, 125, 115, 40};

   private int[] xWindow = {95, 105, 110, 90};
   private int[] yWindow = {45, 45, 70, 70};

   private int[] xFlame = {70, 70, 75, 80, 90, 100, 110, 115, 120, 130, 130};
   private int[] yFlame = {155, 170, 165, 190, 170, 175, 160, 185, 160, 175, 155};

   //-----------------------------------------------------------------
   // Sets up the panel characteristics.
   //-----------------------------------------------------------------
   public RocketPanel()
   {
      setBackground(Color.black);
      setPreferredSize(new Dimension(200, 200));
   }
```

Listing 8.4 (continued)

```
//----------------------------------------------------------------------
// Draws a rocket using polygons and polylines.
//----------------------------------------------------------------------
public void paintComponent(Graphics gc)
{
   super.paintComponent(gc);

   gc.setColor(Color.cyan);
   gc.fillPolygon(xRocket, yRocket, xRocket.length); // rocket body

   gc.setColor(Color.gray);
   gc.fillPolygon(xWindow, yWindow, xWindow.length); // window

   gc.setColor(Color.red);
   gc.drawPolyline(xFlame, yFlame, xFlame.length); // flame
   }
}
```

The xFlame and yFlame arrays define the points of a polyline used to depict the flame shooting out of the rocket. Because it is drawn as a polyline, and not a polygon, the flame is not closed or filled.

TRY THIS!

6. Modify the Rocket program so that the flame is drawn as a filled polygon.

7. Modify the Rocket program so that the shape of the rocket and the window are different.

8. Modify the Rocket program so that the shapes are drawn using a Polygon object.

Arrays as Parameters

An entire array can be passed as a parameter to a method. When it is, because an array is an object, it is a copy of the reference to the original array that is passed.

> ▶ An entire array can be passed as a parameter, making the formal parameter an alias of the original.

A method that receives an array as a parameter can permanently change an element of the array because it is referring to the original element value. However, the method cannot permanently change the reference to the array itself because a copy of the original reference is sent to the method. These rules are consistent with the rules that govern any object type.

An element of an array can be passed to a method as well. If the element type is a primitive type, a copy of the value is passed. If the element is a reference to an object, a copy of the object reference is passed. As always, the impact of changes made to a parameter inside the method depends on the type of the parameter.

Arrays of Objects

In the previous examples in this chapter, we used arrays to store primitive types such as integers and characters. Arrays can also store elements that are references to objects. Fairly complex information management structures can be created using only arrays and other objects. For example, an array could contain objects, and each of those objects could consist of several variables and the methods that use them. Those variables could themselves be arrays, and so on. The design of a program should capitalize on the ability to combine these constructs to create the most appropriate representation for the information.

Keep in mind that an array is an object. So if we have an array of `int` values called `weight`, we are actually dealing with an object reference variable that holds the address of the array, which can be depicted as follows:

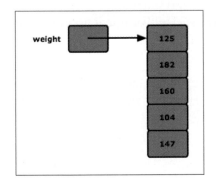

Furthermore, when we store objects in an array, each element is a separate object. That is, an array of objects is really an array of object references. Consider the following declaration:

```
String[] words = new String[5];
```

The array `words` holds references to `String` objects. The `new` operator in the declaration instantiates the array object and reserves space for five `String` references. But this declaration does not create any `String` objects; it merely creates an array that holds references to `String` objects. Initially, the array looks like this:

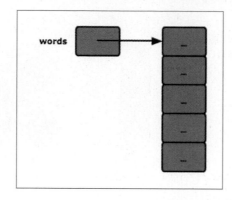

After a few `String` objects are created and put in the array, it might look like this:

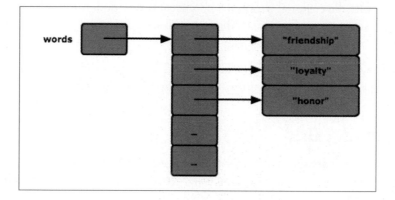

The `words` array is an object, and each character string it holds is its own object. Each object contained in an array has to be instantiated separately.

Keep in mind that `String` objects can be represented as string literals. So the following declaration creates an array called `verbs` and uses an initializer list to populate it with several `String` objects, each instantiated using a string literal:

> ▶ Instantiating an array of objects reserves room to store references only. The objects that are stored in each element must be instantiated separately.

```
String[] verbs = {"play", "work", "eat", "sleep"};
```

8.4 Two-Dimensional Arrays

The arrays we've examined so far have all been *one-dimensional arrays* in the sense that they represent a simple list of values. As the name implies, a *two-dimensional array* has values in two dimensions, which are often thought of as the rows and columns of a table. Figure 8.6 graphically compares a one-dimensional array with a two-dimensional array. To refer to a value in a two-dimensional array, you use two indexes, one specifying the row and another the column.

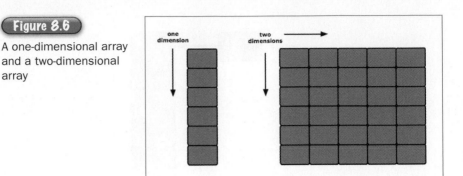

Figure 8.6

A one-dimensional array
and a two-dimensional
array

Brackets are used to represent each dimension in the array. Therefore the type of a two-dimensional array that stores integers is `int[][]`. Technically, Java represents a two-dimensional array as an array of arrays. So a two-dimensional integer array is really a one-dimensional array of references to one-dimensional integer arrays. In most cases it's easier to think about a two-dimensional array as a table with rows and columns.

Nested loops are often helpful when processing a two-dimensional array. The outer loop controls the row value, and the inner loop controls the column value.

The ThunkIt Grid

The main playing area in the ThunkIt game is a grid. Every game object, including the player, obstacles, collectables, and other items are in one of these grid locations at any point in time.

The ThunkIt `Grid` class contains a two-dimensional array of `Cell` objects. Each cell is defined by a `Location` object, which establishes the row and column of that cell. A cell can contain multiple elements, because it is possible to have more than one element at the same location (such as a block sitting on a button).

The grid represents the current status of a game as its being played. As elements move around the playing area, their representations are changed in the grid array. The grid is also used when the user is creating a custom level. The grid locations are explicitly visible in the level editor screen.

Review the `Grid` class to see how the 2D array it contains is represented and used. It is in many ways the heart of the ThunkIt game.

Multidimensional Arrays

An array can have one, two, three, or even more dimensions. Any array with more than one dimension is called a *multidimensional array*.

It's fairly easy to picture a two-dimensional array as a table. A three-dimensional array could be drawn as a cube. However, once you are past three dimensions, multidimensional arrays might seem hard to visualize. But consider that each subsequent dimension is simply a subdivision of the previous one. It is often best to think of larger multidimensional arrays in this way.

For example, suppose we wanted to store the number of students attending universities across the United States, broken down in a meaningful way. We might represent it as a four-dimensional array of integers. The first dimension represents the state. The second dimension represents the universities in each state. The third dimension represents the colleges in each university. Finally, the fourth dimension represents departments in each college. The value stored at each location is the number of students in one particular department. Figure 8.7 shows these subdivisions.

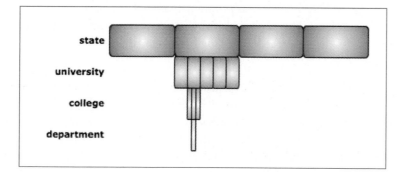

Figure 8.7

Visualizing a multidimensional array

Two-dimensional arrays are fairly common and useful. However, care should be taken when deciding to create multidimensional arrays in a program. Dealing with large amounts of data that are managed at multiple levels will probably require additional information and the methods to manage that information. It is far more likely, for instance, that in the student example each state would be represented by an object, which may contain, among other things, an array to store information about each university, and so on.

> ▶ Using an array with more than two dimensions is rare in an object-oriented system.

There is one other important characteristic of Java arrays to consider. Java does not directly support multidimensional arrays. Instead, as we have seen, they are represented as arrays of references to array objects. Those array objects could themselves contain references to other arrays. This layering could continue for as many dimensions as required. Because of this technique for representing each dimension, the arrays in any one dimension could be of different lengths. These are sometimes called *ragged arrays*. For example, the number of elements in each row of a two-dimensional array may not be the same. In such situations, care must be taken to make sure the arrays are managed appropriately.

8.5 More to Explore

Other Collections Lists are only the beginning of collections. The Java Collections API has several other classes that represent collections. These include stacks, queues, trees, sets, and maps. Each type of collection manages its data in a particular way and can often be used to strong advantage in specific situations.

Command-Line Arguments The formal parameter to the main method of a Java program is always an array of String objects. That parameter, which we typically call args, represents *command-line arguments* that are provided when the interpreter is invoked. This technique is another way to provide input to a program, but it is usually reserved for setting major parameters that determine how a program functions.

Variable-Length Parameter Lists Java provides a way to define methods that accept variable-length parameter lists. By using some special syntax in the formal parameter list of the method, we can define the method to accept any number of parameters. The parameters are automatically put into an array for easy processing in the method. This is helpful when dealing with an unknown amount of data.

Summary of Key Concepts

- A list is just one of several types of collections available in the Java API.

- Generic classes ensure type compatibility among the objects stored by the collection.

- The capacity of an `ArrayList` object changes dynamically as needed.

- An array of size N is indexed from 0 to N–1.

- In Java, an array is an object and therefore must be instantiated.

- Bounds checking ensures that an index used to refer to an array element is in range.

- An initializer list can be used to instantiate an array object instead of using the `new` operator.

- An entire array can be passed as a parameter, making the formal parameter an alias of the original.

- Instantiating an array of objects reserves room to store references only. The objects that are stored in each element must be instantiated separately.

- Using an array with more than two dimensions is rare in an object-oriented system.

Exercises

EX 8.1 Describe four programs that would be difficult to implement without using a list or an array.

EX 8.2 Compare and contrast an array and an `ArrayList`.

EX 8.3 Write code that creates an array capable of storing 1,000 `Student` objects. Explain your code.

EX 8.4 Write code that creates an `ArrayList` capable of storing 1,000 `Student` objects. Explain your code.

EX 8.5 Write code that prints the values stored in an array called `names` backwards.

EX 8.6 Write code that sets each element of a `boolean` array called `flags` to alternating values (`true` at index 0, `false` at index 1, etc.).

EX 8.7 Write a method called `sumArray` that accepts an array of floating point values as a parameter and returns the sum of those values.

EX 8.8 Find and describe four places where an `ArrayList` is used in the ThunkIt program.

EX 8.9 Describe the properties (instance data) of the `Grid` class in ThunkIt. How does the `Location` class relate to the `Grid`?

EX 8.10 Compare and contrast the `Grid` and `Level` classes from ThunkIt, particularly in their use of arrays and `ArrayList` objects.

Programming Projects

PP 8.1 Create a class called `Octagon` that represents an octagon of a particular size, color, and location. Then make a driver program that creates and displays three octagons with varying characteristics.

PP 8.2 Create a program that draws a bar chart corresponding to integer data stored in an array. The height of each bar should correspond to the corresponding value in each element of the array. Draw and label a vertical axis for the chart.

PP 8.3 Create an alternate version of the solution to the Programming Project 2 so that the range of the values in the array is not assumed. Make the tallest bar correspond to the highest data value, and size all others accordingly.

PP 8.4 Create a program that reads an arbitrary number of integers that are in the range 0 to 50, inclusive, and counts how many occurrences of each are entered. After all input has been processed, print all of the values that were entered one or more times with the number of occurrences of each.

PP 8.5 Create a class called `Car` that graphically represents a car. Use polylines and polygons to draw the car in any graphics context and any location. Then create a driver program to display the car.

PP 8.6 Create a class called `Checkerboard` that graphically represents a standard checkerboard using a two-dimensional array that holds `Checker` objects. Include a method to add a checker to a particular location. Create and display a checkerboard containing five red and three black checkers in various locations.

PP 8.7 Using a modified version of the `Circle` class from Chapter 6, create a program that draws 20 circles with random size and location. If a circle does not overlap any other circle, draw that circle in black. If a circle overlaps one or more other circles, draw it in cyan. Use an `ArrayList` to hold the 20 `Circle` objects and set the color of each appropriately (add a `setColor` method to the `Circle` class to do this). *Hint*: Two circles overlap if the distance between their center points is less than the sum of their radii.

PP 8.8 Create a class called `Card` that represents a standard playing card with a suit, rank, and basic graphic representation. Then create class called `DeckOfCards` that represents a standard deck of 52 cards. Include a `shuffle` method to randomize the order of the cards in the deck, and a `deal` method that returns one card, removing it from the deck. Create a driver program that deals and displays five cards.

PP 8.9 Create a program that allows the user to make a polyline shape dynamically using mouse clicks. Each mouse click adds a new line segment from the previous point to the location of the mouse click. Include a button below the drawing area to clear the current polyline and begin another.

PP 8.10 Create a simple version of the Snake game in which a snake moves around the screen guided by the user using the arrow keys. The user tries to direct the snake to "berries" that appear in random locations without running into a wall or its own body. When a berry is eaten, the snake gets longer and another berry appears somewhere else. Use the `Timer` class to keep the snake always moving forward in the current direction at a steady pace. Use an array or `ArrayList` to hold the location of each section of the snake. As the snake moves, each section moves into the location previously occupied by the section in front of it.

Inheritance

CHAPTER OBJECTIVES

In this chapter you will:

- ▸ Derive new classes from existing ones.
- ▸ Explore the design of class hierarchies.
- ▸ Learn the concept and purpose of method overriding.
- ▸ Use abstract classes to enhance program design.
- ▸ Explore the protected visibility modifier.
- ▸ Examine polymorphism and its benefits.
- ▸ Explore processing threads and their creation.
- ▸ See how inheritance and polymorphism are used in ThunkIt.

This chapter explains inheritance, a fundamental technique for organizing and creating classes. We've seen inheritance used in basic ways in previous chapters, and now we can delve into the details. Inheritance is a simple but powerful idea that influences the way we design object-oriented software. In this chapter we explore the technique for creating subclasses and class hierarchies, and we discuss ways to tailor the derived classes to suit specific needs. We also explore polymorphism, another fundamental object-oriented concept, and see how both inheritance and polymorphism are used in ThunkIt.

9.1 Creating Subclasses

We know that a class represents the type of an object. Classes are the plan, and objects are the embodiment of that plan. A class is like a blueprint from which we can make as many objects (houses) as we'd like.

Now suppose you want a house that is similar to another but with some different or additional features. You could start with the blueprint of the other house, then modify it to suit your new, slightly different, needs.

> ▶ Inheritance is the process of deriving a new class from an existing one.

Creating a new blueprint that is based on an existing blueprint is analogous to the object-oriented concept of *inheritance*, which is the process of deriving a new class from an existing one. Inheritance is a powerful software development technique and a defining characteristic of object-oriented programming.

The derived class automatically contains the variables and methods in the original class. Then, to tailor the class as needed, the programmer can add new variables and methods to the derived class or modify the inherited ones.

> ▶ One purpose of inheritance is to reuse existing software.

In general, new classes can be created via inheritance more quickly, easily, and cheaply than by writing them from scratch. Inheritance is one way to support the idea of *software reuse*. By using existing software components to create new ones, we capitalize on the effort that went into the design, implementation, and testing of the existing software.

Keep in mind that the word *class* comes from the idea of classifying groups of objects with similar characteristics. Classification schemes often use levels of classes that relate to each other. For example, all mammals share certain characteristics: They are warm-blooded, have hair, and bear live offspring. Now consider a subset of mammals, such as horses. All horses are mammals and have all of the characteristics of mammals, but they also have unique features that make them different from other mammals such as dogs.

If we translate this idea into software terms, an existing class called `Mammal` would have certain variables and methods that describe the state and behavior of mammals. A `Horse` class could be derived from the existing `Mammal` class, automatically inheriting the variables and methods contained in `Mammal`. The `Horse` class can refer to the inherited variables and methods as if they had been declared locally in that class. New variables and methods can then be added to the derived class to distinguish a horse from other mammals.

The original class that is used to derive a new one is called the *parent class*, *superclass*, or *base class*. The derived class is called a *child class*, or *subclass*. An inheritance relationship can be shown graphically with an arrow with an open arrowhead pointing from the child class to the parent, as shown in Figure 9.1. In this case, a class called `Dictionary` is being derived from a class called `Book`.

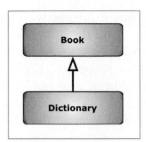

Figure 9.1

An inheritance relationship deriving Dictionary from Book

The process of inheritance should establish an *is-a relationship* between two classes. That is, the child class should be a more specific version of the parent. A horse is a mammal, but not all mammals are horses. A dictionary is a book, but not all books are dictionaries. For any class X that is derived from class Y, you should be able to say that "X is a Y." If such a statement doesn't make sense, then that relationship is probably not an appropriate use of inheritance.

> ▶ Inheritance creates an "is-a" relationship between the parent and child classes.

Java uses the reserved word `extends` to indicate that a new class is being derived from an existing class. Once the `Book` class has been defined, the `Dictionary` class can be defined as follows:

```
public class Dictionary extends Book
{
    //  contents of Dictionary
}
```

Simply by using the `extends` clause in the header of `Dictionary`, you cause the `Dictionary` class to automatically inherit the definitions of methods and variables declared in the `Book` class. For example, if the `Book` class contains an integer variable called `pages`, then the `Dictionary` class automatically has an integer variable called `pages` too, as if it were declared in `Dictionary` explicitly.

Although the `Book` class is needed to create the definition of `Dictionary`, a `Book` object is not needed in order to create a `Dictionary` object. An instance of a child class does not rely on an instance of the parent class.

Inheritance is a one-way street. The `Book` class cannot use variables or methods that are declared explicitly in the `Dictionary` class. This restriction makes sense because a child class is a more specific version of the parent class. A dictionary has pages because all books have pages; but even though a dictionary has definitions, not all books do.

The protected Modifier

As we've seen, visibility modifiers are used to control access to the members of a class. Visibility plays an important role in the process of inheritance as well. Any public method or variable in a parent class can be explicitly referenced by name in the child class, and through objects of that child class. On the other hand, private methods and variables of the parent class cannot be referenced in the child class or through an object of the child class.

This situation causes a dilemma. If we declare a variable with public visibility so that a derived class can reference it, we violate the principle of encapsulation. Therefore, Java provides a third visibility modifier: `protected`. Protected visibility allows the class to retain some encapsulation properties. The encapsulation with protected visibility is not as tight as it would be if the variable or method were declared private, but it is better than if it were declared public. Specifically, a variable or method declared with protected visibility may be accessed by any class in the same package. The relationships among all Java modifiers are explained completely in Appendix E.

> ▶ Protected visibility provides the best possible encapsulation that permits inheritance.

Let's be clear about our terms. All methods and variables, even those declared with private visibility, are inherited by the child class. That is, their definitions exist and memory space is reserved for the variables. It's just that they can't be referenced by name.

Constructors are not inherited. Constructors are special methods that are used to set up a particular type of object, so it doesn't make sense for a class called `Dictionary` to have a constructor called `Book`. But you can imagine that a child class may want to refer to the constructor of the parent class, which is one of the reasons for the `super` reference, described next.

The `super` Reference

The reserved word `super` can be used in a class to refer to its parent class. A common use of the `super` reference is to invoke a parent's constructor. Suppose the constructor of `Dictionary` contained the following call:

```
super();
```

> ▶ A parent's constructor can be invoked using the `super` reference.

This call explicitly calls the `Book` constructor. If the constructor accepts parameters, they can be passed in the `super` call.

The child's constructor could go ahead and deal with the initializations as the parent's constructor does. However, it is good practice to let each class "take care of itself." That way, when changes are made in one class, it's not necessary to remember to make the changes in its children.

A child's constructor is responsible for calling its parent's constructor. Generally, the first line of a constructor should use the `super` reference to call a constructor of the parent class. If no such call exists, Java will automatically make a call to `super` with no parameters at the beginning of the constructor. This rule ensures that a parent class initializes its variables before the child class constructor begins to execute. Using the `super` reference to invoke a parent's constructor can be done only in the child's constructor (not any other method), and if included, it must be the first line of the constructor.

The `super` reference can also be used to reference other variables and methods defined in the parent's class, if needed.

Overriding Methods

When a child class defines a method with the same name and signature as a method in the parent class, we say that the child's version *overrides* the parent's version in favor of its own. The need for overriding occurs often in inheritance situations.

▶ A child class can override (redefine) the parent's definition of an inherited method.

A method can be defined with the `final` modifier. A child class cannot override a final method. This technique is used to ensure that a derived class uses a particular definition of a method.

Method overriding is a key element in object-oriented design. It allows two objects that are related by inheritance to use the same naming conventions for methods that accomplish the same general task in different ways. Overriding becomes even more important when it comes to polymorphism, which is discussed later in this chapter.

 ## Class Hierarchies

A child class derived from one parent can be the parent of its own child class. Furthermore, multiple classes can be derived from a single parent. Therefore, inheritance relationships often develop into *class hierarchies*. The diagram in Figure 9.2 shows a class hierarchy that includes the inheritance relationship between the `Mammal` and `Horse` classes, discussed earlier.

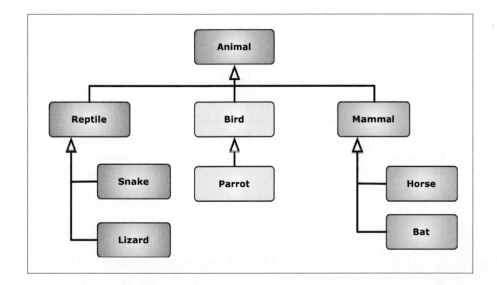

Figure 9.2

A class hierarchy of animals

There is no limit to the number of children a class can have or to the number of levels to which a class hierarchy can extend. Two children of the same parent are called *siblings*. Although siblings share the characteristics passed on by their common parent, they are not related by inheritance because one is not used to derive the other.

▶ The child of one class can be the parent of one or more other classes, creating a class hierarchy.

> ▶ Common features should be located as high in a class hierarchy as is reasonably possible.

In class hierarchies, common features should be kept as high in the hierarchy as reasonably possible. That way, the only characteristics explicitly established in a child class are those that make the class distinct from its parent and from its siblings. This approach maximizes the potential to reuse classes. It also facilitates maintenance activities because when changes are made to the parent, they are automatically reflected in the descendants. Always remember to maintain the "is-a" relationship when building class hierarchies.

The inheritance mechanism is transitive. That is, a parent passes along a trait to a child class, and that child class passes it along to its children, and so on. An inherited feature might have originated in the immediate parent or possibly several levels higher in a more distant ancestor class.

There is no single best hierarchy for all situations. The decisions you make when you are designing a class hierarchy restrict and guide more detailed design decisions and implementation options, so you must make them carefully.

The class hierarchy shown in Figure 9.2 organizes animals by their major biological classifications, such as `Mammal`, `Bird`, and `Reptile`. In a different situation, however, it may be better to organize the same animals in a different way. For example, as shown in Figure 9.3, the class hierarchy might be organized around a function of the animals, such as their ability to fly. In this case, a `Parrot` class and a `Bat` class would be siblings derived from a general `FlyingAnimal` class. This class hierarchy is as valid and reasonable as the original one. The goals of the programs that use the classes are the determining factor, guiding the programmer to a hierarchy design that is best for the situation.

Figure 9.3

An alternative hierarchy for organizing animals

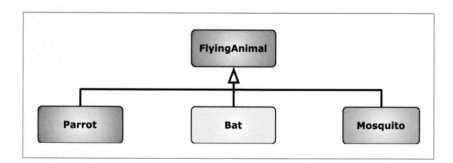

The Object Class

In Java, all classes are derived ultimately from the `Object` class. If a class definition doesn't use the `extends` clause to derive itself explicitly from another class, then that class is automatically derived from the `Object` class by default. Therefore, the following two class definitions are equivalent:

```
class Thing
{
   // whatever
}
```

and

```
class Thing extends Object
{
    // whatever
}
```

Because all classes are derived from `Object`, all public methods of `Object` are inherited by every Java class. They can be invoked through any object created in any Java program. The `Object` class is defined in the `java.lang` package of the Java standard class library. Figure 9.4 lists some of the methods of the `Object` class.

> ▶ All Java classes are derived, directly or indirectly, from the `Object` class.

```
boolean equals (Object obj)
    Returns true if this object is an alias of the specified object.

String toString ()
    Returns a string representation of this object.

Object clone ()
    Creates and returns a copy of this object.
```

Figure 9.4

Some methods of the `Object` class

As it turns out, we've been using `Object` methods quite often in our examples. The `toString` method, for instance, is defined in the `Object` class, so the `toString` method can be called on any object. As we've seen several times, when a `println` method is called with an object parameter, `toString` is called to determine what to print.

So when we define a `toString` method in a class, we are actually overriding an inherited definition. The definition for `toString` that is provided by the `Object` class returns a string containing the object's class name followed by a numeric value that is unique for that object. Usually, we override the `Object` version of `toString` to fit our own needs. The `String` class has overridden the `toString` method so that it returns its stored string value.

> ▶ The `toString` and `equals` methods are inherited by every class in every Java program.

We are also overriding an inherited method when we define an `equals` method for a class. The purpose of the `equals` method is to determine whether two objects are equal. The definition of the `equals` method provided by the `Object` class returns true if the two object references actually refer to the same object (that is, if they are aliases). Classes often override the inherited definition of the `equals` method in favor of a more appropriate definition. For instance, the `String` class overrides `equals` so that it returns true only if both strings contain the same characters in the same order.

Abstract Classes

An *abstract class* represents a generic concept in a class hierarchy. As the name implies, an abstract class represents something that is usually too incompletely defined to be useful by itself. Instead, an abstract class may contain a partial description that is inherited by all of its descendants in the class hierarchy. An abstract class is just like any other class, except that it may have some methods that have not been defined yet. Its children, which are more specific, fill in the gaps.

> An abstract class cannot be instantiated. It represents a concept on which other classes can build their definitions.

An abstract class cannot be instantiated and usually contains one or more *abstract methods*, which have no definition (like in an interface). That is, there is no body of code defined for an abstract method, and therefore it cannot be invoked. An abstract class might also contain methods that are not abstract, meaning that the method definition is provided as usual. And an abstract class can contain data declarations as usual.

A class is declared as abstract by including the `abstract` modifier in the class header. Any class that contains one or more abstract methods must be declared as abstract. In abstract classes, the `abstract` modifier must be applied to each abstract method. A class declared as abstract does not have to contain abstract methods, however.

Consider the class hierarchy shown in Figure 9.5. The `Vehicle` class at the top of the hierarchy may be too generic for a particular application. Therefore we may choose to implement it as an abstract class. In diagrams, the names of abstract classes and abstract methods are usually shown in italics.

Figure 9.5

A class hierarchy of vehicles

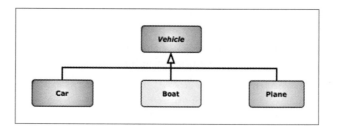

Concepts that apply to all vehicles can be represented in the `Vehicle` class and are inherited by its descendants. That way, each of its descendants doesn't have to define the same concept redundantly (and perhaps inconsistently). For example, suppose we declare a variable called `speed` in the `Vehicle` class, and therefore all specific vehicles below it in the hierarchy automatically have that variable because of inheritance. Any change we make to the representation of the speed of a vehicle is automatically reflected in all descendant classes. Similarly, in `Vehicle` we could declare an abstract method called `fuelConsumption`, whose purpose is to calculate how quickly fuel is being consumed by a particular vehicle. The `Vehicle` class establishes that all vehicles consume fuel and provides a consistent method interface for computing that value. But the implementation of the `fuelConsumption` method is left up to each subclass of `Vehicle`, which can tailor its method accordingly.

Some concepts don't apply to all vehicles, so we wouldn't represent those concepts at the `Vehicle` level. For instance, we wouldn't include a variable called `numberOfWheels` in the `Vehicle` class, because not all vehicles have wheels. The child classes for which wheels are appropriate can add that concept at the appropriate level in the hierarchy.

There are no restrictions as to where in a class hierarchy an abstract class can be defined. Usually they are located at the upper levels of a class hierarchy. However, it is possible to derive an abstract class from a non-abstract parent.

Usually, a child of an abstract class will provide a specific definition for an abstract method inherited from its parent. This is really just a specific case of overriding a method, giving a different definition than the one the parent provides. If a child of an abstract class does not give a definition for every abstract method that it inherits from its parent, then the child class is also considered abstract.

> ▶ A class derived from an abstract parent must override all of its parent's abstract methods, or the derived class will also be considered abstract.

It would be a contradiction for an abstract method to be modified as `final` or `static`. Because a final method cannot be overridden in subclasses, an abstract final method would have no way of being given a definition in subclasses. A static method can be invoked using the class name without declaring an object of the class. Because abstract methods have no implementation, an abstract static method would make no sense.

Choosing which classes and methods to make abstract is an important part of the design process. You should make such choices only after careful consideration. By using abstract classes wisely, you can create flexible, extensible software designs.

ShapeMaker

Let's look at an example that makes use of inheritance. A screen shot of the `ShapeMaker` program is shown in Figure 9.6. It allows the user to draw various shapes, filled or unfilled, using the mouse. The shapes are retained on the drawing surface, allowing the user to create a complete picture made up of many shapes.

Figure 9.6

A screen shot of the
`ShapeMaker` program

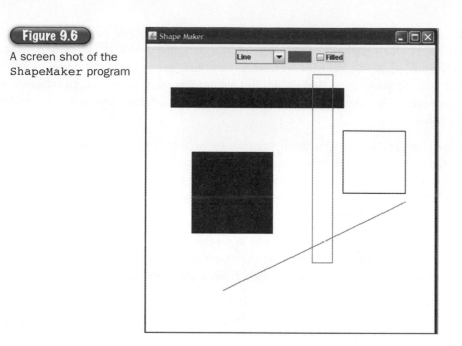

The shape to be drawn is determined by a drop-down menu. The color of the shape is shown in a small panel that also serves as a button. When it is pressed, a color chooser dialog box appears, as shown in Figure 9.7, to allow the user to select the color (which is then displayed in the color panel). If the check box labeled "Filled" is selected, the shape will be drawn solid; otherwise it will be drawn as an outline only. These controls will be discussed further in the next section.

Figure 9.7

A `ColorChooser`
dialog box

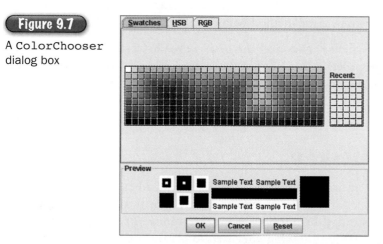

As the mouse is dragged across the window, the shape grows and shrinks accordingly. This is a technique called *rubberbanding*, as if the mouse were stretching the shape into its final position.

In the `ShapeMaker` program, each type of figure is represented by a class. These classes are related by inheritance as shown in Figure 9.8. The `Shape` and `BoundedShape` classes are abstract.

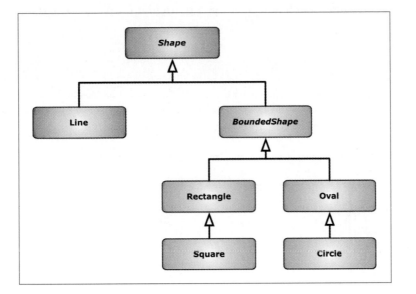

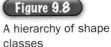

Figure 9.8

A hierarchy of shape classes

The `Shape` class is shown in Listing 9.1. It contains only a data value to store the shape's color, and an abstract method for drawing the shape. Note that the `color` variable is declared with protected visibility. The `draw` method must be implemented by all of the non-abstract descendants of the `Shape` class.

Listing 9.1

```
//********************************************************************
//   Shape.java          Programming with Alice and Java
//
//   Represents an abstract shape that can be drawn.
//********************************************************************

import java.awt.*;

public abstract class Shape
{
    protected Color color;

    //----------------------------------------------------------------
    //   Descendants of this class implement the draw method to draw the
    //   particular shape in the specified graphics context.
    //----------------------------------------------------------------
    public abstract void draw(Graphics gc);
}
```

The Line class, for instance, is not abstract, and is shown in Listing 9.2. It defines two Point objects to represent the two endpoints of the line segment. The Line constructor sets these two points, and sets the value of the shape's color, a variable inherited from the Shape class. The Line class also defines (overrides) the draw method to draw the line segment in a particular graphics context.

Listing 9.2

```java
//*************************************************************************
//  Line.java        Programming with Alice and Java
//
//  Represents a line segment that can be drawn in a particular graphics
//  context.
//*************************************************************************

import java.awt.*;

public class Line extends Shape
{
   protected Point start, end;

   //-------------------------------------------------------------------
   //  Sets up the line characteristics.
   //-------------------------------------------------------------------
   public Line(Point p1, Point p2, Color shade)
   {
      start = p1;
      end = p2;
      color = shade;
   }

   //-------------------------------------------------------------------
   // Draws the line in the specified graphics context.
   //-------------------------------------------------------------------
   public void draw(Graphics gc)
   {
      gc.setColor(color);
      gc.drawLine((int) start.getX(), (int) start.getY(),
      (int) end.getX(), (int) end.getY());
   }
}
```

The BoundedShape class, shown in Listing 9.3, is derived from Shape and is also abstract. It represents all shapes that can be defined by a bounding rectangle. It stores data that represents the upper-left corner point, the width and height of the bounding rectangle, and a boolean value that represents whether the figure is filled or not. None of these values were put in the Shape class because some classes (particularly Line) do not need these values.

Listing 9.3

```java
//*****************************************************************************
//  BoundedShape.java          Programming with Alice and Java
//
//  Represents an abstract shape defined by a bounding rectangle.
//*****************************************************************************

import java.awt.*;

public abstract class BoundedShape extends Shape
{
    protected Point upperLeft;
    protected int width, height;
    protected boolean filled;

    //-----------------------------------------------------------------------
    //  Creates and returns a point representing the upper-left corner of a
    //  bounding rectangle based on two points.
    //-----------------------------------------------------------------------
    protected Point determineUpperLeft(Point p1, Point p2)
    {
        int x = (int) Math.min(p1.getX(), p2.getX());
        int y = (int) Math.min(p1.getY(), p2.getY());
        return new Point(x, y);
    }
}
```

The BoundedShape class also contains a method used by its descendants to determine which point is the upper-left corner. As the user drags the mouse across the screen, the starting point and the current point might "switch places." That is, whichever point is higher and to the left is considered the upper-left corner of the bounding rectangle.

The Rectangle class, shown in Listing 9.4, contains only the instance data it inherits from its ancestors. The Rectangle constructor uses the determine-UpperLeft method to determine the upper-left corner, and then computes the width and height. The draw method draws the rectangle, filled or unfilled, in the appropriate color.

Listing 9.4

```java
//**************************************************************************
//   Rectangle.java          Programming with Alice and Java
//
//   Represents a rectangle that can be drawn in a particular graphics context.
//**************************************************************************

import java.awt.*;

public class Rectangle extends BoundedShape
{
   //--------------------------------------------------------------------
   //  Sets the characteristics of the rectangle based on two points.
   //--------------------------------------------------------------------
   public Rectangle(Point p1, Point p2, Color shade, boolean isFilled)
   {
      upperLeft = determineUpperLeft(p1, p2);
      width = (int) Math.abs(p1.getX()-p2.getX());
      height = (int) Math.abs(p1.getY()-p2.getY());
      filled = isFilled;
      color = shade;
   }

   //--------------------------------------------------------------------
   //  Draws the rectangle in the specified graphics context.
   //--------------------------------------------------------------------
   public void draw(Graphics gc)
   {
      gc.setColor(color);

      int x = (int) upperLeft.getX();
      int y = (int) upperLeft.getY();

      if (filled)
         gc.fillRect(x, y, width, height);
      else
         gc.drawRect(x, y, width, height);
   }
}
```

The Square class, shown in Listing 9.5, is derived from Rectangle. After all, a square is a rectangle with equal sides. The Square constructor calls its parent's constructor using the super reference. Then it ensures that both the width and height are equal. The Square class uses the version of the draw method that it inherits from Rectangle.

```
//************************************************************************
//   Square.java        Programming with Alice and Java
//
//   Represents a square (a rectangle with equal width and height).
//************************************************************************

import java.awt.*;

public class Square extends Rectangle
{
   //-----------------------------------------------------------------
   //   Sets up the square, ensuring an equal width and height based on the
   //   two points used to determine the rectangle size.
   //-----------------------------------------------------------------
   public Square(Point p1, Point p2, Color shade, boolean isFilled)
   {
      super(p1, p2, shade, isFilled);

      int potentialWidth - (int) Math.abs(p1.gctX() p2.getX());
      int potentialHeight = (int) Math.abs(p1.getY()-p2.getY());
      int min = (int) Math.min(potentialWidth, potentialHeight);
      width = min;
      height = min;
   }
}
```

The `Oval` and `Circle` classes shown in the inheritance hierarchy in Figure 9.8 are not included in this version of the `ShapeMaker` program. You'll be asked to add them in section 9.3. Before we explore more details of `ShapeMaker`, let's look at how class hierarchies come into play in ThunkIt.

Class Hierarchies in ThunkIt

Inheritance plays a role in various places throughout the ThunkIt code, but one place that stands out is the hierarchy of classes representing the elements that appear on the playing board. A portion of that hierarchy is shown in Figure 9.9.

Part of the element
hierarchy in ThunkIt

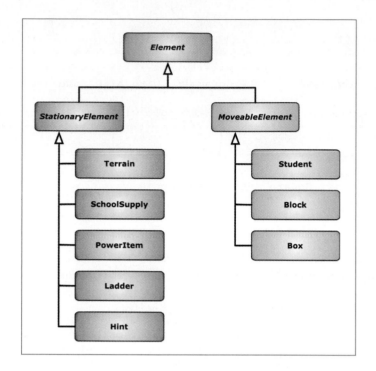

All game elements are derived from a common Element class, which is abstract. The two main divisions under that distinguish between stationary and moveable elements. This distinction focuses on whether an element can move from one cell of the playing grid to another. Both stationary and moveable elements can have an animated representation.

Some classes represent multiple elements. Terrain, for instance, represents the basic support surfaces (grass, ice, sand, etc.). The SchoolSupply class represents any of the school supplies that the student must collect (pencil, calculator, etc.). In these cases, it is sufficient to have a single class whose attributes determine all important differences. For example, other than a different graphical representation, there is no difference between a pencil and a calculator, for instance.

In other cases, a class represents a single type of element. Many of the moveable elements have their own classes due to the way they uniquely interact with other elements as they move around the board.

9.3 Polymorphism

Often, the type of a reference variable exactly matches the class of the object to which it refers. For example, consider the following reference:

```
ChessPiece bishop;
```

The bishop variable may be used to point to an object that is created by instantiating the ChessPiece class. However, it doesn't have to. The variable type and the object it refers to must be compatible, but their types need not be exactly the same. The relationship between a reference variable and the object it refers to is more flexible than that.

The term *polymorphism* can be defined as "having many forms." A *polymorphic reference* is a reference variable that can refer to different types of objects at different points in time. The specific method invoked through a polymorphic reference (the actual code executed) can change from one invocation to the next.

> ▶ A polymorphic reference can refer to different types of objects over time.

Consider the following line of code:

```
obj.doIt();
```

If the reference `obj` is polymorphic, it can refer to different types of objects at different times. So if that line of code is in a loop, or if it's in a method that is called more than once, that line of code could call a different version of the `doIt` method each time it is invoked.

At some point, the commitment is made to execute certain code to carry out a method invocation. This commitment is referred to as *binding* a method invocation to a method definition. In many situations, the binding of a method invocation to a method definition can occur at compile time. For polymorphic references, however, the decision cannot be made until run time. The method definition that is used is determined by the type of the object being referenced at the moment of invocation. This deferred commitment is called *late binding* or *dynamic binding*. It is slightly less efficient than binding at compile time because the decision is made during the execution of the program. But this overhead is generally acceptable in light of the flexibility that a polymorphic reference provides.

> ▶ The binding of a method invocation to its definition is performed at run time for a polymorphic reference.

Polymorphism via Inheritance

When we declare a reference variable using a particular class name, it can be used to refer to any object of that class. In addition, it can also refer to any object of any class that is related to its declared type by inheritance. For example, if the class `Mammal` is the parent of the class `Horse`, then a `Mammal` reference can be used to refer to an object of class `Horse`. This ability is shown in the following code segment:

```
Mammal pet;
Horse secretariat = new Horse();
pet = secretariat; // a valid assignment
```

The ability to assign an object of one class to a reference of another class may seem like a deviation from the concept of strong typing discussed in Chapter 6, but it's not. Strong typing asserts that a variable can only be assigned a value consistent with its declared type. Well, that's what's happening here. Remember, inheritance establishes an "is-a" relationship. A horse is a mammal. Therefore, assigning a `Horse` object to a `Mammal` reference is perfectly reasonable.

▶ A reference variable can refer to any object created from any class related to it by inheritance.

The reverse operation, assigning the `Mammal` object to a `Horse` reference, can also be done but it requires an explicit cast. Assigning a reference in this direction is generally less useful and more likely to cause problems because although a horse has all the functionality of a mammal, the reverse is not necessarily true.

This relationship works throughout a class hierarchy. If the `Mammal` class were derived from a class called `Animal`, the following assignment would also be valid:

```
Animal creature = new Horse();
```

Carrying this idea to the limit, an `Object` reference can be used to refer to any object because ultimately all classes are descendants of the `Object` class.

The reference variable `creature` can be used polymorphically because at any point in time it can refer to an `Animal` object, a `Mammal` object, or a `Horse` object. Suppose that all three of these classes have a method called `move` that is implemented in different ways (because the child classes overrode the definitions they inherited). The following invocation calls the `move` method, but the particular version of the method it calls is determined at run time:

```
creature.move();
```

▶ The type of the object, not the type of the reference, determines which version of a method is invoked.

When this line is executed, if `creature` currently refers to an `Animal` object, the `move` method of the `Animal` class is invoked. Likewise, if `creature` currently refers to a `Mammal` object, the `Mammal` version of `move` is invoked. Similarly, if it currently refers to a `Horse` object, the `Horse` version of `move` is invoked.

Because `Animal` and `Mammal` represent general concepts, they may be defined as abstract classes. This situation does not eliminate the ability to have polymorphic references. Suppose the `move` method in the `Mammal` class is abstract, and is given unique definitions in the `Horse`, `Dog`, and `Whale` classes (all derived from `Mammal`). A `Mammal` reference variable can be used to refer to any objects created from any of the `Horse`, `Dog`, and `Whale` classes, and can be used to execute the `move` method on any of them, even though `Mammal` itself is abstract.

ShapeMaker Revisited

Now let's return to the `ShapeMaker` example and see how polymorphism plays a role in it. The `ShapeMakerPanel` class, shown in Listing 9.6, represents the surface on which the shapes are drawn and holds the control panel that allows the user to determine what is drawn. It also contains all listeners (as inner classes) needed in the program.

Listing 9.6

```java
//***************************************************************************
//   ShapeMakerPanel.java          Programming with Alice and Java
//
//   Represents the main panel for the ShapeMaker program.
//***************************************************************************

import java.awt.*;
import javax.swing.*;
import java.awt.event.*;
import java.util.*;

public class ShapeMakerPanel extends JPanel
{
   private JComboBox shapeCombo;
   private JPanel colorPanel, controlPanel;
   private JCheckBox filled;
   private ArrayList<Shape> shapes;
   private Point point1, point2;
   private Color color;
   private Shape currentShape;

   //-----------------------------------------------------------------------
   //   Sets up the interface and drawing region.
   //-----------------------------------------------------------------------
   public ShapeMakerPanel()
   {
      shapes = new ArrayList<Shape>();
      point1 = null;
      point2 = null;
      color = Color.black;

      String[] shapeNames = {"Line", "Rectangle", "Square"};
      shapeCombo = new JComboBox(shapeNames);

      colorPanel = new JPanel();
      colorPanel.setPreferredSize(new Dimension(40, 20));
      colorPanel.setBackground(color);
      colorPanel.addMouseListener(new ColorListener());

      filled = new JCheckBox("Filled");

      controlPanel = new JPanel();
      controlPanel.add(shapeCombo);
      controlPanel.add(colorPanel);
      controlPanel.add(filled);
      controlPanel.setPreferredSize(new Dimension(500, 40));

      add(controlPanel);
      addMouseListener(new ShapeListener());
      addMouseMotionListener(new ShapeDragListener());
```

(continued)

Listing 9.6 (continued)

```java
        setBackground(Color.white);
        setPreferredSize(new Dimension(500, 500));
    }

    //-----------------------------------------------------------------
    // Creates a shape based on the current interface settings.
    //-----------------------------------------------------------------
    private Shape makeShape()
    {
        Shape shape = null;

        switch (shapeCombo.getSelectedIndex())
        {
            case 0:
                shape = new Line(point1, point2, color);
                break;
            case 1:
                shape = new Rectangle(point1, point2, color, filled.isSelected());
                break;
            case 2:
                shape = new Square(point1, point2, color, filled.isSelected());
                break ;
        }

        return shape;
    }

    //-----------------------------------------------------------------
    // Paints the panel by drawing all previously created shapes and the
    // current shape.
    //-----------------------------------------------------------------
    public void paintComponent(Graphics gc)
    {
        super.paintComponent(gc);

        for (Shape shape : shapes)
            shape.draw(gc);

        if (currentShape != null)
            currentShape.draw(gc);
    }

    //*****************************************************************************
    // The listener for the custom color button.
    //*****************************************************************************
    private class ColorListener extends MouseAdapter
    {
        public void mouseClicked(MouseEvent event)
        {
            color = JColorChooser.showDialog(colorPanel, "Pick a Color", color);
```

Listing 9.6 (continued)

```java
            colorPanel.setBackground(color);
      }
   }

   //************************************************************
   // The listener for starting a new shape (mouse pressed) and ending the
   // current shape (mouse released).
   //************************************************************
   private class ShapeListener extends MouseAdapter
   {
      public void mousePressed(MouseEvent event)
      {
         point1 = event.getPoint();
      }

      public void mouseReleased(MouseEvent event)
      {
         point2 = event.getPoint();
         shapes.add(makeShape());
         currentShape = null;
         repaint();
      }
   }

   //************************************************************
   // The listener for "stretching" the shape to the correct size.
   //************************************************************
   private class ShapeDragListener extends MouseMotionAdapter
   {
      public void mouseDragged(MouseEvent event)
      {
         point2 = event.getPoint();
         currentShape = makeShape();
         repaint();
      }
   }
}
```

The controls are put on a separate panel, which is then added to the main panel. They include a JComboBox, which serves as the drop-down menu providing the choices of shapes to drawn. Its options are determined by an array of strings passed to the JComboBox constructor.

Another small panel is used to show the shape color and to serve as a button to bring up the color chooser. This is an example of a *custom button*. A mouse listener created from the ColorListener inner class is used to capture the user clicking the mouse on the color panel and display the dialog box. Once the color is retrieved, the background of the color panel is set accordingly.

The check box indicating whether the shape should be filled or not does not have its own listener. Instead, when the shape is drawn, the component is consulted directly to see if the box is selected.

As they are being created, all the shapes are drawn based on two points—the point where the mouse was initially clicked, and the point to where the mouse has currently been dragged. The ShapeListener inner class handles the initial click and the final release. When the mouse button is initially pressed down, the first point is captured. When it finally released, the second point is captured a final time, the shape is made and added to the list, and the panel is repainted.

The ShapeDragListener class redraws the panel as the user drags the mouse. The drag event fires so quickly and so often, the illusion of pulling the shape into place is reasonable.

The paintComponent method draws all of the shapes. The following loop retrieves each shape from the list and calls its draw method:

```
for (Shape shape : shapes)
    shape.draw(gc);
```

This call to the draw method is polymorphic. One time through the loop, the shape might be a Line object. The next time, it might be a Square, or a Rectangle. But because they are all shapes, they can all be drawn. Each call invokes the appropriate version of the draw method, depending on the class of the object.

TRY THIS!

1. Add Oval and Circle classes to the ShapeMaker program as depicted in Figure 9.8 and modify the controls to allow them to be drawn.

2. Add a button to the control panel in the ShapeMaker program to clear the drawing surface.

9.4 Threads

In Alice, we had statements such as Do together that allowed us to have multiple actions happening at once. In Java, concurrency is accomplished using multiple execution *threads*. A class can be defined so that it runs in its own thread. Multiple threads of execution can be running at the same time.

A thread can be created using inheritance, as shown in Figure 9.10. If you use the Thread class, which is part of the java.lang package, as the parent of a new class, the child class is a thread. The child class should override a method called run to define what that thread should do when it executes. When the thread is started, control returns immediately to the caller, which can then go on to start other threads of execution.

> ▶ A thread can be created using inheritance.

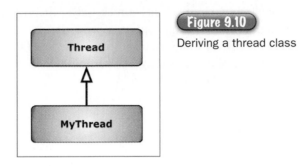

Figure 9.10

Deriving a thread class

A thread can also be created by implementing the `Runnable` interface. When a `Thread` object is created using the `new` operator, the class that implements `Runnable` is passed as a parameter to the `Thread` constructor.

Threads in ThunkIt

Threads are used in the ThunkIt program in some key places. Chief among them is in handling the elements' graphical animation (movement, rotations, etc.). Every element that can appear on the game board has the potential of running in its own thread.

Recall that the `Element` class, discussed earlier in this chapter, is the parent of all elements in the game. `Element` is derived from the `Thread` class, making it and all of its children runnable. The `run` method in each is set up to execute the appropriate animation. Each thread is started and stopped as needed to create the desired visual effect.

By making each element a separate thread, we can start a hint element spinning and forget about it until the student character moves onto it. To show an element moving from one cell to another, its thread is started, the appropriate animation is played, and then the thread is stopped.

9.5 More to Explore

Visibility We noted in this chapter that the visibility modifier used on a variable or method determines how it can be accessed in child classes. As you explore this issue in more detail, subtle aspects of the situation will arise. Even when a variable is declared with private visibility, memory space for it is allocated in the child class as well. The derived class cannot refer tot that variable by name, but it could call a method (perhaps inherited from the parent) that does. Consult Appendix E for more details.

Synchronization Threads are introduced briefly in the last section of this chapter as the way Java allows concurrent processing. Threads are created using inheritance, and the ThunkIt application relies on them, so this was an appropriate point to introduce them. But be aware that the concept of threads opens the door to many issues. Chief among them is synchronization — the need to carefully control access to shared data so that inappropriate operations do not take place. Since ThunkIt uses treads mainly for animation purposes, the need for synchronization is minimal. But as you explore threading further, be aware that they create the need for additional levels of data security.

Summary of Key Concepts

- Inheritance is the process of deriving a new class from an existing one.

- One purpose of inheritance is to reuse existing software.

- Inheritance creates an "is-a" relationship between the parent and child classes.

- Protected visibility provides the best possible encapsulation that permits inheritance.

- A parent's constructor can be invoked using the `super` reference.

- A child class can override (redefine) the parent's definition of an inherited method.

- The child of one class can be the parent of one or more other classes, creating a class hierarchy.

- Common features should be located as high in a class hierarchy as is reasonably possible.

- All Java classes are derived, directly or indirectly, from the `Object` class.

- The `toString` and `equals` methods are inherited by every class in every Java program.

- An abstract class cannot be instantiated. It represents a concept on which other classes can build their definitions.

- A class derived from an abstract parent must override all of its parent's abstract methods, or the derived class will also be considered abstract.

- A polymorphic reference can refer to different types of objects over time.

- The binding of a method invocation to its definition is performed at run time for a polymorphic reference.

- A reference variable can refer to any object created from any class related to it by inheritance.

- The type of the object, not the type of the reference, determines which version of a method is invoked.

- A thread can be created using inheritance.

Exercises

EX 9.1 Would an inheritance hierarchy be well suited to represent a family tree? Explain.

EX 9.2 Draw an inheritance hierarchy containing classes that represent different types of clocks.

EX 9.3 In contrast to your answer to the previous exercise, draw an alternate hierarchy for classes that represent clocks. Discuss situations in which one might be better or worse than the other.

EX 9.4 Draw an inheritance hierarchy containing classes that represent different types of cars, organized first by manufacturer.

EX 9.5 In contrast to your answer in the previous exercise, draw an alternate hierarchy for classes the represent cars, organized first by type (sports car, sedan, SUV, etc.).

EX 9.6 Draw an inheritance hierarchy containing classes that represent different types of vehicles that travel in the air.

EX 9.7 Draw an inheritance hierarchy containing classes that represent different types of trees (oak, elm, etc.).

EX 9.8 Draw an inheritance hierarchy containing classes that represent different types of payment transactions at a store (cash, credit card, etc.).

EX 9.9 Draw an inheritance hierarchy containing classes that represent different types of animals in a zoo. Explain how polymorphism could play a role in guiding the feeding of the animals.

EX 9.10 Explain how a call to the `addMouseListener` method on a panel represents a polymorphic situation.

Programming Projects

PP 9.1 Create classes that represent a `Book` and a `Dictionary` as shown in Figure 9.1. Have a `Book` keep track of its number of pages and a `Dictionary` keep track of the number of definitions it contains. Include constructors in both classes. Create a method called `computeRatio` in the `Dictionary` class that returns its average number of definitions per page. Create a driver class whose `main` method instantiates a `Dictionary` object and prints its definition ratio.

PP 9.2 Create a class called `MonetaryCoin` that is derived from the `Coin` class presented in Chapter 6. Store a value in the monetary coin that represents its value and add a method that returns its value. Create a driver class whose `main` method instantiates several `MonetaryCoin` objects and computes their total value. Demonstrate that a monetary coin inherits its parent's ability to be flipped.

PP 9.3 Create a set of classes that represent the employees at a company, including salaried employees, hourly employees, executives, and volunteers. Form appropriate inheritance relationships. Have each class implement a method called `pay` that returns the payment amount for that employee. Create a class called `Staff` that holds a list of various types of employees, and includes a method called `payday` that pays the entire staff.

PP 9.4 Create a set of classes that represent the employees of a hospital: doctor, nurse, surgeon, anesthesiologist, etc. Form appropriate inheritance relationships. Include methods in each class that are named according to the services they provide and that print an appropriate message. Create a driver class whose `main` method instantiates and exercises several of the classes.

PP 9.5 Create a hierarchy of classes that keep track of various sports statistics. Have each specific class (low in the hierarchy) represent a particular sport. Tailor the services of the classes to the appropriate sport and move common attributes to the higher-level classes. Create a driver class whose `main` method instantiates and exercises several of the classes.

PP 9.6 Create a hierarchy of classes that represent various types of electronics equipment (computers, cell phones, pagers, cameras, etc.). Include data values that describe various attributes of the devices, such as weight, cost, power usage, and manufacturer. Include methods that are named appropriately for each class and that print an appropriate message. Create a driver class whose `main` method instantiates and exercises several of the classes.

PP 9.7 Create a hierarchy of classes that represent courses in a specific curriculum. Include information about each course such as the title, number, description, and department. Categorize classes in appropriate ways when designing the inheritance structure. Create a driver class whose `main` method instantiates and exercises several of the classes.

PP 9.8 Create a hierarchy of classes that represent various types of reading material: books, magazines, technical journals, etc. Include data values that describe appropriate attributes of the material. Include methods that are named appropriately and that print an appropriate message. Create a driver class whose `main` method instantiates and exercises several of the classes.

PP 9.9 Create a hierarchy of classes that represent various kinds of spaceships. Provide a `draw` method for each class that allows it to be drawn in a particular graphics context. Include differentiating characteristics among the spaceships as appropriate. Create a driver program whose `main` method instantiates and draws several types of spaceships.

PP 9.10 Create a hierarchy of classes that represent various kinds of human faces. Design your hierarchy carefully, making some distinctions via class differences and others by the instance data they hold. Provide a draw method for each class that allows it to be drawn in a particular graphics context. Create a driver program whose `main` method instantiates and draws several faces.

Exceptions and I/O

CHAPTER OBJECTIVES

In this chapter you will:

- ▶ Explore the purpose of exceptions.
- ▶ Examine exception messages and the call stack trace.
- ▶ Examine the `try-catch` statement for handling exceptions.
- ▶ Explore the concept of exception propagation.
- ▶ Identify I/O streams and discuss their use.
- ▶ Explore exceptions that occur during I/O operations.
- ▶ Read and write text files.

Exception handling is an important part of an object-oriented software system. Exceptions represent problems or unusual situations that may occur in a program. Java provides various ways to handle exceptions when they occur. In this chapter we explore how exceptions arise and how we can handle them when they do. This chapter also discusses Java input and output in more detail, with a focus on its use of exception processing.

10.1 Exception Handling

> ▶ Errors and exceptions are objects that represent unusual or invalid processing.

Problems that arise in a Java program may generate exceptions or errors. An *exception* is an object that defines an unusual or erroneous situation. An exception is thrown by a program or the run-time environment and can be caught and handled appropriately if desired. An *error* is similar to an exception except that an error generally represents an unrecoverable situation and should not be caught.

Java has a predefined set of exceptions and errors that may occur during the execution of a program. If the predefined exceptions don't suffice, a programmer may choose to design a new class to represent an exception specific to a particular situation.

Problem situations represented by exceptions and errors can have various kinds of root causes. Here are some examples of situations that cause exceptions to be thrown:

- Attempting to divide by zero

- An array index that is out of bounds

- A specified file that could not be found

- A requested I/O operation that could not be completed normally

- Attempting to follow a null reference

- Attempting to execute an operation that violates some kind of security measure

These are just a few examples. There are dozens of other exceptions that address very specific situations.

As some of these examples show, an exception can represent a truly erroneous situation. But an exception may also simply represent a situation that won't occur under usual conditions. Exception handling is set up to be an efficient way to deal with such situations, especially given that they don't happen too often.

We have several options when it comes to dealing with exceptions. A program can be designed to process an exception in one of three ways. It can:

- not handle the exception at all,

- handle the exception where it occurs, or

- handle the exception at another point in the program.

We explore each of these approaches in the following sections.

Uncaught Exceptions

If a program does not handle the exception at all, it will terminate abnormally and produce a message that describes the exception that occurred and where in the code it was produced. The information in an exception message is often helpful in tracking down the cause of a problem. For example, the following output is produced when the `main` method in a class called `Zero` attempts to divide by zero:

```
Exception in thread "main" java.lang.ArithmeticException: / by
zero at Zero.main(Zero.java:19)
```

The first line of the exception output indicates which exception was thrown and provides some information about why it was thrown. The remaining lines are the *call stack trace*; they indicate where the exception occurred. In this case, there is only one line in the call stack trace, but there may be several depending on where the exception originated. The first trace line indicates the method, file, and line number where the exception occurred. The other trace lines, if present, indicate the methods that were called to get to the method that produced the exception.

> ▶ The messages printed when an exception is thrown provide a method call stack trace.

You can also obtain the call stack trace information by calling methods of the exception class being thrown. The method `getMessage` returns a string explaining the reason the exception was thrown. The method `printStackTrace` prints the call stack trace.

The `try-catch` Statement

Let's now examine how we catch and handle an exception when it is thrown. The `try-catch` statement identifies a block of statements that may throw an exception. A *catch clause*, which follows a `try` block, defines how a particular kind of exception is handled. A `try` block can have several `catch` clauses associated with it. Each `catch` clause is called an *exception handler*.

When a `try-catch` statement is executed, the statements in the `try` block are executed. If no exception is thrown during the execution of the `try` block, processing continues with the statement following the `try-catch` statement (after all of the `catch` clauses). This situation is the normal execution flow and should occur most of the time.

If an exception is thrown at any point during the execution of the `try` block, control is immediately transferred to the appropriate `catch` handler if it is present. That is, control transfers to the first `catch` clause whose exception corresponds to the class of the exception that was thrown. After executing the statements in the `catch` clause, control transfers to the statement after the entire `try-catch` statement.

> ▶ Each `catch` clause handles a particular kind of exception that may be thrown within the `try` block.

Let's look at an example. Suppose a hypothetical company uses codes to represent its various products. A product code includes, among other information, a character in the tenth position that represents the zone from which that product was made, and a four-digit integer in positions 4 through 7 that represents the district in which it will be sold. Due to some reorganization, products from zone R are banned from being sold in districts with a designation of 2000 or higher. The program shown in Listing 10.1 reads product codes from the user and counts the number of banned codes entered.

Listing 10.1

```java
//**************************************************************************
//   ProductCodes.java          Programming with Alice and Java
//
//   Demonstrates the use of a try-catch block.
//**************************************************************************
import java.util.Scanner;

public class ProductCodes
{
   // ----------------------------------------------------------------
   // Counts the number of product codes that are entered with
   // a zone of R and a district greater than 2000.
   // ----------------------------------------------------------------
   public static void main (String[] args)
   {
      String code;
      char zone;
      int district, valid = 0, banned = 0;
      Scanner scan = new Scanner(System.in);

      System.out.print("Enter product code (STOP to quit): ");
      code = scan.nextLine();

      while (!code.equals("STOP"))
      {
         try
         {
            zone = code.charAt(9);
            district = Integer.parseInt(code.substring(3, 7));
            valid++;
            if (zone == 'R' && district > 2000)
               banned++;
         }
         catch (StringIndexOutOfBoundsException exception)
         {
            System.out.println("Improper code length: " + code);
         }
         catch (NumberFormatException exception)
```

Listing 10.1 (continued)

```
        {
            System.out.println("District is not numeric: " + code);
        }

        System.out.print("Enter product code (STOP to quit): ");
        code = scan.nextLine();
    }

    System.out.println("# of valid codes entered: " + valid);
    System.out.println("# of banned codes entered: " + banned);
    }
}
```

Figure 10.1 shows the prompts and output of a sample execution of the ProductCodes program. You can see where the exception processing produces error messages in various situations.

```
Enter product code (STOP to quit): TRV2475A5R-14
Enter product code (STOP to quit): TRD1704A7R-12
Enter product code (STOP to quit): TRL2k74A5R-11
District is not numeric: TRL2k74A5R-11
Enter product code (STOP to quit): TRQ2949A6M-04
Enter product code (STOP to quit): TRV2105A2
Improper code length: TRV2105A2
Enter product code (STOP to quit): TRQ2778A7R-19
Enter product code (STOP to quit): STOP
# of valid codes entered: 4
# of banned codes entered: 2
```

Figure 10.1

A sample run of the ProductCodes program

The programming statements in the try block attempt to pull out the zone and district information, and then determine whether it represents a banned product code. If there is any problem extracting the zone and district information, the product code is considered to be invalid and is not processed further. For example, a StringIndexOutOfBoundsException could be thrown by either the charAt or substring methods. Furthermore, a NumberFormatException will be thrown by the parseInt method if the substring does not contain a valid integer. A particular message is printed depending on which exception is thrown. In either case, because the exception is caught and handled, processing continues normally.

Note that, for each code examined, the integer variable valid is incremented only if no exception is thrown. If an exception is thrown, control transfers immediately to the appropriate catch clause. Likewise, the zone and district are tested by the if statement only if no exception is thrown.

TRY THIS!

1. Add a third `catch` clause to the `try-catch` statement in the `ProductCodes` program so that an appropriate message is printed if any other exception occurs.

2. Modify the `ProductCodes` program so that the exception object is printed before the error message in both cases.

Exception Handling in ThunkIt

As you might expect, ThunkIt is sufficiently complex that there are a number of locations where we need to catch exceptions that might arise. One such situation occurs when we attempt to load the user's preferences. Anytime the ThunkIt options are modified, the program automatically saves the user's preferences in a file named `.thunkit.props`. During the game's start up, we attempt to load the file, if present, so that the user's preferences can be set as they wish.

Listing 10.2 shows the `loadOptions` method that resides in the `OptionsManager` class. In its `try` block, the method attempts to create a new `File` object based on the storage location and name of the properties file. Then, assuming we have a

Listing 10.2

```
/***************************************************************************
 *  Loads the game option preferences from the saved file, if present.
 ***************************************************************************
public static void loadoptions()
{
   try
   {
      File loadFile = new File(Constants.USER_HOME, Constants.PROPSFILE);
      FileInputStream is = new FileInputStream(loadFile);
      options.loadFromXML(is);
      is.close();
   }
   catch (FileNotFoundException fnfException)
   {
      // Use default properties
   }
   catch (Exception exception)
   {
      exception.printStackTrace();
   }
}
```

valid `File` object to work with, the method constructs a `FileInputStream` object from which the properties can be read. The last two statements read the contents of the file and then close the file.

During the call to the `FileInputStream`'s constructor, there is a chance that the constructor cannot find the specified file. The very first time the user runs the program, we don't expect to find this file, as the user has not had a chance to change any options. And even if the file had been created in the past, it might have been deleted or moved for some reason. If the options file cannot be found, the `FileInputStream` constructor will throw a `FileNotFoundException`. To handle this situation when it occurs, we surround the appropriate statements with a `try` block.

The first `catch` clause handles a `FileNotFoundException` if one arises. Notice that the body of this clause is empty, indicating that nothing special should be done when this exception occurs. When the options file cannot be found, the `loadFile` variable will be null and a default set of options will be used. So this exception handler exists only to acknowledge the situation and to keep the program from terminating because of the missing file.

The second `catch` clause catches all other exceptions raised elsewhere in the four statements in the `try` block. There are a number of other situations that may arise from these statements, including:

- The `File` constructor may throw a `NullPointerException` if the second parameter (the filename) is null.

- The `FileInputStream` constructor may throw a `SecurityException` to indicate that the application does not have suitable permission to read the options file.

- The `options` object (an object of the `java.util.Properties` class) may throw a `NullPointerException` if the parameter is null, an `IOException` if reading from the input file causes problems (the reading fails or is interrupted), or an `InvalidPropertiesFormatException` if the options file is not in valid XML format (a specific text-based data format).

If any of the above occurs, the second `catch` clause will print a call stack trace (information about where the error occurred) to the screen. These situations should be rare, if they occur at all, so we chose not to deal with them (in terms of attempting to handle and correct them in the program) at this time.

The `finally` Clause

A `try-catch` statement can have an optional *finally clause*. The `finally` clause defines a section of code that is executed no matter how the `try` block is exited. Most often, a `finally` clause is used to manage resources or to guarantee that particular parts of an algorithm are executed.

> ▶ The `finally` clause is executed whether the `try` block is exited normally or because of a thrown exception.

If no exception is generated, the statements in the `finally` clause are executed after the `try` block is complete. If an exception is generated in the `try` block, control first transfers to the appropriate `catch` clause. After executing the exception-handling code, control transfers to the `finally` clause and its statements are executed. A `finally` clause, if present, must be listed after the `catch` clauses.

Note that a `try` block does not need to have a `catch` clause at all. If there are no `catch` clauses, a `finally` clause may be used by itself if that is appropriate for the situation.

10.2 Exception Propagation

We can design our software so that an exception is caught and handled at an outer level in the method-calling hierarchy. If an exception is not caught and handled in the method where it occurs, control is immediately returned to the method that invoked the method that produced the exception. If it isn't caught there, control returns to the method that called it, and so on. This process is called *exception propagation*.

> ▶ If an exception is not caught and handled where it occurs, it is propagated to the calling method.

An exception will be propagated until it is caught and handled or until it is passed out of the `main` method, which causes the program to terminate and produces an exception message. To catch an exception at any level, the method that produces the exception must be invoked inside a `try` block that has `catch` clauses to handle it.

The `Propagation` program shown in Listing 10.3 succinctly demonstrates the process of exception propagation. The output of the program is shown in Figure 10.2.

Listing 10.3

```java
//********************************************************************
//   Propagation.java          Programming with Alice and Java
//
//   Demonstrates exception propagation.
//********************************************************************

public class Propagation
{
    //-----------------------------------------------------------------
    // Invokes the level1 method to begin the exception demonstration.
    //-----------------------------------------------------------------
    public static void main(String[] args)
    {
        ExceptionScope demo = new ExceptionScope();
```

Listing 10.3 (continued)

```
        System.out.println("Program beginning.");
        demo.level1();
        System.out.println("Program ending.");
    }
}
```

```
Program beginning.
Level 1 beginning.
Level 2 beginning.
Level 3 beginning.

The exception message is: / by zero

The call stack trace:
java.lang.ArithmeticException: / by zero
        at ExceptionScope.level3(ExceptionScope.java:54)
        at ExceptionScope.level2(ExceptionScope.java:41)
        at ExceptionScope.level1(ExceptionScope.java:18)
        at Propagation.main(Propagation.java:17)

Level 1 ending.
Program ending.
```

Figure 10.2

Output of the Propagation program

The main method of the Propagation class invokes method level1 in the ExceptionScope class (see Listing 10.4), which invokes level2, which invokes level3, which produces an exception. Method level3 does not catch and handle the exception, so control is transferred back to level2. The level2 method does not catch and handle the exception either, so control is transferred back to level1. Because the invocation of level2 is made inside a try block (in method level1), the exception is caught and handled at that point.

Listing 10.4

```
//********************************************************************************
// ExceptionScope.java           Programming with Alice and Java
//
// Demonstrates exception propagation.
//********************************************************************************

public class ExceptionScope
{
    //------------------------------------------------------------------------
    // Catches and handles the exception that is thrown in level3.
    //------------------------------------------------------------------------
```

Listing 10.4 (continued)

```java
public void level1()
{
   System.out.println("Level 1 beginning.");
   try
   {
      level2();
   }
   catch (ArithmeticException problem)
   {
      System.out.println();
      System.out.println("The exception message is: " +
         problem.getMessage());
      System.out.println();
      System.out.println("The call stack trace:");
      problem.printStackTrace();
      System.out.println();
   }
   System.out.println("Level 1 ending.");
}

//-----------------------------------------------------------------------
// Serves as an intermediate level. The exception propagates through
// this method back to level1.
//-----------------------------------------------------------------------
public void level2()
{
   System.out.println("Level 2 beginning.");
   level3();
   System.out.println("Level 2 ending.");
}

//-----------------------------------------------------------------------
// Performs a calculation to produce an exception. It is not caught and
// handled at this level.
//-----------------------------------------------------------------------
public void level3()
{
   int numerator = 10, denominator = 0;

   System.out.println("Level 3 beginning.");
   int result = numerator / denominator;
   System.out.println("Level 3 ending.");
}
}
```

Note that the program output does not include the messages indicating that the methods level3 and level2 are ending. These println statements are never executed because an exception occurred and had not yet been caught. However, after method level1 handles the exception, processing continues normally from that point, printing the messages indicating that method `level1` and the program are ending.

Note also that the `catch` clause that handles the exception uses the `getMessage` and `printStackTrace` methods to output that information. The stack trace shows the methods that were called when the exception occurred.

> ▶ A programmer must carefully consider how and where exceptions should be handled, if at all.

A programmer must pick the most appropriate level at which to catch and handle an exception. There is no single best answer as to how to do this. It depends on the situation and the design of the system. Sometimes the right approach will be not to catch an exception at all and let the program terminate.

Checked and Unchecked Exceptions

Some exceptions are checked, whereas others are unchecked. A *checked exception* must either be caught by a method or be listed in the *throws clause* of any method that may throw or propagate it. A `throws` clause is appended to the header of a method definition to formally acknowledge that the method will throw or propagate a particular exception if it occurs. An *unchecked* exception requires no `throws` clause.

> ▶ The `throws` clause in a method header must be included for checked exceptions that are not caught and handled in the method.

The only unchecked exceptions in Java are objects of type `RuntimeException` or any of its descendants. All other exceptions are considered checked exceptions.

The `RuntimeException` class is a direct descendent of the `Exception` class in the Java API. We can define our own exceptions by deriving a new class from Exception or one of its descendents. The class we choose as the parent depends on the situation or condition the new exception represents. We explicitly throw an exception using the `throw` statement.

The `main` method of the `CreatingExceptions` program, shown in Listing 10.5, has a `throws` clause, indicating that it may throw an `OutOfRangeException`. A sample run of the program that causes the exception to be thrown is shown in Figure 10.3.

Listing 10.5

```
//********************************************************************
//  CreatingExceptions.java       Programming with Alice and Java
//
//  Demonstrates the ability to define an exception via inheritance.
//********************************************************************
import java.util.Scanner;

public class CreatingExceptions
{
```

Listing 10.5 (continued)

```java
//----------------------------------------------------------------------
// Creates an exception object and possibly throws it.
//----------------------------------------------------------------------
public static void main (String[] args) throws OutOfRangeException
{
    final int MIN = 25, MAX = 40;

    Scanner scan = new Scanner(System.in);

    OutOfRangeException problem =
            new OutOfRangeException("Input value is out of range.");

    System.out.print("Enter an integer value between " + MIN +
                        " and " + MAX + ", inclusive: ");
    int value = scan.nextInt();

    // Determine if the exception should be thrown
    if (value < MIN || value > MAX)
        throw problem;

    System.out.println("End of main method."); // May never reach
    }
}
```

Figure 10.3

A sample run of the `CreatingExceptions` program

```
Enter an integer value between 25 and 40, inclusive: 69
Exception in thread "main" OutOfRangeException: Input value is out of range.
        at CreatingExceptions.main(CreatingExceptions.java:20)
```

The `OutOfRangeException`, shown in Listing 10.6, is not a predefined class in the Java API—we created it specifically for this situation. The `throws` clause is required because the `OutOfRangeException` was derived from the `Exception` class, making it a checked exception.

Listing 10.6

```java
//*****************************************************************************
//   OutOfRangeException.java          Programming with Alice and Java
//
//   Represents an exceptional condition in which a value is out of some
//   particular range.
//*****************************************************************************
```

Listing 10.6 (continued)

```java
public class OutOfRangeException extends Exception
{
   //-----------------------------------------------------------------
   // Sets up the exception object with a particular message.
   //-----------------------------------------------------------------
   OutOfRangeException (String message)
   {
      super (message);
   }
}
```

3. Modify the `Propagation` program to catch the exception in the `level2` method.

4. Modify the `CreatingExceptions` program to catch the exception and issue an error message.

TRY THIS!

(10.3) Java File I/O

Processing input and output often produces error situations, given that it relies on external resources such as user data and files. These resources can have various problems that lead to exceptions being thrown. Let's explore input/output (I/O) processing and the problems that may arise.

A *stream* is an ordered sequence of bytes. The term stream comes from the analogy that as we read and write information, the data flows from a source to a destination (or *sink*) as water flows down a stream. The source of the information is like a spring filling the stream, and the destination is like a cave into which the stream flows.

> ▶ A stream is a sequential sequence of bytes; it can be used as a source of input or a destination for output.

In a program, we treat a stream as either an *input stream*, from which we read information, or as an *output stream,* to which we write information. A program can deal with multiple input and output streams at one time.

A particular store of data, such as a file, can serve either as an input stream or as an output stream to a program, but it generally cannot be both at the same time.

> ▶ Three public reference variables in the System class represent the standard I/O streams.

There are three streams that are referred to as the standard I/O streams. They are listed in Table 10.1. The System class contains three object reference variables (in, out, and err) that represent the three standard I/O streams. These references are declared as both public and static, which allows them to be accessed directly through the System class.

Table 10.1

Standard I/O Streams

Standard I/O Stream	Description
System.in	Standard input stream.
System.out	Standard output stream.
System.err	Standard error stream (output for error messages)

We've been using the standard output stream, with calls to System.out.println for instance, in examples throughout this book. We've also used the standard input stream to create a Scanner object when we want to process input read interactively from the user. The Scanner class manages the input read from the standard input stream in various ways that makes our programming tasks easier. It also processes various I/O exceptions internally, producing an InputMismatchException when needed.

The standard I/O streams, by default, represent particular I/O devices. System.in typically represents keyboard input, whereas System.out and System.err typically represent a particular window on the monitor screen. The System.out and System.err streams write output to the same window by default (usually the one in which the program was executed), though they could be set up to write to different places. The System.err stream is usually where error messages are sent. A Java program can make use of all three of these streams simultaneously, if needed (see Figure 10.4).

Figure 10.4

The default streams available in Java

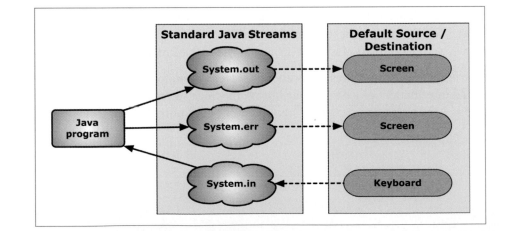

In addition to the standard input streams, the `java.io` package of the Java standard class library provides many classes that let us define streams with particular characteristics. Some of the classes deal with files, others with memory, and others with strings. Some classes assume that the data they handle consists of characters, whereas others assume the data consists of raw bytes of binary information. Some classes provide a means of manipulating the data in the stream in some way, such as buffering the information or numbering it. By combining classes in appropriate ways, we can create objects that represent a stream of information with the exact characteristics we want for a particular situation.

> ▶ The Java class library contains many classes for defining I/O streams with various characteristics.

The breadth of the topic and the sheer number of classes in the `java.io` package prohibit us from covering Java I/O in detail in this book. Our focus for the moment is on I/O exceptions.

Many operations performed by I/O classes can potentially throw an `IOException`. The `IOException` class is the parent of several exception classes that represent problems when trying to perform I/O.

An `IOException` is a checked exception. As described earlier in this chapter, that means that either the exception must be caught or all methods that propagate it must list it in a `throws` clause of the method header.

Because I/O often deals with external resources, many problems can arise in programs that attempt to perform I/O operations. For example, a file from which we want to read might not exist; when we attempt to open the file, an exception will be thrown because that file can't be found. In general, we should try to design programs to be as robust as possible when dealing with potential problems.

Reading Text Files

Reading data from an input file is a common programming task. In addition to manipulating the file (opening it as a stream for reading), we need to be concerned with the contents of the file and translating it to a usable form in our program.

Fortunately, we can use the `Scanner` class again to read from a file that contains text. Suppose we have an input file called `websites.inp` that contains a list of Web page addresses (Uniform Resource Locators, or URLs) that we want to process in some fashion. The following are the first few lines of `websites.inp`:

```
www.alice.org
newsyllabus.com/about
java.sun.com/j2se/6.0
www.linux.org/info/gnu.html
technorati.com/search/java/
cs.tcnj.edu/faculty_fulltime.php
```

The program shown in Listing 10.7 reads the URLs from this file and dissects them to show the various parts of the path. It uses a `Scanner` object to process the input. In fact, the program uses multiple `Scanner` objects—one to read the lines of the data file and another to process each URL string. The output is shown in Figure 10.5.

Listing 10.7

```java
//*****************************************************************************
//  URLDissector.java          Programming with Alice and Java
//
//  Demonstrates the use of Scanner to read file input and parse it using
//  alternative delimiters.
//*****************************************************************************

import java.util.Scanner;
import java.io.*;

public class URLDissector
{
   // -----------------------------------------------------------------------
   // Reads URLs from a file and prints their path components.
   // -----------------------------------------------------------------------
   public static void main (String[] args)
   {
      String url;
      Scanner fileScan = null, urlScan = null;
      boolean found = true;

      try
      {
         fileScan = new Scanner (new File ("websites.inp"));
      }
      catch (FileNotFoundException exception)
      {
         System.out.println ("The input file was not found.");
         found = false;
      }

      if (found)
      {
         // Read and process each line of the file
         while (fileScan.hasNext ())
         {
            url = fileScan.nextLine ();
            System.out.println ("URL: " + url);

            urlScan = new Scanner (url);
            urlScan.useDelimiter ("/");

            // Print each part of the url
            while (urlScan.hasNext ())
            System.out.println ("  " + urlScan.next ());
            System.out.println ();
         }
      }
   }
}
```

```
URL: www.alice.org
   www.alice.org

URL: newsyllabus.com/about
   newsyllabus.com
   about

URL: java.sun.com/j2se/6.0
   java.sun.com
   j2se
   6.0

URL: www.linux.org/info/gnu.html
   www.linux.org
   info
   gnu.html

URL: technorati.com/search/java/
   technorati.com
   search
   java

URL: cs.tcnj.edu/faculty_fulltime.php
   cs.tcnj.edu
   faculty_fulltime.php
```

Figure 10.5

Output from the URLDissector program

If for some reason there is a problem finding or opening the input file, the attempt to create a File object will throw an IOException. The exception will be caught by the catch clause that follows the try block. In the event of the exception being thrown (also known as *raised*), a message is printed to the screen for the user and a boolean flag variable—found—is set to false, preventing the remainder of the program from executing.

Writing Text Files

Now let's explore an example that writes data to a text output file. Writing output to a text file requires simply that we use the appropriate classes to create the output stream, then call the appropriate methods to write the data.

Suppose we want to test a program we are writing, but don't have the real data available. We could write a program that generates a test data file that contains random values. The program shown in Listing 10.8 generates a file that contains random integer values within a particular range. It also writes one line of standard output, confirming that the data file has been written.

Listing 10.8

```java
//****************************************************************************
//  TestData.java          Programming with Alice and Java
//
//  Demonstrates I/O exceptions and the use of a character file output stream.
//****************************************************************************

import java.util.Random;
import java.io.*;

public class TestData
{
   //--------------------------------------------------------------------------
   // Creates a file of test data that consists of ten lines each containing
   // ten integer values in the range 10 to 99.
   //--------------------------------------------------------------------------
   public static void main (String[] args) throws IOException
   {
      final int MAX = 10;

      int value;
      String file = "test.dat";

      Random rand = new Random ();

      FileWriter fw = new FileWriter (file);
      BufferedWriter bw = new BufferedWriter (fw);
      PrintWriter outFile = new PrintWriter (bw);

      for (int line=1; line <= MAX; line++)
      {
         for (int num=1; num <= MAX; num++)
         {
            value = rand.nextInt (90) + 10;
            outFile.print (value + " ");
         }
         outFile.println ();
      }

      outFile.close ();
      System.out.println ("Output file has been created: " + file);
   }
}
```

The `FileWriter` class represents a text output file, but has minimal method support for manipulating data. The `PrintWriter` class provides `print` and `println` methods similar to the standard I/O `PrintStream` class.

Although we do not need to do so for the program to work, we have added a layer in the file stream configuration to include a `BufferedWriter`. This addition simply gives the output stream buffering capabilities, which makes the processing more efficient. While buffering is not crucial in this situation, it is usually a good idea when writing text files.

Note that in the `TestData` program, we have eliminated explicit exception handling. That is, if something goes wrong, we simply allow the program to terminate instead of specifically catching and handling the problem. Because all `IOExceptions` are checked exceptions, we must include the `throws` clause in the method header to indicate that they may be thrown. For each program, we must carefully consider how best to handle the exceptions that may be thrown. This requirement is especially important when dealing with I/O, which is fraught with potential problems that cannot always be foreseen.

The `TestData` program uses nested `for` loops to compute random values and write them to the output file. After all values are printed, the file is closed. Output files must be closed explicitly to ensure that the data is retained. In general, it is good practice to close all file streams explicitly when they are no longer needed.

> ▶ Output file streams should be explicitly closed or they may not correctly retain the data written to them.

The data that is contained in the file `test.dat` after the `TestData` program is run might look like this:

85	90	93	15	82	79	52	71	70	98
74	57	41	66	22	16	67	65	24	84
86	61	91	79	18	81	64	41	68	81
98	47	28	40	69	10	85	82	64	41
23	61	27	10	59	89	88	26	24	76
33	89	73	36	54	91	42	73	95	58
19	41	18	14	63	80	96	30	17	28
24	37	40	64	94	23	98	10	78	50
89	28	64	54	59	23	61	15	80	88
51	28	44	48	73	21	41	52	35	38

File Processing in ThunkIt

ThunkIt uses files extensively throughout the program. Audio and graphic files are loaded at start up, so they are ready for use when needed. Game level files need to be loaded when a player selects a level and begins to play the game. Additionally, the level editor permits the user to save their newly created levels to files for sharing or later play. There is also the game options file, which stores the user's game preferences. This file is utilized each time the application starts or the user preferences are changed.

Audio and graphic files are binary files, which are unreadable by humans. Binary files require special processing, a discussion which is beyond the scope of this chapter. The preference files are text files, but they are encoded using the eXtensible Markup Language (XML). XML uses a special format and extra characters that will make our processing of the file with a `Scanner` object challenging. Instead, we'll rely on API-provided objects and methods to read the level files.

Each level of the ThunkIt game is represented as a text file. Figure 10.6 shows an example of a level file.

Figure 10.6

Part of a ThunkIt level file

```
First Things First
blueMoonBackground
17      1       grass
17      2       grass
17      3       grass
17      4       grass
17      5       grass
17      6       grass
17      7       grass
17      8       grass
16      3       pencil
16      7       block
15      7       box
16      5       ladder
15      5       ladder
14      5       ladder
13      5       ladder
12      5       ladder
11      5       ladder
10      5       ladder
9       5       ladder
8       5       ladder
```

The first line of a level file contains the level's title. The second line indicates which background image should be used when this level is played. The remaining lines in a level file define the location and element type present in the level's grid. We use a `Scanner` object to read each level file.

There are actually two different types of level files in ThunkIt, "standard" files (which we have created and provided with the game) and "custom" files (which users can create and save to their local file system). Standard files use the same text-based format that the custom files use, but are stored as a resource in the application itself, much as the images are.

Custom level files are written by using the `PrintWriter`, `BufferedWriter`, and `FileWriter` classes (all of which can be found in the `java.io` package). Similar to the `File` constructor we saw earlier, the `FileWriter` constructor may throw an `IOException`. As we have seen previously, we handle this situation by adding the `throws IOException` clause to the method's header, thereby causing the exception to propagate upward.

10.4 More to Explore

Exception Hierarchy We briefly touched on the notion of the exception classes forming a hierarchy through the use of inheritance. As you begin to use exceptions and design exception handling in your programs, be sure to thoroughly investigate how inheritance plays a role in the exception classes.

Exceptions and the Java API By now you should be familiar with the Java API documentation and how to navigate your way through the information. Because exception classes play a special role in our Java programs, the API lists the exception classes for each package toward the end of the navigation listing in the lower-left corner of the API window. Be sure to look for this section and the exception classes present in any package you work with.

Creating Your Own Exceptions Exception classes are not really that different from regular classes that you have been creating. In fact, implementing your own exceptions is quite straightforward. Be sure to look at the API documentation for the `java.lang.Exception` and `java.lang.RunTimeException` classes and try creating your own exceptions.

Summary of Key Concepts

- Errors and exceptions are objects that represent unusual or invalid processing.

- The messages printed when an exception is thrown provide a method call stack trace.

- Each `catch` clause handles a particular kind of exception that may be thrown within the `try` block.

- The `finally` clause is executed whether the `try` block is exited normally or because of a thrown exception.

- If an exception is not caught and handled where it occurs, it is propagated to the calling method.

- A programmer must carefully consider how and where exceptions should be handled, if at all.

- The `throws` clause in a method header must be included for checked exceptions that are not caught and handled in the method.

- A stream is a sequential sequence of bytes; it can be used as a source of input or a destination for output.

- Three public reference variables in the `System` class represent the standard I/O streams.

- The Java class library contains many classes for defining I/O streams with various characteristics.

- Output file streams should be explicitly closed or they may not correctly retain the data written to them.

Exercises

EX 10.1 What is the difference between an error and an exception?

EX 10.2 What is a checked exception? An unchecked exception?

EX 10.3 Describe the output of the `ProductCodes` program if a `finally` clause that printed the string `"Got here!"` were added to the `try` statement.

EX 10.4 Look up the following exception classes in the online Java API documentation and describe their purpose.

    a. `ArithmeticException`

    b. `ArrayStoreException`

    c. `IndexOutOfBoundsException`

    d. `NullPointerException`

EX 10.5 Describe the output file used in the `TestData` program in terms of the classes that were used to create it.

EX 10.6 What exception will the following source code throw?

```
for (int i = 0; i <= myArray.length; i++)
    System.out.println(myArray[i])
```

EX 10.7 From what classes can the custom exceptions you create be derived?

EX 10.8 Identify all of the source files in the ThunkIt `net.thunkit.gui` package that use `try-catch` clauses. What exceptions are thrown in these cases?

EX 10.9 Find your ThunkIt properties file and open it in a text editor of your choice. Describe the data portions of the file that store the preferences.

EX 10.10 Identify the places in ThunkIt where any of the three standard I/O streams are used.

Programming Projects

PP 10.1 Design and implement a program that reads a series of 10 integers from the user and prints their average. Read each input value as a string, then attempt to convert it to an integer using the `Integer.parseInt` method. If this process throws a `NumberFormatException` (meaning the input is not a valid number), print an appropriate error message and prompt for the number again. Continue reading values until 10 valid integers have been entered.

PP 10.2 Write a program that reads strings from the user and writes them to an output file called `userStrings.dat`. Terminate processing when the user enters the string `"DONE"`. Do not write the sentinel string (`"DONE"`) to the output file.

PP 10.3 Design and implement a program that counts the number of integer values in a text input file. Produce a table listing the values you identify as integers from the input file.

PP 10.4 Modify your solution to Programming Project 10.3 so that if the Scanner object throws an exception while attempting to read an integer, you catch the exception, inform the user with a message, and continue reading the contents of the input file. The nextInt method of the Scanner may throw any of three exceptions. Be sure to write three catch clauses to catch each of them and provide a different message for each.

PP 10.5 Design and implement a program that creates an exception class called StringTooLongException, designed to be thrown when a string is discovered that has too many characters in it. In the main method of the program, read strings from the user until the user enters "DONE". If a string is entered that has too many characters (say 20), throw the exception. Allow the thrown exception to terminate the program.

PP 10.6 Modify the solution to Programming Project 10.5 such that it catches and handles the exception if it is thrown. Handle the exception by printing an appropriate message, and then continue processing more strings.

PP 10.7 Design and implement a program that creates an exception class called InvalidDocumentCodeException, designed to be thrown when an improper designation for a document is encountered during processing. Suppose in a particular business all documents are given a two-character designation starting with U, C, or P, standing for unclassified, confidential, or proprietary. If a document designation is encountered that doesn't fit that description, the exception is thrown. Create a driver program to test the exception, allowing it to terminate the program.

PP 10.8 Suppose a library is processing an input file containing the titles of books in order to remove duplicates. Write a program that reads all of the titles from an input file called bookTitles.inp and writes them to an output file called noDuplicates.out. When complete, the output file should contain all unique titles found in the input file.

PP 10.9 Write a program that will read in a file of student academic credit data and create a list of students on academic warning. The list of students on warning will be written to an output file. Each line of the input file contains the student name, the number of semester hours earned, and the total quality points earned. The following shows part of a typical data file:

```
Bob Smith 27 83.7
Jason Jones 21 28.35
Sarah Walker 96 182.4
Mary Doe 60 150
```

The program should compute the GPA (grade point or quality point average) for each student (the total quality points divided by the number of semester hours), then write the student information to the output file if that student should be put on academic warning. A student is on warning if he/she has a GPA less than 1.5 for students with fewer than 30 semester hours of credit,

1.75 for students with fewer than 60 semester hours of credit, and 2.0 for all other students.

PP 10.10 Write a small program that determines whether the water used to brew coffee is the correct temperature. Create a simple GUI with a slider to enter the water temperature and a button to check the temperature.

If the water is less than 190° F, the program should throw a `TooColdException`. The program should catch the exception and show a message in a `JOptionPane` stating that the temperature should be at least 190° F. If the water is between 190° F and 200° F, show a message stating that the temperature is fine for brewing. If the water is above 200° F, throw a `TooHotException` and show a message in a `JOptionPane` stating that the temperature should be less than 200° F.

CHAPTER 11

Software Design Revisited

CHAPTER OBJECTIVES

In this chapter you will:

- ▶ Explore the software development process.
- ▶ Identify several software development models.
- ▶ Explore the use of UML class and sequence diagrams.
- ▶ Define the notion of dependency and aggregation between and among classes.

Throughout this book our focus has been on the design of software—particularly the issues related to the design of object-oriented software. We saw how such software came to life in Alice worlds, then how the flexibility of Java gives you much more control over the details of the design. Even so, we've only scratched the surface of software design issues. In this chapter, we step back to review the entire development process and explore various aspects of and techniques used in software design.

11.1 The Development Process

Any proper software development effort consists of four basic *development activities*:

- Establishing the requirements
- Creating a design
- Implementing the design
- Testing

It would be nice if these activities, in this order, defined a step-by-step approach for developing software. Although they may seem to be sequential, they are in fact almost never completely linear. They overlap and interact. Let's discuss each development activity briefly.

Software requirements specify *what* a program must accomplish. They indicate the tasks that a program should perform, not how it performs them. Often, requirements are expressed in a document called a *functional specification*.

Requirements are a clear expression of the problem to be solved. Until we truly know what problem we are trying to solve, we can't actually solve it.

In a classroom setting, students are generally provided the software requirements in the form of the problem assignment. However, even when they are provided, such requirements need to be discussed and clarified. In professional development, the person or group who wants a software product developed (the *client*) will often provide an initial set of requirements. However, these initial requirements are often incomplete, ambiguous, and perhaps even contradictory. The software developer must work with the client to refine the requirements until all key decisions about what the system will do have been addressed.

Requirements often address user interface issues such as output format, screen layouts, and graphical interface components. Essentially, the requirements establish the characteristics that make the program useful for the end user. They may also apply constraints to your program, such as how fast a task must be performed.

A *software design* indicates *how* a program will accomplish its requirements. The design specifies the classes and objects needed in a program and defines how they interact. It also specifies the relationships among the classes. Low-level design issues deal with how individual methods accomplish their tasks.

A civil engineer would never consider building a bridge without designing it first. The design of software is no less essential. Many problems that occur in software are directly attributable to poor design. It has been shown time and again that the effort spent on the design of a program is well worth it, saving both time and money in the long run.

During software design, alternatives need to be considered and explored. Often, the first attempt at a design is not the best solution. Fortunately, changes are relatively easy to make during the design stage.

> ▶ The effort put into design is both crucial and cost effective.

Implementation is the process of writing the source code that will solve the problem. More precisely, implementation is the act of translating the design into a particular programming language. Too many programmers focus on implementation exclusively when, actually, it should be the least creative of all development activities. The important decisions should be made when establishing the requirements and creating the design.

Testing is the act of ensuring that a program will solve the intended problem given all of the constraints under which it must perform. Testing includes running a program multiple times with various inputs and carefully scrutinizing the results. But it means far more than that. Testing in one form or another should be a part of every stage of development. The accuracy of the requirements, for instance, should be tested by reviewing them with the client.

Software Development Models

A *software development model* is an organized strategy for executing the steps necessary to create high-quality software. All development models incorporate, in various ways, the basic development activities of establishing requirements, creating a design, implementing the design, and testing the implementation.

Too often, however, programmers follow the build-and-fix approach depicted in Figure 11.1. In this approach, a programmer creates an initial version of a program, then continually modifies it until it has reached some level of acceptance. Often, testing activities are not systematic or carefully planned, so problems go undiscovered. In a build-and-fix approach, the programmer is reacting to problems as opposed to participating in an effort to create a quality product in the first place.

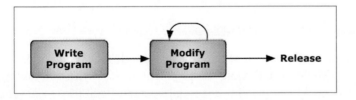

> **Figure 11.1**
>
> The build-and-fix approach to software development

In the build-and-fix approach, although some problems might be eliminated during development, the overall quality of the product is never really addressed. Defects that still exist in the software will be difficult to isolate and correct. Enhancements to the program will be challenging because the system is not designed well.

> ▶ A program produced using the build-and-fix approach is a product of ad hoc, reckless activities.

A program produced using the build-and-fix approach is a product of ad hoc, reckless activities. It is reactive rather than proactive. Therefore, the build-and-fix approach is not really a development model at all.

One of the first true development process models, called the *waterfall model*, was introduced in the early 1970s. It is depicted in Figure 11.2. The waterfall model is linear, with one stage followed directly by the next. In fact, the model gets its name from the implication that development flows in one direction from stage to stage until the final release is created. This model does not allow for an earlier stage to be revisited after a new stage is begun any more than water can be made to flow up a waterfall.

Figure 11.2

The waterfall software development model

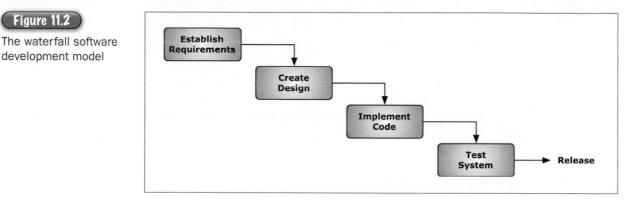

Although the waterfall model formalizes the stages of development, it ultimately is not realistic because it does not acknowledge the fact that developers sometimes need to revisit previous stages. It would be nice if all program requirements were completely specified and analyzed before design activities started. Likewise, it would be nice to have all design decisions made before implementation begins. Unfortunately, it almost never works out that way. No matter how carefully the requirements are established or how carefully the design is created, it is impossible to consider every eventuality, and there will always come a time when the developer realizes that an earlier decision was in error.

> ▶ The waterfall model does not recognize the inherently iterative nature of development activities.

Iterative Development

A realistic model must take into account that development activities are somewhat overlapping. We need a flexible development model with interacting activities. However, we need to be careful not to allow such flexibility to degenerate into a build-and-fix approach. We must focus rigorous attention on each stage to ensure the quality of the overall product.

> ▶ Added flexibility in the development process must not be allowed to degenerate into a build-and-fix approach.

An *iterative development process* is one that allows a software developer to cycle through the different development activities. Earlier stages can be formally revisited, allowing proper changes to be made. Figure 11.3 shows an initial version of an iterative development process.

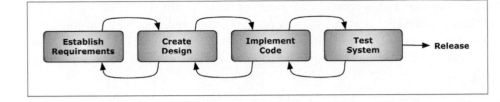

Figure 11.3

An iterative
development process

The process in Figure 11.3 is essentially the waterfall model leveled out to permit backtracking. That is, when new information is uncovered that changes the requirements or design, we have a way to formally go back and modify the affected stages. The appropriate documents are updated to reflect these new decisions.

The danger of backtracking is that the developer might rely on it too much. This model is not intended to reduce the amount of effort that goes into developing the initial requirements before starting on the design. Likewise, the design of a program should still be well established before beginning implementation. Backtracking activity should primarily be used to correct problems uncovered in later stages.

Any realistic development model will include the prospect of revisiting previous activities in some iterative manner, as well as formal test strategies.

Identifying Classes and Objects

A fundamental part of object-oriented software design is determining which classes should be created to define the program. We have to carefully consider how we want to represent the various elements that make up the overall solution. These classes determine the objects that we will manage in the system.

One way to identify potential classes is to identify the objects discussed in the program requirements. Objects are generally nouns. You literally may want to scrutinize a problem description, or a functional specification if available, to identify the nouns found in it. For example, Figure 11.4 shows part of a problem description with the nouns circled.

```
The user must be allowed to specify each
product by its primary characteristics,
including its name and product number. If the
bar code does not match the product, then an
error should be generated to the message window
and entered into the error log. The summary
report of all transactions must be structured
as specified in section 7.A.
```

Figure 11.4

Finding potential objects
in a problem description

Of course, not every noun in the problem specification will correspond to a class in a program. Some nouns may be represented as attributes of other objects, and the designer may decide not to represent other nouns explicitly in the program at all. This activity is just a starting point that allows a developer to think about the types of objects a program will manage.

 The nouns in a problem description may indicate some of the classes and objects needed in a program.

Remember that a class represents a group of objects with similar behavior. A plural noun in the specification, such as products, may indicate the need for a class that represents one of those items, such as `Product`. Even if there is only one of a particular kind of object needed in your system, it may best be represented as a class.

Classes that represent objects should generally be given names that are singular nouns, such as `Coin`, `Student`, and `Message`. A class represents a single item from which we are free to create as many instances as we choose.

Another key decision is whether to represent something as an object or as a primitive attribute of another object. For example, we may initially think that an employee's salary should be represented as an integer, and that may work for much of the system's processing. But upon further reflection we might realize that the salary is based on the person's rank, which has upper and lower salary bounds that must be managed with care. Therefore the final conclusion may be that we'd be better off representing all of that data and the associated behavior as a separate class.

Given the needs of a particular program, we want to strike a good balance between classes that are too general and those that are too specific. For example, it may complicate our design unnecessarily to create a separate class for each type of appliance that exists in a house. It may be sufficient to have a single `Appliance` class, with perhaps a piece of instance data that indicates what type of appliance it is. Then again, this may not be an adequate solution. It all depends on what the software is going to accomplish.

In addition to classes that represent objects from the problem domain, we likely will need classes that support the work necessary to get the job done. For example, in addition to `Member` objects, we may want a separate class to help us manage all of the members of a club.

Keep in mind that when producing a real system, some of the classes we identify during design may already exist. Even if nothing matches exactly, there may be an old class that's similar enough to serve as the basis for our new class. The existing class may be part of the Java standard class library, part of a solution to a problem we've solved previously, or part of a library that can be bought from a third party. These are all examples of software reuse.

Assigning Responsibilities

Part of the process of identifying the classes needed in a program is the process of assigning responsibilities to each class. Each class represents an object with certain behaviors that are defined by the methods of the class. Any activity that the program must accomplish must be represented somewhere in the behaviors of the classes. That is, each class is responsible for carrying out certain activities, and those responsibilities must be assigned as part of designing a program.

The behaviors of a class perform actions that make up the functionality of a program. Thus we generally use verbs for the names of behaviors and the methods that accomplish them.

Sometimes it is challenging to determine which is the best class to carry out a particular responsibility. A good designer considers multiple possibilities. Sometimes such analysis makes you realize that you could benefit from defining another class to shoulder the responsibility.

It's not necessary in the early stages of a design to identify all the methods that a class will contain. It is often sufficient to assign primary responsibilities, and consider how those responsibilities translate to particular methods.

 **UML**

As our programs become more complex, containing multiple classes, it's helpful to make use of a graphical notation to capture, visualize, and communicate the program design. Throughout the remainder of this book we use *UML diagrams* for this purpose. UML stands for the *Unified Modeling Language*, which has become the most popular notation for representing the design of an object-oriented program.

Class Diagrams

Several types of UML diagrams exist; each is designed to show specific aspects of object-oriented programs. We focus primarily on UML *class diagrams* to show the contents of classes and the relationships among them.

> ▶ A UML class diagram helps us visualize the contents of and relationships among the classes of a program.

In a UML diagram, each class is represented as a rectangle, possibly containing three sections to show the class name, its attributes (data), and its operations (methods). Figure 11.5 shows a class diagram containing the classes of the PushCounter program introduced in Chapter 7.

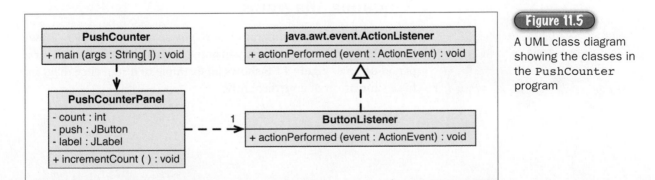

Figure 11.5

A UML class diagram showing the classes in the PushCounter program

UML is not designed specifically for Java programmers. It is language independent. Therefore the syntax used in a UML diagram is not necessarily the same as Java. For example, a variable's type is shown after the variable name, separated by a colon. Method return types are shown the same way. The + and − notations in front of variables and methods indicate their visibility: + for public and − for private.

A dashed line with an open arrowhead connecting two classes in a UML diagram indicates that a relationship of one kind or another exists between the two classes. These lines are called associations, and indicate that one class "knows about" and uses the other in some way. For example, an association might indicate that one class creates an object of the other, and/or that one class invokes a method of the other. Associations can be labeled to indicate the details of the association.

A directed association uses an arrowhead to indicate that the association is particularly one-way. For example, the arrow connecting the PushCounter-Panel and ButtonListener classes in Figure 11.5 indicates that the PushCounterPanel class "knows about" and uses the ButtonListener class, but not vice versa.

An association can show *multiplicity* by annotating the ends of the connection with numeric values. In this case, the diagram indicates that PushCounter-Panel is associated with exactly one ButtonListener object. Both ends of an association can show multiplicity values, if desired. Multiplicity also can be expressed in terms of a range of values and by using wildcards for unknown values.

UML diagrams are versatile. We can include whatever appropriate information is desired, depending on what we are trying to convey in a particular diagram. We might leave out the data and method sections of a class, for instance, if those details aren't relevant for a particular diagram. For example, the fact that the PushCounterPanel class makes use of the JButton and JLabel classes from the Java API is indicated in Figure 11.5, but the details of these classes are not provided.

> ▶ A UML sequence diagram helps us visualize the exchange of messages between objects over time.

Sequence Diagrams

Another type of UML diagram is a *sequence diagram*, which shows the exchange of messages between active objects in a program over a period of time. Figure 11.6 shows an example of a sequence diagram for a simulation of a medical office.

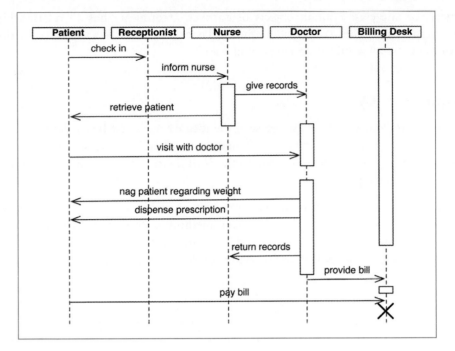

Figure 11.6

A UML sequence diagram showing the exchange of messages in a medical office simulation

In a sequence diagram, each object is represented by a rectangle or square with the object's name near the top of the diagram. Each object has a vertical line (called a timeline) that runs down from it, parallel to the vertical lines from other objects.

Horizontal arrow lines running from the vertical line of the source to the vertical line of the destination represent the messages exchanged between objects. The notion of time is represented on the vertical axis. That is, we read the diagram in a top-to-bottom fashion noting the sending of messages (one object calling a method in another object), and the response messages (if any).

Message lines have the name of the message written above them, in order to clearly identify what message is being sent. To indicate that a method is being performed in response to a received message, *activation boxes* are drawn over the vertical lines. Finally, we can indicate that an object has been removed from memory, or destroyed, by placing an X on its vertical timeline at the point at which it is removed.

11.3 Class Relationships

The classes in a software system have various types of relationships to each other. Three of the more common relationships are dependency, aggregation, and inheritance.

We've seen dependency relationships in many examples in which one class "uses" another. This section revisits the dependency relationship and explores the situation where a class depends on itself. We then explore aggregation, in which the objects of one class contain objects of another, creating a "has-a" relationship. Inheritance is another relationship among classes, as discussed in Chapter 8, that creates an "is-a" relationship between classes.

Dependency

In many previous examples, we've seen the idea of one class being dependent on another. This means that one class relies on another in some sense. Often the methods of one class will invoke the methods of the other class. This establishes a "uses" relationship.

Generally, if class A uses class B, then one or more methods of class A invoke one or more methods of class B. If an invoked method is static, then A merely references B by name. If the invoked method is not static, then A must have access to a specific instance of class B in order to invoke the method. That is, A must have a reference to an object of class B.

The way in which one object gains access to an object of another class is an important design decision. It occurs when one class instantiates the objects of another, but the access can also be accomplished by passing one object to another as a method parameter.

In general, we want to minimize the number of dependencies among classes. The less dependent our classes are on each other, the less impact changes and errors will have on the system.

Dependencies Among Objects of the Same Class

In some cases, a class depends on itself. That is, an object of one class interacts with another object of the same class. To accomplish this, a method of the class may accept an object of the same class as a parameter.

The `concat` method of the `String` class is an example of this situation. The method is executed through one `String` object and is passed another `String` object as a parameter. For example:

```
str3 = str1.concat (str2);
```

The `String` object executing the method (`str1`) appends its characters to those of the `String` passed as a parameter (`str2`). A new `String` object is returned as a result and stored as `str3`.

The `RationalTester` program shown in Listing 11.1 demonstrates a similar situation. A rational number is a value that can be represented as a ratio of two integers (a fraction). The `RationalTester` program creates two objects representing rational numbers and then performs various operations on them to produce new rational numbers.

Listing 11.1

```java
//***************************************************************************
//   RationalTester.java         Programming with Alice and Java
//
//   Driver to exercise the use of multiple RationalNumber objects.
//***************************************************************************

public class RationalTester
{
   //-----------------------------------------------------------------------
   // Creates some RationalNumber objects and performs various operations on
   // them.
   //-----------------------------------------------------------------------
   public static void main (String[] args)
   {
      RationalNumber r1 = new RationalNumber (6, 8);
      RationalNumber r2 = new RationalNumber (1, 3);
      RationalNumber r3, r4, r5, r6, r7;

      System.out.println ("First rational number: " + r1);
      System.out.println ("Second rational number: " + r2);

      if (r1.isLike (r2))
         System.out.println ("r1 and r2 are equal.");
      else
         System.out.println ("r1 and r2 are NOT equal.");

      r3 = r1.reciprocal ();
      System.out.println ("The reciprocal of r1 is: " + r3);

      r4 = r1.add (r2);
      r5 = r1.subtract (r2);
      r6 = r1.multiply (r2);
      r7 = r1.divide (r2);

      System.out.println ("r1 + r2: " + r4);
      System.out.println ("r1 - r2: " + r5);
      System.out.println ("r1 * r2: " + r6);
      System.out.println ("r1 / r2: " + r7);
   }
}
```

Figure 11.7

Output from the
`RationalTester`
program

```
First rational number: 3/4
Second rational number: 1/3
r1 and r2 are NOT equal.
The reciprocal of r1 is: 4/3
r1 + r2: 13/12
r1 - r2: 5/12
r1 * r2: 1/4
r1 / r2: 9/4
```

The `RationalNumber` class is shown in Listing 11.2. Keep in mind as you examine this class that each object created from the `RationalNumber` class represents a single rational number. The `RationalNumber` class contains various operations on rational numbers, such as addition and subtraction.

Listing 11.2

```java
//************************************************************************
//   RationalNumber.java        Programming with Alice and Java
//
//   Represents one rational number with a numerator and denominator.
//************************************************************************

public class RationalNumber
{
    private int numerator, denominator;

    //---------------------------------------------------------------------
    // Sets up the rational number by ensuring a nonzero denominator and
    // making only the numerator signed.
    //---------------------------------------------------------------------
    public RationalNumber (int numer, int denom)
    {
        if (denom == 0)
            denom = 1;

        // Make the numerator "store" the sign
        if (denom < 0)
        {
            numer = numer * -1;
            denom = denom * -1;
        }

        numerator = numer;
        denominator = denom;
```

Listing 11.2 (continued)

```java
      reduce ();
   }

   //----------------------------------------------------------------------
   // Returns the numerator of this rational number.
   //----------------------------------------------------------------------
   public int getNumerator ()
   {
      return numerator;
   }

   //----------------------------------------------------------------------
   // Returns the denominator of this rational number.
   //----------------------------------------------------------------------
   public int getDenominator ()
   {
      return denominator;
   }

   //----------------------------------------------------------------------
   // Returns the reciprocal of this rational number.
   //----------------------------------------------------------------------
   public RationalNumber reciprocal ()
   {
      return new RationalNumber (denominator, numerator);
   }

   //----------------------------------------------------------------------
   // Adds this rational number to the one passed as a parameter. A common
   // denominator is found by multiplying the individual denominators.
   //----------------------------------------------------------------------
   public RationalNumber add (RationalNumber op2)
   {
      int commonDenominator = denominator * op2.getDenominator ();
      int numerator1 = numerator * op2.getDenominator ();
      int numerator2 = op2.getNumerator () * denominator;
      int sum = numerator1 + numerator2;

      return new RationalNumber (sum, commonDenominator);
   }

   //----------------------------------------------------------------------
   // Subtracts the rational number passed as a parameter from this rational
   // number.
   //----------------------------------------------------------------------
   public RationalNumber subtract (RationalNumber op2)
   {
      int commonDenominator = denominator * op2.getDenominator ();
      int numerator1 = numerator * op2.getDenominator ();
```

(continued)

Listing 11.2 (continued)

```java
      int numerator2 = op2.getNumerator () * denominator;
      int difference = numerator1 - numerator2;

      return new RationalNumber (difference, commonDenominator);
   }

   //-----------------------------------------------------------------
   // Multiplies this rational number by the one passed as a parameter.
   //-----------------------------------------------------------------
   public RationalNumber multiply (RationalNumber op2)
   {
      int numer = numerator * op2.getNumerator ();
      int denom = denominator * op2.getDenominator ();

      return new RationalNumber (numer, denom);
   }

   //-----------------------------------------------------------------
   // Divides this rational number by the one passed as a parameter by
   // multiplying by the reciprocal of the second rational number.
   //-----------------------------------------------------------------
   public RationalNumber divide (RationalNumber op2)
   {
      return multiply (op2.reciprocal ());
   }

   //-----------------------------------------------------------------
   // Determines if this rational number is equal to the one passed as a
   // parameter. Assumes they are both reduced.
   //-----------------------------------------------------------------
   public boolean isLike (RationalNumber op2)
   {
      return (numerator == op2.getNumerator () &&
              denominator == op2.getDenominator ());
   }

   //-----------------------------------------------------------------
   // Returns this rational number as a string.
   //-----------------------------------------------------------------
   public String toString ()
   {
      String result;

      if (numerator == 0)
         result = "0";
      else
         if (denominator == 1)
            result = numerator + "";
         else
            result = numerator + "/" + denominator;
```

Listing 11.2 (continued)

```java
      return result;
   }

   //-----------------------------------------------------------------
   // Reduces this rational number by dividing both the numerator and the
   // denominator by their greatest common divisor.
   //-----------------------------------------------------------------
   private void reduce ()
   {
      if (numerator != 0)
      {
         int common = gcd (Math.abs (numerator), denominator);

         numerator = numerator / common;
         denominator = denominator / common;
      }
   }

   //-----------------------------------------------------------------
   // Computes and returns the greatest common divisor of the two positive
   // parameters. Uses Euclid's algorithm.
   //-----------------------------------------------------------------
   private int gcd (int num1, int num2)
   {
      while (num1 != num2)
         if (num1 > num2)
            num1 = num1 - num2;
         else
            num2 = num2 - num1;

      return num1;
   }
}
```

The methods of the RationalNumber class, such as add, subtract, multiply, and divide, use the RationalNumber object that is executing the method as the first (left) operand and the RationalNumber object passed as a parameter as the second (right) operand.

The isLike method of the RationalNumber class is used to determine if two rational numbers are essentially equal. It's tempting, therefore, to call that method equals, similar to the method used to compare String objects. But we chose a different name so as not to be confused with overriding the equals method from the Object class.

Note that some of the methods in the RationalNumber class, including reduce and gcd, are declared with private visibility. These methods are private because we don't want them executed directly from outside a RationalNumber object. They exist only to support the other services of the object.

Aggregation

Some objects are made up of other objects. A car, for instance, is made up of its engine, its chassis, its wheels, and several other parts. Each of these other parts could be considered a separate object. Therefore we can say that a car is an *aggregation*—it is composed, at least in part, of other objects. Aggregation is sometimes described as a *has-a relationship*. For instance, a car has a chassis.

> ▶ An aggregate object is composed of other objects, forming a *has-a* relationship.

In the software world, we define an *aggregate object* as any object that contains references to other objects as instance data. For example, an Account object contains, among other things, a String object that represents the name of the account owner. We sometimes forget that strings are objects, but technically that makes each Account object an aggregate object.

Aggregation is a special type of dependency. That is, a class that is defined in part by another class is dependent on that class. The methods of the aggregate object generally invoke the methods of the objects from which it is composed.

The more complex an object, the more likely it will need to be represented as an aggregate object. In UML, aggregation is represented by a connection between two classes, with an open diamond at the end near the class that is the aggregate. Figure 11.8 shows a UML class diagram that contains an aggregation relationship; a Student can have more than one Address.

Figure 11.8

A UML class diagram showing an aggregation relationship

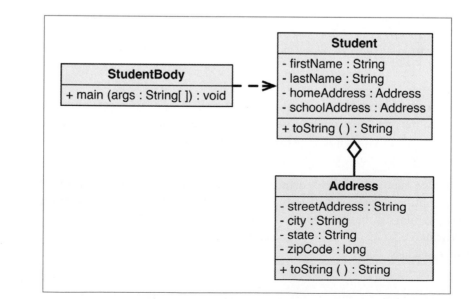

Note that strings are not represented as separate classes with aggregation relationships in a UML diagram, though technically they could be. Strings are so fundamental to programming that they are often represented in UML as if they were a primitive type.

11.4 More to Explore

Use Case Diagrams UML class diagrams are just one type of diagram programmers use to represent their systems. A use case diagram shows how users of the system (both human and non-human), known as actors, interact with the system and achieve their goals. In essence, the use case diagram will show a representation of the major functionality of the system as a series of actor goals.

Agile Software Development Agile software development is a relatively new development process model. It involves teams of developers iterating very quickly through the development process to create releases of a software product. It is noted for having highly aggressive techniques that treat each iteration (lasting one to four weeks) as an individual software project. Consider exploring the agile approach, as it is gaining in popularity with professional software developers and corporations.

Test-Driven Software Development Yet another type of software development process is the test-driven development model. This approach encourages programmers to adopt a style in which they write their testing routines (test cases) first. Then they implement only enough of the program so that the test case will pass. The programmer will then repeat this process over and over as the program develops. Investigate this approach to explore the fine points of this development process.

Summary of Key Concepts

- The effort put into design is both crucial and cost effective.

- A program produced using the build-and-fix approach is a product of ad hoc, reckless activities.

- The waterfall model does not recognize the inherently iterative nature of development activities.

- Added flexibility in the development process must not be allowed to degenerate into a build-and-fix approach.

- The nouns in a problem description may indicate some of the classes and objects needed in a program.

- A UML class diagram helps us visualize the contents of and relationships among the classes of a program.

- A UML sequence diagram helps us visualize the exchange of messages between objects over time.

- An aggregate object is composed of other objects, forming a *has-a* relationship.

Exercises

EX 11.1 What are the four basic software development activities?

EX 11.2 What is an aggregate object?

EX 11.3 What are UML class diagrams designed to do?

EX 11.4 Describe a dependency relationship between two classes.

EX 11.5 List some attributes and operations that might be defined for a class called `Meeting` that represents a business meeting.

EX 11.6 List some attributes and operations that might be defined for a class called `PictureFrame` that represents a picture frame.

EX 11.7 Create a UML class diagram of the ThunkIt `net.thunkit.game` package.

EX 11.8 Create a UML class diagram of the ThunkIt `net.thunkit.gui` package.

EX 11.9 Create a UML use case diagram of the ThunkIt game.

EX 11.10 Explore the World Wide Web for a discussion of other software development approaches. Summarize each of the approaches you are able to locate.

Programming Projects

PP 11.1 Design and implement a software program to perform library book management. The system should be able to catalog all books, record books being borrowed and returned, and deal with associated fines related to books returned late.

    a. Identify the objects and classes in your system.

    b. Identify the relationships between the classes and objects.

    c. Draw a UML class diagram for your solution.

    d. Implement your solution.

PP 11.2 Expand on the implementation of your solution to PP 11.1.

    a. Identify several possible refinements, such as book borrowing, for the system.

    b. Identify several objects and classes for the book-borrowing refinement.

    c. Identify possible relationships between classes and objects in the book-borrowing refinement.

    d. Draw a UML class diagram for the book-borrowing refinement.

    e. Implement your solution.

PP 11.3 Implement a software program that simulates an airport. The system should be able to simulate airplane takeoffs, landings on various runways, and air-traffic control, and allow an operator to control the takeoff, landing, and flying attributes of planes (such as course and speed).

    a. Identify the objects and classes in your system.

    b. Identify the relationships between the classes and objects.

    c. Draw a UML class diagram for your solution.

    d. Implement your solution.

PP 11.4 Consider several possible refinements to your solution to PP 11.3.

    a. Identify changes to the objects, classes, and relationships required to implement your changes.

    b. Revise your earlier UML class diagram of the original system to account for your modifications.

PP 11.5 Design and implement a program that will manage a cell phone contact / address book. Include those data fields that are most common in the contact list (not just names and phone numbers anymore). Draw a UML use case diagram and class diagram of your proposed solution, then implement your design.

PP 11.6 Design a program that will manage cars and trucks at a two-way intersection with a stoplight. Identify the objects and classes required to implement this simulation. Assume that all cars and trucks can travel through the intersection at the same speed. Draw a UML class diagram of your proposed solution and use the diagram as the basis for your implementation.

PP 11.7 Refine your solution to PP 11.6. Expand the intersection to a four-way intersection. Allow the cars and trucks to travel through the intersection at different speeds. How does your UML class diagram change?

PP 11.8 Design a program that will simulate a movie theater box office. Your solution should include customers, two ticket windows, and three movies that begin at 10-minute intervals. Draw a UML class diagram of your proposed solution and use the diagram as the basis for your implementation.

PP 11.9 Explore the `ImageManager` class in ThunkIt and the classes that the `ImageManager` utilizes. Be sure to understand how images load into the game, how they are scaled, and how they are retrieved elsewhere in the program. Then, try adding or replacing some of the images with a few of your own. Summarize the interactions surrounding the `ImageManager` class with a UML sequence diagram.

PP 11.10 Explore the `AudioManager` class in ThunkIt and the classes that the manager utilizes. Then, try adding or replacing some of the sound effects or music tracks (loops) in the program with ones that you find on the Internet. A good source for sound effects and loops is www.soundsnap.com. Summarize the `AudioManager` and related classes with a UML class diagram.

CHAPTER 12

Recursion

CHAPTER OBJECTIVES

In this chapter you will:

- ▶ Explore the underlying concepts of recursion.

- ▶ Examine recursive methods and unravel their processing steps.

- ▶ Define infinite recursion.

- ▶ Demonstrate the use of recursion to solve problems.

- ▶ Explore when recursion should and should not be used.

- ▶ Explore the use of recursion in graphics-based programs.

- ▶ Define the concept of a fractal and its relationship to recursion.

Recursion is a powerful programming technique that can be used to create elegant solutions to certain types of problems. This chapter explains the basic concept of recursion, then explores the use of recursion in programming. Recursive solutions to several specific problems are presented to demonstrate recursion's versatility, simplicity, and elegance.

12.1 Recursive Thinking

> ▶ Recursion is a programming technique in which a method calls itself. To program recursively, you must be able to think recursively.

We've seen many times in previous examples that one method can call another method to accomplish its goal. What we haven't seen yet, however, is that a method can call itself. *Recursion* is a programming technique in which a method calls itself in order to fulfill its purpose. Before we get into the details of how we use recursion in a program, however, we need to explore the general concept of recursion. The ability to think recursively is essential to being able to use recursion as a programming technique.

In general, recursion is the process of defining something in terms of itself. For example, consider the following definition of the word *decoration*:

decoration: n. any ornament or adornment used to decorate something

The word *decorate* is used to define the word *decoration*. You may recall your grade school teacher telling you to avoid such recursive definitions when explaining the meaning of a word. In many situations, however, recursion is an appropriate way to express an idea or definition.

For example, suppose we wanted to formally define a list of one or more numbers, separated by commas. Such a list can be defined recursively as either a number or as a number followed by a comma followed by a list. This definition can be expressed as follows:

A LIST is a: `number`

or a: `number  comma  LIST`

This recursive definition of LIST applies to each of the following lists of numbers:

24, 88, 40, 37

96, 43

14, 64, 21, 69, 32, 93, 47, 81, 28, 45, 81, 52, 69

70

No matter how long a list is, the recursive definition describes it. A list of one element, such as in the last example, is defined completely by the first (non-recursive) part of the definition. For any list longer than one element, the recursive part of the definition (the part which refers to itself) is used as many times as necessary, until the last element is reached. The last element in the list is always defined by the non-recursive part of the definition. Figure 12.1 shows how one particular list of numbers corresponds to the recursive definition of LIST.

```
LIST: number   comma   LIST
        24        ,     88,  40,  37
                        number   comma   LIST
                          88        ,     40,  37
                                    number   comma   LIST
                                      40        ,     37
                                                number
                                                  37
```

Figure 12.1

Tracing the recursive definition of a LIST

Infinite Recursion

Note that the definition of LIST contains one option that is recursive, and one option that is not. The part of the definition that is not recursive is called the *base case*. The base case of the LIST definition is a single number that is not followed by anything. In other words, when the last number in the list is reached, the base case option terminates the recursive path.

If all options had a recursive component, then the recursion would never end. For example, if the definition of a LIST was simply "a number followed by a comma followed by a LIST," then no list could ever end. This problem is called *infinite recursion*. It is similar to an infinite loop, except that the "loop" occurs in the definition itself.

> ▶ Any recursive definition must have a non-recursive part, called the base case, which permits the recursion to eventually end.

As with infinite loops, a programmer should be careful to design algorithms so that they avoid infinite recursion. Any recursive definition must have a base case that does not include a recursive component.

Recursion in Math

Let's look at an example of recursion in mathematics. The value referred to as $N!$ (which is pronounced N *factorial*) is defined for any positive integer N as the product of all integers between 1 and N inclusive. Therefore:

$$3! = 3 * 2 * 1 = 6$$

and

$$5! = 5 * 4 * 3 * 2 * 1 = 120.$$

Mathematical formulas are often expressed recursively. The definition of $N!$ can be expressed recursively as:

$$1! = 1$$

$$N! = N * (N-1)! \text{ for } N > 1$$

> ▶ Mathematical problems and formulas are often expressed recursively.

The first part of this definition establishes that 1! is 1. This is the base case, which has no recursive element. The second part of this definition establishes that $N!$ is N times $(N - 1)!$ for all values of N greater than 1. In this recursive part of the definition, the factorial function is defined in terms of the factorial function.

Using this definition, 50! is equal to 50 * 49!. And 49! is equal to 49 * 48!. And 48! is equal to 48 * 47!. This process continues until we get to the base case of 1. Because $N!$ is defined only for positive integers, this definition is complete and will always conclude with the base case.

The next section describes how recursion is accomplished in programs.

12.2 Recursive Programming

Let's use a simple mathematical operation to demonstrate the concepts of recursive programming. Suppose we want to compute the sum of the values between 1 and N inclusive, where N is any positive integer. The sum of the values between 1 and 8 is

$$1 + 2 + 3 + 4 + 5 + 6 + 7 + 8 = 36.$$

The sum of the values from 1 to N can be expressed recursively as N plus the sum of the values from 1 to $N - 1$. Figure 12.2 shows how that recursive expression unfolds.

Figure 12.2

The sum of the numbers 1 through N, expressed recursively

$$
\sum_{i=1}^{N} i = N + \sum_{i=1}^{N-1} i = N + N - 1 + \sum_{i=1}^{N-2} i
$$

$$
= N + N - 1 + N - 2 + \sum_{i=1}^{N-3} i
$$

$$
\vdots
$$

$$
= N + N - 1 + N - 2 + \cdots + 2 + 1
$$

For example, the sum of the values from 1 to 20 is equal to 20 plus the sum of the values from 1 to 19. Continuing this approach, the sum of the values from 1 to 19 is equal to 19 plus the sum of the values from 1 to 18. Although this is a strange way to think about this problem, it is a straightforward example that demonstrates how recursion is programmed.

In Java, as in many other programming languages, a method can call itself. Each call to the method creates a new environment in which to work. That is, all local variables and parameters are newly created with their own unique data space every time the method is called. Each parameter is given an initial value based on the new call. Each time a method terminates, processing returns to the method that called it (which may be an earlier invocation of the same method). These rules are no different from those governing any "regular" method invocation.

> ▶ Each recursive call to a method creates new local variables and parameters.

The following method, called sum, implements a recursive solution to the problem of computing the sum of the values from 1 to the number passed in as a parameter:

```java
// This method returns the sum of 1 to num
public int sum(int num)
{
    int result;
    if (num == 1)
        result = 1;
    else
        result = num + sum(num-1);
    return result;
}
```

This method essentially embodies our recursive definition that the sum of the numbers between 1 and N is equal to N plus the sum of the numbers from 1 to $N - 1$. The sum method is recursive because sum calls itself. The parameter passed to sum is decremented each time sum is called, until it reaches the base case of 1 (we're assuming it's initially called with a positive parameter in this case). Recursive methods often contain an if-else statement, with one of the branches, usually the first one, representing the base case.

Suppose the main method calls sum, passing it an initial value of 1, which is stored in the parameter num. Because num is equal to 1, the result of 1 is returned to main and no recursion occurs.

Now let's trace the execution of the sum method when it is passed an initial value of 2. Since num does not equal 1, sum is called again with an argument of num − 1, or 1. This is a new call to the method sum, with a new parameter num and a new local variable result. Since num is equal to 1 in this invocation, the result of 1 is returned without further recursive calls. Control returns to the first version of sum that was invoked. The return value of 1 is added to the initial value of num in that call to sum, which is 2. Therefore, result is assigned the value 3, which is returned to the main method. The method called from main correctly calculates the sum of the integers from 1 to 2, returning the result of 3.

> ▶ A careful trace of recursive processing can provide insight into the way it is used to solve a problem.

The base case in the summation example is when N equals 1, at which point no further recursive calls are made. The recursion begins to fold back into the earlier versions of the sum method, returning the appropriate value each time. Each return value contributes to the computation of the sum at the higher level. Without the base case, infinite recursion would result. Each call to a method requires additional memory space; therefore infinite recursion often results in a run-time error indicating that memory has been exhausted.

Trace the sum function with different initial values of num until this processing becomes familiar. Figure 12.3 illustrates the recursive calls when main invokes sum to determine the sum of the integers from 1 to 4. Each box represents a copy of the method as it is invoked, indicating the allocation of space to store the formal parameters and any local variables. Invocations are shown as solid lines, and returns as dotted lines. The return value result is shown at each step. The recursive path is followed repeatedly until the base case is reached; then the calls begin to return their result up through the chain.

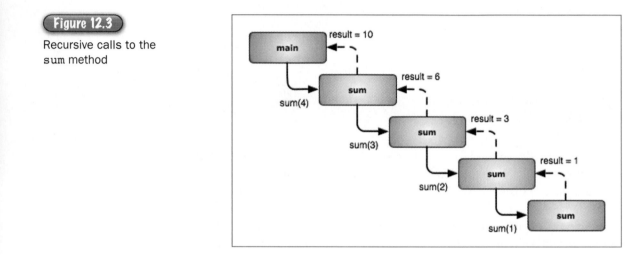

Figure 12.3

Recursive calls to the sum method

Recursion vs. Iteration

Of course, there is a non-recursive solution to the summation problem we just explored. One way to compute the sum of the numbers from 1 to num in an iterative manner is as follows:

```
sum = 0;
for (int number=1; number <= num; number++)
   sum += number;
```

> Recursion is the most elegant and appropriate way to solve some problems, but for others it is less intuitive than an iterative solution.

This solution is certainly more straightforward than the recursive version. We used the summation problem to demonstrate recursion because it is simple, not because you would use recursion to solve it under normal conditions. Recursion has the overhead of multiple method invocations and, in this case, presents a more complicated solution than its iterative counterpart.

A programmer must learn when to use recursion and when not to use it. Determining which approach is best depends on the problem being solved. All problems can be solved in an iterative manner, but in some cases the iterative version is much more complicated. Recursion, for some problems, allows us to create relatively short, elegant programs.

Direct vs. Indirect Recursion

Direct recursion occurs when a method invokes itself, such as when sum calls sum. *Indirect recursion* occurs when a method invokes another method, eventually resulting in the original method being invoked again. For example, if method m1 invokes method m2, and m2 invokes method m1, we can say that m1 is indirectly recursive. The amount of indirection could be several levels deep, as when m1 invokes m2, which invokes m3, which invokes m4, which invokes m1. Figure 12.4 depicts a situation with indirect recursion. Method invocations are shown with solid lines, and returns are shown with dotted lines. The entire invocation path is followed, and then the recursion unravels following the return path.

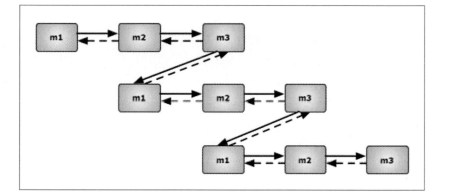

Indirect recursion

Indirect recursion requires all of the same attention to base cases that direct recursion requires. Furthermore, indirect recursion can be more difficult to trace because of the intervening method calls. Therefore, extra care is warranted when designing or evaluating indirectly recursive methods. When designing a program, ensure that the indirection is truly necessary and clearly explained in documentation.

 **Using Recursion**

Let's now turn our attention to several examples that use recursion to solve a problem. For each one, we examine exactly how recursion plays a role in the solution and how a base case is used to terminate the recursion. As you explore these examples, consider how complicated a non-recursive solution for each problem would be.

Note that none of the following examples involve ThunkIt. In previous chapters, in addition to exploring smaller examples, we discussed how particular concepts are embodied in the ThunkIt application. In this chapter, ThunkIt does not help us, as it does not make use of recursion. As we discussed previously, a software developer must learn to recognize when recursion is helpful and when it is not. In the case of ThunkIt, there is simply no situation in the program that requires recursion.

Traversing a Maze

> ▶ A backtracking algorithm, which solves a problem using trial and error, is often implemented using recursion.

Solving a maze involves a great deal of trial and error: following a path, backtracking when you cannot go farther, and trying other untried options. Such activities often are handled nicely using recursion. The program shown in Listing 12.1 creates a `Maze` object and attempts to traverse it.

Listing 12.1

```java
// ****************************************************************
//  MazeSearch.java          Programming with Alice and Java
//
//  Demonstrates the use of recursion to search a maze.
// ****************************************************************

public class MazeSearch
{
   //--------------------------------------------------------------
   // Creates a new maze, prints its original form, attempts to solve it,
   // and prints out its final form.
   //--------------------------------------------------------------
   public static void main(String[] args)
   {
      Maze labyrinth = new Maze();

      System.out.println(labyrinth);

      if (labyrinth.traverse (0, 0))
         System.out.println("The maze was successfully traversed!");
      else
         System.out.println("There is no possible path.");

      System.out.println(labyrinth);
   }
}
```

The `Maze` class, shown in Listing 12.2, uses a two-dimensional array of integers to represent the maze. The goal is to move from the top-left corner (the entry point) to the bottom-right corner (the exit point). Initially, a 1 indicates a clear path, and a 0 indicates a blocked path. As the maze is solved, these array elements are changed to other values to indicate attempted paths and, ultimately, a successful path through the maze if one exists.

Listing 12.2

```java
//**************************************************************************
//  Maze.java          Programming with Alice and Java
//
//  Represents a maze using a 2D array of characters. The goal is to get from
//  the top-left corner to the bottom-right corner. A 1 represents an open
//  path and a 0 represents a wall. Diagonal moves are not allowed.
//**************************************************************************

public class Maze
{
   private final int TRIED = 3;
   private final int PATH = 7;

   private int[][] grid = { {1,1,1,0,1,1,0,0,0,1,1,1,1},
                            {1,0,1,1,1,0,1,1,1,1,0,0,1},
                            {0,0,0,0,1,0,1,0,1,0,1,0,0},
                            {1,1,1,0,1,1,1,0,1,0,1,1,1},
                            {1,0,1,0,0,0,0,1,1,1,0,0,1},
                            {1,0,1,1,1,1,1,1,1,0,1,1,1,1},
                            {1,0,0,0,0,0,0,0,0,0,0,0,0},
                            {1,1,1,1,1,1,1,1,1,1,1,1,1} };

   //-----------------------------------------------------------------------
   // Attempts to recursively traverse the maze. Inserts special characters
   // indicating locations that have been tried and that eventually become
   // part of the solution.
   //-----------------------------------------------------------------------
   public boolean traverse(int row, int column)
   {
      boolean done = false;

      if (valid(row, column))
      {
         grid[row][column] = TRIED; // This cell has been tried

         if (row == grid.length-1 && column == grid[0].length-1)
            done = true; // The maze is solved
         else
         {
            done = traverse(row+1, column); // down
            if (!done)
               done = traverse(row, column+1); // right
            if (!done)
```

(continued)

Listing 12.2 (continued)

```java
            done = traverse(row-1, column); // up
        if (!done)
            done = traverse(row, column-1); // left
    }

    if (done) // This location is part of the final path
        grid[row][column] = PATH;
    }

    return done;
}

//----------------------------------------------------------------------------
// Determines if a specific location is valid. A location is valid if it
// is in the bounds of the matrix and is open (not blocked and not
// previously tried).
//----------------------------------------------------------------------------
private boolean valid(int row, int column)
{
    boolean result = false;

    if (row >= 0 && row < grid.length &&
        column >= 0 && column < grid[row].length)
        if (grid[row][column] == 1)
            result =true ;

    return result;
}

//----------------------------------------------------------------------------
// Creates a string representation of the maze, showing tried and
// successful paths if the maze has been attempted.
//----------------------------------------------------------------------------
public String toString()
{
    String result = "\n";

    for (int row=0; row < grid.length; row++)
    {
        for (int column=0; column < grid[row].length; column++)
            result += grid[row][column] + " ";
        result += "\n";
    }

    return result;
}
}
```

The only valid moves through the maze are in the four primary directions: down, right, up, and left. No diagonal moves are allowed. In this example, the maze is 8 rows by 13 columns, although the code is designed to handle a maze of any size.

Let's think this problem through recursively. The maze can be traversed successfully if it can be traversed successfully from position (0, 0). Therefore, the maze can be traversed successfully if it can be traversed successfully from any positions adjacent to (0, 0), namely position (1, 0), position (0, 1), position (−1, 0), or position (0, −1). Picking a potential next step, say (1, 0), we find ourselves in the same type of situation we did before. To successfully traverse the maze from the new current position, we must successfully traverse it from an adjacent position. At any point, some of the adjacent positions may be invalid, may be blocked, or may represent a possible successful path. We continue this process recursively. If the base case, position (7, 12) is reached, the maze has been traversed successfully.

The recursive method in the `Maze` class is called `traverse`. It returns a `boolean` value that indicates if a solution path was found. First the method determines if a move to the specified row and column is valid. A move is considered valid if it stays within the grid boundaries and if the grid contains a 1 in that location, indicating that a move in that direction is not blocked. The initial call to `traverse` passes in the upper-left location (0, 0), the starting point of the maze.

If a move is valid, the grid entry is changed from a 1 to a 3, marking this location as visited so that later we don't retrace our steps. The `traverse` method then determines whether the maze has been completed (e.g., the move has reached the bottom-right location). So for this problem there are actually three base cases that will terminate any particular recursive path:

- an invalid move because the move is out of bounds,
- an invalid move because the move has been tried before, and
- a move that arrives at the final location.

If the current location is not the bottom-right corner, we search for a solution in each of the primary directions, if necessary. First, we look down by recursively calling the `traverse` method and passing in the new location. The logic of the `traverse` method starts all over again using this new position. A solution is either ultimately found by first attempting to move down from the current location, or it's not found. If it's not found, we try moving right. If that fails, we try up. Finally, if no other direction has yielded a correct path, we try left. If no direction from the current location yields a correct solution, then there is no path from this location, and `traverse` returns false.

If a solution is found from the current location, then the grid entry is changed to a 7. In this example, the first 7 is placed in the bottom-right corner. The next 7 is placed in the location that led to the bottom-right corner, and so on until the final 7 is placed in the upper-left corner. Therefore, when the final maze is printed, the zeros still indicate a blocked path, a 1 indicates an open path that was never tried, a 3 indicates a path that was tried but failed to yield a correct solution, and a 7 indicates a part of the final solution of the maze. The output for this example is shown in Figure 12.5.

Figure 12.5

Output from the
`MazeSearch` program

```
1110110001111
1011101111001
0000101010100
1110111010111
1010000111001
1011111101111
1000000000000
1111111111111

The maze was successfully traversed!

7770110001111
3077707771001
0000707070300
7770777070333
7070000773003
7077777703333
7000000000000
7777777777777
```

Note that there are several opportunities for recursion in each call to the `traverse` method. Any or all of them might be followed, depending on the maze configuration. Although there may be many paths through the maze, the recursion terminates when a path is found. Carefully trace the execution of this code while following the maze array to see how the recursion solves the problem. Then consider the difficulty of producing a non-recursive solution.

TRY THIS!

1. Modify `MazeSearch` so that it prints out the path of the final solution as it is discovered without storing it.

2. Design a new maze for the `MazeSearch` program. Trace the recursive processing as it applies to your new maze.

3. Modify the `MazeSearch` program so that, from each location, it first searches up, then right, then down, and finally left.

The Towers of Hanoi

The *Towers of Hanoi* puzzle was invented in the 1880s by Edouard Lucas, a French mathematician. It has become a favorite among computer scientists because its solution is an excellent demonstration of recursive elegance.

The puzzle consists of three upright pegs and a set of disks with holes in the middle so that they slide onto the pegs. Each disk has a different diameter. Initially, all of the disks are stacked on one peg in order of size such that the largest disk is on the bottom, as shown in Figure 12.6.

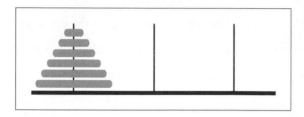

The Towers of Hanoi puzzle

The goal of the puzzle is to move all of the disks from their original (first) peg to the destination (third) peg. To solve the puzzle, we can use the "extra" peg as a temporary place to put disks, and we must obey the following three rules:

- We can move only one disk at a time.

- We cannot place a larger disk on top of a smaller disk.

- All disks must be on some peg except for the disk in transit between pegs.

These rules imply that we must move smaller disks "out of the way" in order to move a larger disk from one peg to another. Figure 12.7 shows the step-by-step solution for the Towers of Hanoi puzzle using three disks. In order to ultimately move all three disks from the first peg to the third peg, we first have to get to the point where the smaller two disks are out of the way on the second peg so that the largest disk can be moved from the first peg to the third peg.

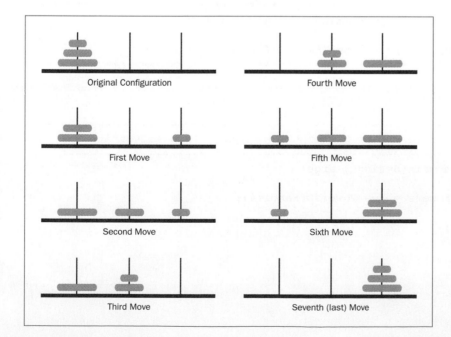

Original Configuration

First Move

Second Move

Third Move

Fourth Move

Fifth Move

Sixth Move

Seventh (last) Move

Figure 12.7

A solution to the three-disk Towers of Hanoi puzzle

The first three moves shown in Figure 12.7 can be thought of as "moving the smaller disks out of the way." The fourth move puts the largest disk in its final place. Then the last three moves put the smaller disks in their final place on top of the largest one.

Let's use this idea to form a general strategy. To move a stack of N disks from the original peg to the destination peg:

- Move the topmost $N - 1$ disks from the original peg to the extra peg.

- Move the largest disk from the original peg to the destination peg.

- Move the $N - 1$ disks from the extra peg to the destination peg.

This strategy lends itself nicely to a recursive solution. The step to move the $N - 1$ disks out of the way is the same problem all over again: moving a stack of disks. For this subtask, though, there is one less disk, and our destination peg is what we were originally calling the extra peg. An analogous situation occurs after we've moved the largest disk, and we have to move the original $N - 1$ disks again.

The base case for this problem occurs when we want to move a "stack" that consists of only one disk. That step can be accomplished directly and without recursion.

The program in Listing 12.3 creates a `TowersOfHanoi` object and invokes its `solve` method. The output is a step-by-step list of instructions that describe how the disks should be moved to solve the puzzle. This example uses four disks, which is specified by a parameter to the `TowersOfHanoi` constructor.

Listing 12.3

```java
//********************************************************************
//  SolveTowers.java          Programming with Alice and Java
//
//  Demonstrates recursion using the Towers of Hanoi puzzle.
//********************************************************************

public class SolveTowers
{
   //-----------------------------------------------------------------
   //  Creates a 4-disk Towers of Hanoi puzzle object, then solves it.
   //-----------------------------------------------------------------
   public static void main(String[] args)
   {
      TowersOfHanoi towers = new TowersOfHanoi(4);

      towers.solve();
   }
}
```

The TowersOfHanoi class, shown in Listing 12.4, uses the solve method to make an initial call to moveTower, the recursive method. The initial call indicates that all of the disks should be moved from peg 1 to peg 3, using peg 2 as the extra position.

Listing 12.4

```java
//*****************************************************************************
//   TowersOfHanoi.java        Programming with Alice and Java
//
//   Represents the classic Towers of Hanoi puzzle.
//*****************************************************************************

public class TowersOfHanoi
{
   private int totalDisks;

   //---------------------------------------------------------------------------
   // Sets up the puzzle with the specified number of disks.
   //---------------------------------------------------------------------------
   public TowersOfHanoi(int disks)
   {
      totalDisks = disks;
   }

   //---------------------------------------------------------------------------
   // Performs the initial call to moveTower to solve the puzzle. Moves the
   // disks from tower 1 to tower 3 using tower 2.
   //---------------------------------------------------------------------------
   public void solve()
   {
      moveTower(totalDisks, 1, 3, 2);
   }

   //---------------------------------------------------------------------------
   // Prints instructions for moving the specified number of disks from the
   // start tower to the end tower. This is accomplished by recursively
   // moving a subtower of n-1 disks out of the way, moving one disk, then
   // moving the subtower back. Base case: 1 disk.
   //---------------------------------------------------------------------------
   private void moveTower(int numDisks, int start, int end, int temp)
   {
      if (numDisks == 1)
         System.out.println("Move one disk from " + start + " to " + end);
      else
      {
         moveTower(numDisks-1, start, temp, end);
         System.out.println("Move one disk from " + start + " to " + end);
         moveTower(numDisks-1, temp, end, start);
      }
   }
}
```

The moveTower method first considers the base case (a "stack" of one disk). When that occurs, it prints a single line describing that particular move. If the stack contains more than one disk, we call moveTower again to get the $N - 1$ disks out of the way, then move the largest disk, then move the $N - 1$ disks to their final destination with yet another call to moveTower.

Note that the parameters to moveTower describing the pegs are switched around as needed to move the partial stacks. This code follows our general strategy, and uses the moveTower method to move all partial stacks.

The only output for this program is produced when a disk is moved. The complete output for this program is shown in Figure 12.8. Trace the recursive processing carefully, comparing it to the output produced, to see how the solution is accomplished.

Figure 12.8

Output from the
SolveTowers program

```
Move one disk from 1 to 2
Move one disk from 1 to 3
Move one disk from 2 to 3
Move one disk from 1 to 2
Move one disk from 3 to 1
Move one disk from 3 to 2
Move one disk from 1 to 2
Move one disk from 1 to 3
Move one disk from 2 to 3
Move one disk from 2 to 1
Move one disk from 3 to 1
Move one disk from 2 to 3
Move one disk from 1 to 2
Move one disk from 1 to 3
Move one disk from 2 to 3
```

> ▶ The Towers of Hanoi solution has exponential complexity, which is very inefficient, but its implementation is remarkably short and elegant.

Contrary to its short and elegant implementation, the solution to the Towers of Hanoi puzzle is terribly inefficient. To solve the puzzle with a stack of N disks, we have to make $2^N - 1$ individual disk moves. This situation is an example of *exponential complexity*. As the number of disks increases, the number of required moves increases exponentially.

Legend has it that priests of Brahma are working on this puzzle in a temple at the center of the world. They are using 64 gold disks, moving them between pegs of pure diamond. The downside is that when the priests finish the puzzle, the world will end. The upside is that even if they move one disk every second of every day, it will take them over 584 billion years to complete it. That's with a puzzle of only 64 disks! It is certainly an indication of just how inefficient an algorithm with exponential complexity is.

TRY THIS!

4. Modify the `SolveTowers` program to count and print the number of disk moves needed to solve a puzzle.

5. Annotate the lines of output of the `SolveTowers` program to show the recursive steps.

Tiled Pictures

Carefully examine the screen shot for the `TiledPictures` program shown in Figure 12.9. There are three unique images in the collage. The entire area is divided into four equal quadrants. A picture of the world (with a circle indicating the Himalayan mountain region) is shown in the bottom-right quadrant. The bottom-left quadrant contains a picture of Mt. Everest. In the top-right quadrant is a picture of a mountain goat.

Figure 12.9

Image produced by the `TiledPictures` program

The interesting part of the picture is the top-left quadrant. It contains a copy of the entire collage, including itself. In this smaller version you can see the three simple pictures in their three quadrants. And again, in the top-left corner, the picture is repeated (including itself). This repetition continues for several levels. It is similar to the effect you can create when looking at a mirror in the reflection of another mirror.

The driver for this application is shown in Listing 12.5. The visual effect is created using recursion in the `TiledPicturesPanel` class, shown in Listing 12.6. The `paintComponent` method paints the panel by making the initial invocation of the recursive `drawPictures` method.

Listing 12.5

```java
//********************************************************************
//  TiledPictures.java          Programming with Alice and Java
//
//  Demonstrates the use of recursion to present a collage of images.
//********************************************************************

import java.io.*;
import javax.swing.*;

public class TiledPictures
{
   //----------------------------------------------------------------
   //  Creates and displays the application frame containing the panel of
   //  tiled images.
   //----------------------------------------------------------------
   public static void main(String[] args) throws IOException
   {
      JFrame frame = new JFrame("Tiled Pictures");
      frame.getContentPane().add(new TiledPicturesPanel());
      frame.setResizable(false);
      frame.setDefaultCloseOperation(JFrame.EXIT_ON_CLOSE);
      frame.pack();
      frame.setVisible(true);
   }
}
```

Listing 12.6

```java
//********************************************************************
//  TiledPicturesPanel.java          Programming with Alice and Java
//
//  Represents a panel divided into four quadrants. Three quadrants contain
//  a single image in each, and the fourth contains a recursive version of the
//  entire panel.
//********************************************************************
```

Listing 12.6 (continued)

```java
import java.io.*;
import java.awt.*;
import javax.swing.*;
import javax.imageio.*;

public class TiledPicturesPanel extends Jpanel
{
   private final int PANEL_SIZE = 480;
   private final int MIN = 20; // smallest picture size

   private Image world, everest, goat;

   //-----------------------------------------------------------------
   //  Loads the images and sets the panel size.
   //-----------------------------------------------------------------
   public TiledPicturesPanel() throws IOException
   {
      world = ImageIO.read(new File("world.gif"));
      everest = ImageIO.read(new File("everest.gif"));
      goat = ImageIO.read(new File("goat.gif"));
      setPreferredSize(new Dimension(PANEL_SIZE, PANEL_SIZE));
   }

   //-----------------------------------------------------------------
   //  Paints this panel by performing the initial call to the drawPictures
   //  method.
   //-----------------------------------------------------------------
   public void paintComponent(Graphics page)
   {
      drawPictures(PANEL_SIZE, page);
   }

   //-----------------------------------------------------------------
   //  Draws the images in three quadrants, then calls itself to draw the
   //  fourth (upper left) quadrant.
   //-----------------------------------------------------------------
   public void drawPictures(int size, Graphics page)
   {
      page.drawImage(everest, 0, size/2, size/2, size/2, this);
      page.drawImage(goat, size/2, 0, size/2, size/2, this);
      page.drawImage(world, size/2, size/2, size/2, size/2, this);

      if (size > MIN)
         drawPictures(size/2, page);
   }
}
```

The drawPictures method accepts a parameter that defines the size of the area in which the pictures are displayed. It draws the three images using the drawImage method, with parameters that scale the picture to the correct size and location. Then the drawPictures method is called recursively to draw the upper-left quadrant.

On each invocation, if the drawing area is large enough, the drawPictures method is invoked again, using a smaller drawing area. Eventually, the drawing area becomes so small that the recursive call is not performed. Thus, the base case of this recursion is a minimum size for the drawing area. Because the size is decreased on each recursive invocation, eventually the base case is reached and the recursion stops. This is the reason that the upper-left corner is empty in the smallest version of the collage.

Carefully examine the parameters to the drawImage method calls. They determine where each image is placed and scale the picture to the appropriate size.

TRY THIS!

6. Modify the TiledPictures program so that the mountain image appears in the upper-left quadrant and the repeated images appear in the lower-left quadrant.

7. Modify the TiledPictures program so that the world image appears in the upper-left quadrant and the repeated images appear in the lower-right quadrant.

Fractals

A *fractal* is a geometric shape that can be made up of the same pattern repeated at different scales and orientations. The nature of a fractal lends itself to a recursive definition. Interest in fractals has grown immensely in recent years, largely due to

> ▶ A fractal is a geometric shape that can be defined naturally in a recursive manner.

Benoit Mandelbrot, a Polish mathematician born in 1924. He demonstrated that fractals occur in many places in mathematics and nature. Computers have made fractals much easier to generate and investigate. Over the past quarter century, the bright, interesting images that can be created with fractals have come to be considered as much an art form as a mathematical interest.

One particular example of a fractal is called the *Koch snowflake,* named after Helge von Koch, a Swedish mathematician. It begins with an equilateral triangle, which is considered to be the Koch fractal of order 1. Koch fractals of higher orders are constructed by repeatedly modifying all of the line segments in the shape.

To create the Koch fractal of the next higher order, each line segment in the shape is modified by replacing its middle third with a sharp protrusion made of two line segments, each having the same length as the replaced portion. Relative to the entire shape, the protrusion on any line segment always points outward. Several orders of Koch fractals are shown in Figure 12.10. As the order increases, the shape begins to look like a snowflake.

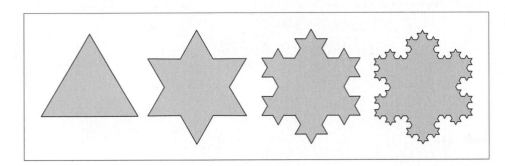

 Figure 12.10

Several orders of the Koch snowflake

Figure 12.11 shows a screen shot of the KochSnowflake program, which allows the user to increase and decrease the order of the fractal using the arrow buttons at the top of the panel. Each time an arrow button is pressed, the fractal image is redrawn.

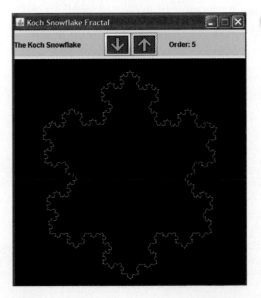

 Figure 12.11

A screen shot of the KochSnowflake program

The main method for the KochSnowflake program is shown in Listing 12.7. The KochSnowflakePanel class, shown in Listing 12.8, contains the button toolbar as well as a separate panel on which the fractal is painted. It also serves as the listener for the two buttons that control the order of the fractal.

Listing 12.7

```java
//***************************************************************************
//  KochSnowflake.java          Programming with Alice and Java
//
//  Demonstrates the use of recursion to draw a Koch Snowflake fractal.
//***************************************************************************

import java.io.*;
import javax.swing.*;

public class KochSnowflake
{
   //--------------------------------------------------------------------
   //  Creates and displays the application frame.
   //--------------------------------------------------------------------
   public static void main (String[] args) throws IOException
   {
      JFrame frame = new JFrame("Koch Snowflake Fractal");
      frame.getContentPane().add(new KochSnowflakePanel());
      frame.setResizable(false);
      frame.setDefaultCloseOperation(JFrame.EXIT_ON_CLOSE);
      frame.pack();
      frame.setVisible(true);
   }
}
```

Listing 12.8

```java
//***************************************************************************
//  KochSnowflakePanel.java         Programming with Alice and Java
//
//  Represents the main panel of the KochSnowflake app, containing the control
//  buttons and the drawing panel. Also serves as a listener for the buttons.
//***************************************************************************

import java.io.*;
import java.awt.*;
import javax.swing.*;
import javax.imageio.*;
import java.awt.event.*;
```

Listing 12.8 (continued)

```java
public class KochSnowflakePanel extends JPanel implements ActionListener
{
    private final int PANEL_WIDTH = 400;
    private final int PANEL_HEIGHT = 440;

    private final int MIN = 1, MAX = 9;

    private JButton increase, decrease;
    private JLabel titleLabel, orderLabel;
    private JPanel tools;
    private KochDrawingPanel drawing;

    //-----------------------------------------------------------------
    // Sets up the toolbar and the drawing panel.
    //-----------------------------------------------------------------
    public KochSnowflakePanel()throws IOException
    {
        tools = new JPanel();
        tools.setLayout(new BoxLayout(tools, BoxLayout.X_AXIS));
        tools.setPreferredSize(new Dimension(PANEL_WIDTH, 40));
        tools.setBackground(Color.yellow);
        tools.setOpaque(true);

        titleLabel = new JLabel("The Koch Snowflake");
        titleLabel.setForeground(Color.black);

        increase = new JButton(new ImageIcon("increase.gif"));
        increase.setPressedIcon(new ImageIcon("increasePressed.gif"));
        increase.setMargin(new Insets(0, 0, 0, 0));
        increase.addActionListener(this);

        decrease = new JButton(new ImageIcon("decrease.gif"));
        decrease.setPressedIcon(new ImageIcon("decreasePressed.gif"));
        decrease.setMargin(new Insets (0, 0, 0, 0));
        decrease.addActionListener(this);

        orderLabel = new JLabel("Order: 1");
        orderLabel.setForeground(Color.black);

        tools.add(titleLabel);
        tools.add(Box.createHorizontalStrut (40));
        tools.add(decrease);
        tools.add(increase);
        tools.add(Box.createHorizontalStrut (20));
        tools.add(orderLabel);

        drawing = new KochDrawingPanel(1);

        add(tools);
        add(drawing);
```

(continued)

Listing 12.8 (continued)

```
        setPreferredSize(new Dimension(PANEL_WIDTH, PANEL_HEIGHT));
    }

    //---------------------------------------------------------------------
    // Determines which button was pushed and sets the new order if it is in
    // range.
    //---------------------------------------------------------------------
    public void actionPerformed(ActionEvent event)
    {
        int order = drawing.getOrder();

        if (event.getSource() == increase)
            order++;
        else
            order--;
        if (order >= MIN && order <= MAX)
        {
            orderLabel.setText("Order: " + order);
            drawing.setOrder(order);
            repaint();
        }
    }
}
```

The fractal image is drawn on an instance of the KochDrawingPanel class, shown in Listing 12.9. The paintComponent method makes the initial calls to the recursive method drawFractal. The three calls to drawFractal in the paint method represent the original three sides of the equilateral triangle that make up a Koch fractal of order 1.

Listing 12.9

```
//********************************************************************
//   KochDrawingPanel.java   Programming with Alice and Java
//
//   Represents the drawing surface on which the Koch fractal is drawn.
//********************************************************************

import java.awt.*;
import javax.swing.JPanel;
```

Listing 12.9 (continued)

```java
public class KochDrawingPanel extends JPanel
{
   private final int PANEL_WIDTH = 400;
   private final int PANEL_HEIGHT = 400;

   private final double SQ = Math.sqrt(3.0) / 6;

   private final int TOPX = 200, TOPY = 20;
   private final int LEFTX = 60, LEFTY = 300;
   private final int RIGHTX = 340, RIGHTY = 300;

   private int current; // Current order

   //-----------------------------------------------------------------
   // Sets the initial fractal order and panel characteristics.
   //-----------------------------------------------------------------
   public KochDrawingPanel(int initialOrder)
   {
      current = initialOrder;
      setBackground(Color.black);
      setPreferredSize(new Dimension(PANEL_WIDTH, PANEL_HEIGHT));
   }

   //-----------------------------------------------------------------
   // Paints the panel by making the initial calls to the drawFractal method.
   //-----------------------------------------------------------------
   public void paintComponent(Graphics gc)
   {
      super.paintComponent(gc);

      gc.setColor(Color.green);

      drawFractal(current, TOPX, TOPY, LEFTX, LEFTY, gc);
      drawFractal(current, LEFTX, LEFTY, RIGHTX, RIGHTY, gc);
      drawFractal(current, RIGHTX, RIGHTY, TOPX, TOPY, gc);
   }

   //-----------------------------------------------------------------
   // Draws the fractal recursively. The base case is order 1 for which a
   // simple line is drawn. Otherwise three intermediate points are computed,
   // and each line segment is drawn as a fractal.
   //-----------------------------------------------------------------
   public void drawFractal (int order, int x1, int y1, int x5, int y5,
            Graphics gc)
   {
      int deltaX, deltaY, x2, y2, x3, y3, x4, y4;

      if (order == 1)
         gc.drawLine(x1, y1, x5, y5);
```

(continued)

Listing 12.9 (continued)

```
        else
        {
            deltaX = x5 - x1; // Distance between end points
            deltaY = y5 - y1;

            x2 = x1 + deltaX / 3; // One-third
            y2 = y1 + deltaY / 3;

            x3 = (int) ((x1+x5)/2 + SQ * (y1-y5)); // tip of projection
            y3 = (int) ((y1+y5)/2 + SQ * (x5-x1));

            x4 = x1 + deltaX * 2/3; // Two-thirds
            y4 = y1 + deltaY * 2/3;

            drawFractal(order-1, x1, y1, x2, y2, gc);
            drawFractal(order-1, x2, y2, x3, y3, gc);
            drawFractal(order-1, x3, y3, x4, y4, gc);
            drawFractal(order-1, x4, y4, x5, y5, gc);
        }
    }

    //-----------------------------------------------------------------
    // Sets the fractal order to the value specified.
    //-----------------------------------------------------------------
    public void setOrder(int order)
    {
        current = order;
    }

    //-----------------------------------------------------------------
    // Returns the current order of the fractal.
    //-----------------------------------------------------------------
    public int getOrder()
    {
        return current;
    }
}
```

The variable current represents the order of the fractal to be drawn. Each recursive call to drawFractal decrements the order by 1. The base case of the recursion occurs when the order of the fractal is 1, which results in a simple line segment between the coordinates specified by the parameters.

If the order of the fractal is higher than 1, three additional points are computed. In conjunction with the parameters, these points form the four line segments of the modified fractal. The transformation is shown in Figure 12.12.

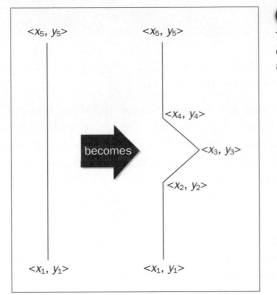

Figure 12.12

The transformation of each line segment of a Koch snowflake

Based on the position of the two end points of the original line segment, a point one-third of the way and a point two-thirds of the way between them are computed. The calculation of $<x_3, y_3>$, the point at the tip of the protrusion, is more convoluted and uses a simplifying constant that incorporates multiple geometric relationships. The calculation to determine protrusion point has nothing to do with the recursive technique used to draw the fractal, and we don't discuss the details of that computation here.

TRY THIS!

> 8. Modify the KochSnowflake program so that the maximum order of the fractal is 15.
>
> 9. Modify the KochSnowflake program so that the two intermediate points $<x_2, y_2>$ and $<x_4, y_4>$ are one-quarter and three-quarters of the distance between end points, respectively.

An interesting mathematical feature of a Koch snowflake is that it has an infinite perimeter, but a finite area. As the order of the fractal increases, the perimeter grows exponentially larger, with a mathematical limit of infinity. However, a rectangle large enough to surround the second order fractal for the Koch snowflake is large enough to contain all higher-order fractals. The shape is restricted forever in area, but its perimeter gets infinitely longer.

12.4 More to Explore

In this final chapter, let's conclude by mentioning a few things that you may encounter if you continue your exploration of Java.

JAR Files   You can bundle your source code, classes, and other files into a single compressed file suitable for email or other types of file transfers. This special type of compressed file is known as a *Java Archive File*, or JAR. JAR files are similar to .zip files, and also provide a mechanism for making your Java program execute when the .jar file containing it is double clicked. You can find more information about creating and using .jar files in the online Java tutorial found at java.sun.com/docs/books/tutorial.

Threads   Programmers will often want to have their programs execute more than one statement at a time. We saw that Alice achieves this through the `Do together` statement. Java accomplishes simultaneous execution using objects known as *threads*. The `Thread` and `Runnable` classes in the `java.lang` package provide the ability to have multiple objects execute their code at the same time.

Data Structures   A data structure is an object designed to store and manage collections of other objects. We explored the `ArrayList` data structure in Chapter 10. The Java API contains a rich collection of data structures that can be used in many situations. Structures such as stacks, queues, trees, and maps manage objects in particular ways and thus help us solve particular kinds of programming problems. Some structures lend themselves to recursive processing. Certainly, any further exploration of programming will involve the use of some of these data structures.

Summary of Key Concepts

- Recursion is a programming technique in which a method calls itself. To program recursively, you must be able to think recursively.

- Any recursive definition must have a non-recursive part, called the base case, which permits the recursion to eventually end.

- Mathematical problems and formulas are often expressed recursively.

- Each recursive call to a method creates new local variables and parameters.

- A careful trace of recursive processing can provide insight into the way it is used to solve a problem.

- Recursion is the most elegant and appropriate way to solve some problems, but for others it is less intuitive than an iterative solution.

- A backtracking algorithm, which solves a problem using trial and error, is often implemented using recursion.

- The Towers of Hanoi solution has exponential complexity, which is very inefficient, but its implementation is remarkably short and elegant.

- A fractal is a geometric shape that can be defined naturally in a recursive manner.

Exercises

EX 12.1 Write a recursive definition of a valid Java identifier.

EX 12.2 Write a recursive definition of x^y (x raised to the power y), where x and y are integers and $y > 0$.

EX 12.3 Write a recursive definition of $i * j$ (integer multiplication), where $i > 0$. Define the multiplication process in terms of integer addition. For example, $4 * 7$ is equal to 7 added to itself 4 times.

EX 12.4 The Fibonacci numbers are a sequence of integers, each of which is the sum of the previous two numbers. The first two numbers in the sequence are 0 and 1. Write a recursive definition of the Fibonacci numbers. Explain why you would not normally use recursion to solve this problem.

EX 12.5 In this chapter we presented a recursive method that calculates the sum of the integers from 1 to N. Create a new version of that method that uses the following recursive definition: The sum of 1 to N is the sum of 1 to ($N/2$) plus the sum of ($N/2 + 1$) to N. Trace your solution using an N of 7.

EX 12.6 Write a recursive method that returns the value of N! (N factorial) using the definition given in this chapter. Explain why you would not normally use recursion to solve this problem.

EX 12.7 Write a recursive method that reverses the characters of a string. Explain why you would not normally use recursion to solve this problem.

EX 12.8 If num1 and num2 are positive integers, what does the following method do?

```
public int doIt(int num1, int num2)
{
   if (num2 == 0)
      result = 0;
   else if (num2% 2 == 0)
      result = doIt(num1+num1, num2/2);
   else
      result = doIt(num1+num1, num2/2) + num1;
   return result;
}
```

EX 12.9 Produce a chart showing the number of moves required to solve the Towers of Hanoi puzzle for each of the following numbers of disks: 2, 3, 4, 5, 6, 7, 8, 9, 10, 15, 20, and 25.

EX 12.10 How many line segments are used to construct a Koch snowflake of order N? Produce a chart showing the number of line segments that make up a Koch snowflake for orders 1 through 9.

Programming Projects

PP 12.1 Design and implement a recursive program that determines if a string is a palindrome. A palindrome is a string that reads the same forward and backward, such as "radar" and "Able was I ere I saw Elba" (if you ignore spaces and differences in case). Create a driver that allows the user to test multiple strings.

PP 12.2 Design and implement a program that implements Euclid's algorithm for finding the greatest common divisor (gcd) of two positive integers. The greatest common divisor is the largest integer that divides both values without producing a remainder. Create a driver to test your implementation. The gcd function can be defined recursively as follows:

- gcd(num1, num2) is num2 if num2 <= num1 and num2 divides num1

- gcd(num1, num2) is gcd(num2, num1) if num1 < num2

- gcd(num1, num2) is gcd(num2, num1%num2) otherwise

PP 12.3 Design and implement a recursive program that traverses a three-dimensional maze in which the goal is to move from one corner of a cube to the opposite corner. Movement can occur in the six primary directions, but not diagonally.

PP 12.4 Design and implement a program that conducts a recursive *binary search* on an array of sorted integers. A binary search examines the middle item of the items being searched. If the target is not found, the search continues with the appropriate half of the remaining items (each comparison eliminates half of the items because they are in sorted order). Create a driver that allows the user to search for multiple values.

PP 12.5 Design and implement a recursive program that solves the Non-Attacking Queens problem. That is, write a program to determine how eight queens can be positioned on an eight-by-eight chessboard so that none of them are in the same row, column, or diagonal as any other queen. There are no other chess pieces on the board.

PP 12.6 In the language of an alien race, all words take the form of Blurbs. A Blurb is a Whoozit followed by one or more Whatzits. A Whoozit is the character "x" followed by zero or more "y" characters. A Whatzit is a "q" followed by either a "z" or a "d", followed by a Whoozit. Design and implement a recursive program that generates random Blurbs in this alien language.

PP 12.7 Design and implement a recursive program to determine if a string is a valid Blurb as defined in the previous programming project.

PP 12.8 Design and implement a recursive program that produces all permutations of a string. Create a driver that allows the user to process multiple strings. *Hint*: Convert the string to an array of characters and recursively process smaller substrings.

PP 12.9 Design and implement a recursive program to determine and print the Nth line of Pascal's Triangle, as shown below. Each interior value is the sum of the two values above it. *Hint*: Use a list or an array to store the values on each line.

```
                        1
                     1     1
                  1     2     1
               1     3     3     1
            1     4     6     4     1
         1     5    10    10     5     1
      1     6    15    20    15     6     1
   1     7    21    35    35    21     7     1
1     8    28    56    70    56    28     8     1
```

PP 12.10 Design and implement a program that draws a *C-curve fractal* whose order
1 is a straight line. Allow the user to increment and decrement the order of
the fractal using buttons (similar to the KochSnowflake example). Each
successive order of the C-curve fractal is created by replacing all line
segments with two line segments, both half of the size of the original, and
which meet at a right angle. Specifically, a C-curve of order N from $<x_1$,
$y_1>$ to $<x_3, y_3>$ is replaced by two C-curves from $<x_1, y_1>$ to $<x_2, y_2>$ and
from $<x_2, y_2>$ to $<x_3, y_3>$ where:

x2 = (x1 + x3 + y1 − y3) / 2;

y2 = (x3 + y1 + y3 − x1) / 2;

Appendix A

This appendix contains succinct instructions for accomplishing particular tasks with the Alice environment.

How To: Install the Alice Environment

Point your web browser to the Alice home page (http://www.alice.org) and look for the download section (http://www.alice.org/index.php?page=downloads/download_alice). Select the version of Alice appropriate for your platform (we'll assume you are using Windows) and the download will begin. Note where your download will be stored and, when it is completed, double click on the downloaded file. The .zip file you downloaded will expand into a temporary folder (under Windows XP) that contains the Alice directory. Drag the Alice directory to the desired location on your computer. To open the directory, double click on its icon. Then, double click on the Alice program (Alice.exe) to start the Alice program.

Figure A.1

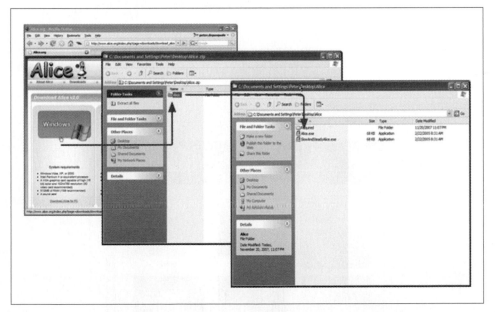

How To: Create a New World

There are two ways to create a new world in Alice. First, you can select New World from the File menu shown in the figure below.

Figure A.2

Second, when Alice starts, you can use the Templates tab of the Welcome to Alice! window to choose a ground surface for your new world, then click the Open button.

Figure A.3

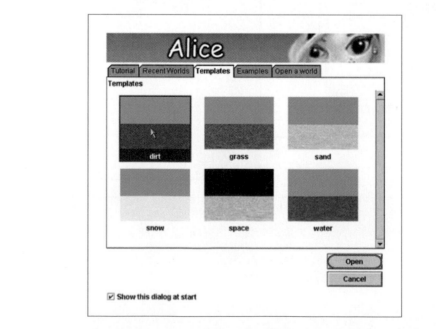

(How To:) Add an Object to a World

To add an object to a world, click the Add Objects button on the toolbar beneath the world view. Then, use the gallery library at the bottom of the Alice window to locate and select the object you wish to add to the world. Click the object's tile once and then click on the Add instance to world button on the window that appears, or drag the object's tile into the world view window. You can now repeat the process to add additional objects to the world or click the Done button to exit the world editor.

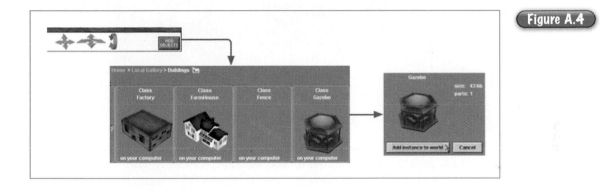

Figure A.4

(How To:) Position and Orient an Object

Click the Add Objects button on the toolbar beneath the world view. Next, click one of the buttons in the Move Objects Freely section of the world editor, then click and drag the object to modify its position or orientation in the world. Each button controls a different aspect of position or orientation.

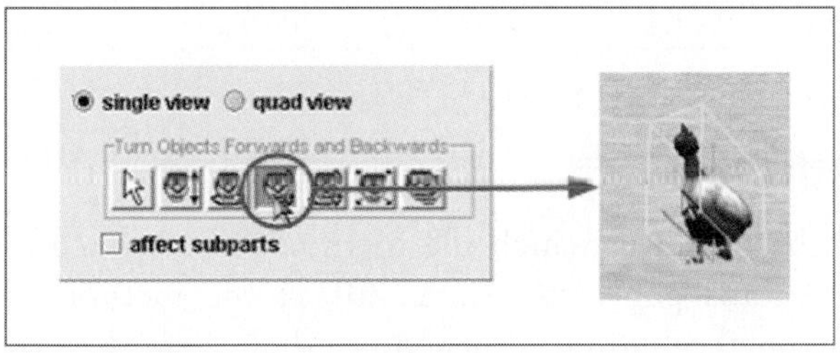

Figure A.5

How To: Duplicate an Object

Enter the world editor by clicking on the Add Objects button on the toolbar beneath the world view in Alice. Click the right-most button (Copy Objects), then click the object you wish to duplicate in the world view window.

Figure A.6

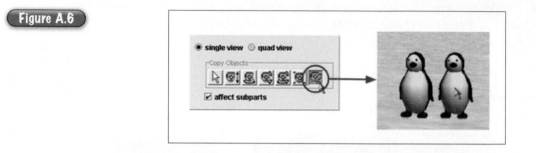

How To: Create a New Method

Select the object that will contain the new method. Then select the methods tab of the details panel. Click the create new method button. A New Method window will open, prompting you to provide a name for your new method. Enter the name in the window's text area and click the OK button. The new method will be displayed in the method editor.

Figure A.7

How To: Edit a Method

To edit a method, select the object in which the method resides, then click on the methods tab of the details panel to display all of the methods for the selected object. Locate the method you wish to edit and click on the edit button to the right of the method's tile. The method will be displayed in the method editor for editing.

Figure A.8

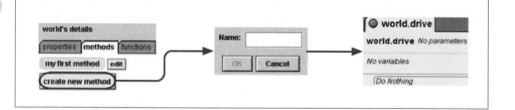

How To: Add a New Statement to a Method

To add a new statement to a method, display the method in the method editor, then drag the statement's tile into the body of the method. For example, if you wish to add a loop statement, drag one of the loop statement tiles (`While` or `Loop`) into the method editor. To add an assignment statement, drag the tile for the variable that will be the recipient of the assignment into the method editor.

Figure A.9

How To: Call One Method or Function from Another

Drag the method or function you wish to call from the details panel into the calling method. If the method or function you are calling contains parameters, a small menu will appear so you can select each value you wish to pass to the method.

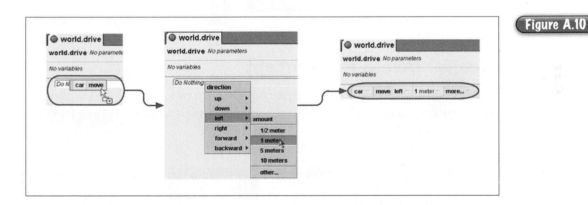

Figure A.10

How To: Delete an Object

Drag the object you wish to delete from the object tree to the trash can icon on the Alice toolbar. You can also right click the object in the world view (or the object tree) and select `delete` from the menu that appears.

Figure A.11

How To: Delete a Method

Select the method you wish to delete and drag its tile from the details panel to the trash can icon on the Alice toolbar.

Figure A.12

How To: Delete a Statement

Drag the statement you wish to delete to the trash can icon on the Alice toolbar. Alternatively, you can right click on the statement's tile and select `delete` from the menu that appears.

Figure A.13

How To: Change the Value Passed to a Method

Use the drop-down menus embedded in the method's tile (in the method editor) to select new parameter values.

Figure A.14

How To: **Add a Parameter to a Method Definition**

Click the `create new parameter` button on the right side of the method editor. A dialog box will appear asking you to name the parameter and declare its type. After you click OK, the parameter appears at the top of the method with an icon indicating its type.

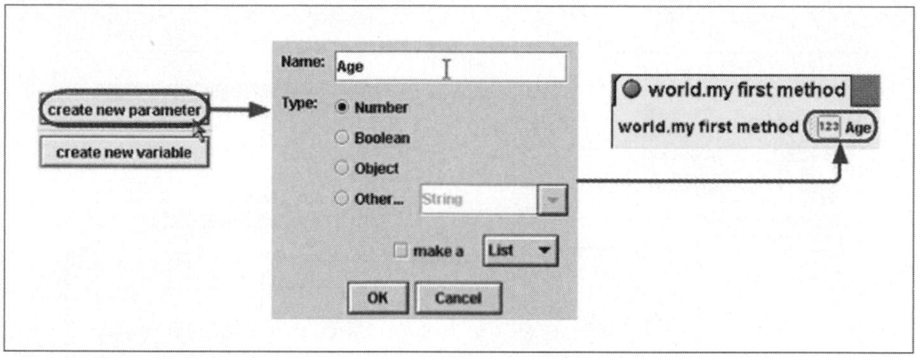

Figure A.15

How To: **Add a Local Variable to a Method**

Click the `create new variable` button on the right side of the method editor. A dialog box will appear asking you to name the variable, declare its type, and give it an initial value. The variable must be given an initial value even if you plan to reset it immediately in the code of the method. (The variable's value may later be set by a function call or other expression, but the initial value cannot be.) After you click OK, the variable appears at the top of the method with an icon indicating its type and a drop-down menu showing its initial value.

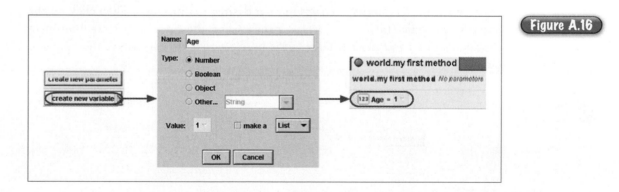

Figure A.16

How To: Set the Value of a Variable

Drag the variable's definition tile in the method header into the method where you wish to change the variable's value. In the menu that appears, select set value to change the variable to a specific value. Alternatively, you can use the increment by 1 and decrement by 1 options on the menu that appears to increment and decrement the value.

Figure A.17

How To: Set an Object's Pose

Position the object and its subparts in their desired orientations. Then click on the object's properties tab in the details panel. Click the capture pose button in the details panel and enter a name in the pose tile that appears above the capture pose button.

Figure A.18

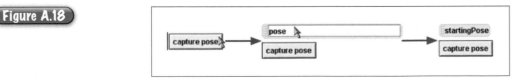

(How To:) **Drop a Dummy Object to
Set a Camera Position**

Press the Add Objects button under the world view window. Click the more controls button to reveal additional options for object and camera control. Now you have two options:

- Click the drop dummy at camera button to place a dummy object at the camera's current location.

- Click on an object in the world view window, then click the drop dummy at selected object button to place a dummy object at the selected object's current location.

In both cases, a dummy object will be created (dummy objects are invisible) and placed in the object tree in a Dummy Objects group folder.

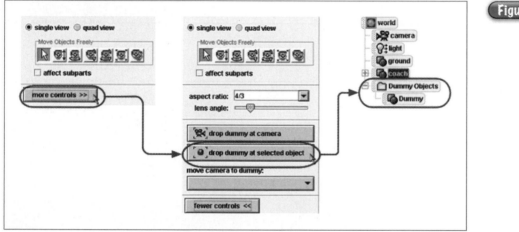

Figure A.19

This appendix is a summary of all the built-in methods and functions found in Alice. Methods and functions of the world object are listed first, followed by methods and functions that are part of almost every other object that can be used in an Alice world. Methods and functions that can be applied to lists are described next. The final section of this appendix describes the parameters common to many of the methods and functions.

 World Methods

my first method
    This is the default method provided by Alice in each new world. It need not be used; other user-defined methods can be created instead.

 World Functions

Boolean Logic Functions

not a
    Returns the logical opposite of the value of a. If a is true, false is returned. If a is false, true is returned.

both a and b
    Returns true if the value of both a and b are true.

either a or b, or both
    Returns true if either a or b are true, or if both are true.

Math Functions

a == b
    Returns true if a and b contain the same value.

a != b
    Returns true if a and b do not contain the same value.

a > b
    Returns true if the value of a is greater than the value of b.

a >= b
    Returns true if the value of a is greater than or equal to the value of b.

```
a < b
```
Returns true if the value of a is less than the value of b.

```
a <= b
```
Returns true if the value of a is less than or equal to the value of b.

Random Functions

```
choose true probabilityOfTrue of the time
```
Returns true randomly a percentage of times based on the percentage set by `probabilityOfTrue`.

```
random number
```
Returns a random floating point number between 0 and 1. Parameters: `integerOnly, minimum, maximum`

String Functions

```
a joined with b
```
Returns a new string containing the contents of both a and b concatenated together. Parameters: `duration, howMuch, style`

```
what as a string
```
Returns a string representation of the value of `what`. `what` can be a numeric value, Boolean, or object reference such as a point of view, pose, etc. Parameters: `duration, howMuch, style`

User-Interaction Functions

```
ask user for a number
```
Creates a dialog window prompting the user to enter a numeric value. The function returns the entered value. Parameters: `question`

```
ask user for yes or no
```
Creates a dialog window prompting the user to choose either a Yes or No value by selecting one of two buttons. The function returns the selected value. Parameters: `question`

```
ask user for a string
```
Creates a dialog window prompting the user to enter a string value. The function returns the entered value. Parameters: `question, title`

Mouse Functions

```
mouse distance from left edge
```
Returns the distance in pixels (a numeric value) of the mouse location from the left edge of the running world window. Parameters: `relativeToRenderTarget`

`mouse distance from top edge`
> Returns the distance in pixels (a numeric value) of the mouse location from the top edge of the running world window. Parameters: `relativeToRenderTarget`

Time Functions

`time elapsed`
> Returns a numeric value of the time elapsed since the world was first executed.

`year`
> Returns the current year as a four-digit numeric value.

`month of year`
> Returns the number of the current month in the year. Month numbering starts from 0 in January and increments by one for each successive month.

`day of year`
> Returns the number of the current day in the year. Day numbering starts from 1 on January first and increments by one for each successive day.

`day of month`
> Returns the number of the current day in the month. Day numbering starts from 1 on the first day of the month and increments by one for each successive day.

`day of week`
> Returns the number of the current day in the week. Day numbering starts from 0 on Sunday and increments by one for each successive day.

`day of week in month`
> Returns the number of occurrences the current weekday has appeared in the current month.

`is AM`
> Returns true if the current time is between midnight and noon, false otherwise.

`is PM`
> Returns true if the current time is between noon and midnight, false otherwise.

`hour of AM or PM`
> Returns the numeric value of the current hour of the day in 12-hour format.

`hour of day`
> Returns the numeric value of the current hour of the day in 24-hour format.

`minute of hour`
> Returns the numeric value of the current minute of the hour.

`second of minute`
> Returns the numeric value of the current second of the minute.

Advanced Math Functions

`minimum of a and b`
Returns the smaller of two values.

`maximum of a and b`
Returns the larger of two values.

`absolute value of a`
Returns the absolute value of a.

`square root of a`
Returns the square root of a.

`floor a`
Returns the largest integer value that is less than a.

`ceiling a`
Returns the smallest integer value that is greater than a.

`sin a`
Returns the sine of a.

`cos a`
Returns the cosine of a.

`tan a`
Returns the tangent of a.

`arccos a`
Returns the arccosine of an angle, a.

`arcsin a`
Returns the arcsine of an angle, a.

`arctan a`
Returns the arctangent of an angle, a.

`arctan2 a b`
Returns the arctangent of the ratio of b / a.

`a raised to the b power`
Returns the numeric value of a^b.

`e raised to the a power`
Returns the numeric value of e^a.

`natural log of a`
Returns the natural logarithm of a, ln a.

`IEEERemainder of a / b`
Returns the remainder of a / b.

`round a`
Returns the integer numeric value closest to a.

`a converted from radians to degrees`
    Converts a from radians to degrees returning the value of a in degrees.

`a converted from degrees to radians`
    Converts a from degrees to radians returning the value of a in radians.

`the bth root of a`
    Returns the b root of a as a numeric value.

Other Functions

`right, up, forward`
    Returns a new position object created from the x (`right`), y (`up`), and z (`forward`) values specified in the function call.

 ## B.3 Object Methods

`move`
    Moves the specified object in one of six directions (left, right, up, down, forward, or backward), relative to the object's point of view. Parameters: `asSeenBy, duration, isScaledBySize, style`

`turn`
    Rotates the specified object about its x-axis (forward or backward turn) or y-axis (left or right turn). The amount of the turn can be any amount of full or partial revolutions. Parameters: `asSeenBy, duration, style`

`roll`
    Rotates the specified object about its z-axis (left or right roll). The amount of the roll can be any amount of full or partial revolutions. Parameters: `asSeenBy, duration, style`

`resize`
    Modifies the size of the specified object. The size of the object can be increased (making the object larger) or decreased (making the object smaller) by any amount. Parameters: `asSeenBy, dimension, duration, howMuch, likeRubber, style`

`say`
    Creates a cartoon-style speech bubble emanating from the object and containing a string of text. The bubble is generally interpreted as a representation of the object speaking the contained text. Parameters: `bubbleColor, duration, fontName, fontSize, textColor`

`think`
    Creates a cartoon-style thought bubble emanating from the object and containing a string of text. The bubble is generally interpreted as a representation of the object thinking the contained text. Parameters: `bubbleColor, duration, fontSize, fontName, textColor`

play sound
>   Causes the object to be responsible for playing a sound clip. The clip played can be one of the provided Alice sound clips, a clip that is imported into the world, or a clip the user can record. Parameters: `duration`, `fromMarker`, `toMarker`, `volumeLevel`

move to
>   Moves the object to the same position as a second, specified object. Parameters: `duration`, `position` (offset), `style`

move toward
>   Moves the object a specified number of meters toward a second, specified object. Parameters: `asSeenBy`, `duration`, `style`

move away from
>   Moves the object a specified number of meters away from a second, specified object. Parameters: `asSeenBy`, `duration`, `style`

orient to
>   Turns the object so that it is pointing (facing) in the same direction as a second, specified object. Parameters: `duration`, `quaternion` (offset), `style`

turn to face
>   Turns the object so that it is pointing (facing) the second, specified object. Parameters: `asSeenBy`, `duration`, `offset`, `style`, `upGuide`

point at
>   Turns the object so that it is pointing (facing) the second, specified object. This method acts similarly to the `turn to face` method, however it will also change the tilt of the object being turned. If the two objects are located in the world at different heights, the effect of the point at method is more noticeable. Parameters: `asSeenBy`, `duration`, `offset`, `style`, `upGuide`

set point of view to
>   Sets the point of view for the object to be identical to the point of view of a second, specified object. Parameters: `affectPosition`, `affectQuaternion`, `duration`, `followHermiteCubic`, `pointOfView`, `style`

set pose
>   Positions the object into a predefined pose. Parameters: `duration`, `style`

stand up
>   Rolls the object into a "standing" position so that its vertical axis is parallel to the world's vertical axis. Parameters: `asSeenBy`, `duration`, `style`

move at speed
>   Moves the object in a specified direction (up, down, left, right, forward, or backward) at a specified rate. Parameters: `asSeenBy`, `duration`, `style`

turn at speed
>   Turns the object in a specified direction (left, right, forward, or backward) at a specified rate. Parameters: `asSeenBy`, `duration`

`roll at speed`
> Rolls the object in a specified direction (left or right) at a specified rate. Parameters: `asSeenBy, duration`

`constrain to face`
> Instantly and abruptly faces the object toward a second, specified object. Parameters: `asSeenBy, duration, offset, upGuide`

`constrain to point at`
> Instantly and abruptly points the object toward a second, specified object. Parameters: `asSeenBy, duration, offset, onlyAffectYaw, upGuide`

B.4 Object Functions

Proximity Functions

`object is within threshold of object`
> Returns true if the object is located within a specified number of meters from a second, specified object. Returns false otherwise. Parameters: `duration, howMuch, style`

`object is at least threshold away from object`
> Returns true value if the object is located at least a specified number of meters from a second, specified object. Returns false otherwise. Parameters: `duration, howMuch, style`

`object distance to`
> Returns the distance in meters of the current object to a second, specified object. Parameters: `duration, howMuch, style`

`object distance to the left of`
> Returns the distance of the current object in meters to the left of a second, specified object. Parameters: `asSeenBy, duration, howMuch, style`

`object distance to the right of`
> Returns the distance of the current object in meters to the right of a second, specified object. Parameters: `asSeenBy, duration, howMuch, style`

`object distance above`
> Returns the distance of the current object in meters above a second, specified object. Parameters: `asSeenBy, duration, howMuch, style`

`object distance below`
> Returns the distance of the current object in meters below a second, specified object. Parameters: `asSeenBy, duration, howMuch, style`

`object distance in front of`
> Returns the distance of the current object in meters in front of a second, specified object. Parameters: `asSeenBy, duration, howMuch, style`

`object distance behind`

Returns the distance of the current object in meters behind a second, specified object. Parameters: `asSeenBy`, `duration`, `howMuch`, `style`

Size Functions

`object's width`

Returns the width in meters of the current object. Parameters: `duration`, `howMuch`, `style`

`object's height`

Returns the height in meters of the current object. Parameters: `duration`, `howMuch`, `style`

`object's depth`

Returns the depth in meters of the current object. Parameters: `duration`, `howMuch`, `style`

`object is smaller than`

Returns true if the current object is smaller (volume is less) than a second, specified object. False is returned otherwise. Parameters: `duration`, `howMuch`, `style`

`object is larger than`

Returns true if the current object is larger (volume is greater) than a second, specified object. False is returned otherwise. Parameters: `duration`, `howMuch`, `style`

`object is narrower than`

Returns true if the current object is narrower (width is less) than a second, specified object. False is returned otherwise. Parameters: `duration`, `howMuch`, `style`

`object is wider than`

Returns true if the current object is wider (width is greater) than a second, specified object. False is returned otherwise. Parameters: `duration`, `howMuch`, `style`

`object is shorter than`

Returns true if the current object is smaller (height is less) than a second, specified object. False is returned otherwise. Parameters: `duration`, `howMuch`, `style`

`object is taller than`

Returns true if the current object is taller (height is greater) than a second, specified object. False is returned otherwise. Parameters: `duration`, `howMuch`, `style`

Spatial Relation Functions

`object is to the left of`

Returns true if the current object is located to the left of a second, specified object. False is returned otherwise. Parameters: `asSeenBy`, `duration`, `howMuch`, `style`

`object is to the right of`
Returns true if the current object is located to the right of a second, specified object. False is returned otherwise. Parameters: `asSeenBy`, `duration`, `howMuch`, `style`

`object is above`
Returns true if the current object is located above a second, specified object. False is returned otherwise. Parameters: `asSeenBy`, `duration`, `howMuch`, `style`

`object is below`
Returns true if the current object is located below a second, specified object. False is returned otherwise. Parameters: `asSeenBy`, `duration`, `howMuch`, `style`

`object is in front of`
Returns true if the current object is located in front of a second, specified object. False is returned otherwise. Parameters: `asSeenBy`, `duration`, `howMuch`, `style`

`object is behind`
Returns true if the current object is located behind a second, specified object. False is returned otherwise. Parameters: `asSeenBy`, `duration`, `howMuch`, `style`

Point of View Functions

`object's point of view`
Returns the current object's point of view as an object. A point of view object defines a location and orientation. Parameters: `asSeenBy`, `duration`, `howMuch`, `style`

`object's position`
Returns a position object representing the current object's position in the world. Parameters: `asSeenBy`, `duration`, `howMuch`, `style`

`object's quaternion`
Returns a quaternion object representing the current object's orientation in three-dimensional space. Parameters: `asSeenBy`, `duration`, `howMuch`, `style`

Other Functions

`object's current pose`
Returns a pose object representing the current object's current pose. Parameters: `duration`, `howMuch`, `style`

`object's part named key`
Returns an object that references a specified part (`key`) from the current object, if key exists. Parameters: `duration`, `howMuch`, `style`

`object's variable named variableName of type valueClass`
Returns the value of the current object's variable (property) named `variableName` that is of type `valueClass`. Parameters: `duration`, `howMuch`, `style`

 **List Methods**

`insert value at beginning of listname`
Inserts the specified `value` at the beginning of the list named `listname`. Parameters: `duration`

`insert value at end of listname`
Inserts the specified `value` at the end of the list named `listname`. Parameters: `duration`

`insert value at position index of listname`
Inserts the specified `value` into the list named `listname` at position `index` of the list. Parameters: `duration`

`remove all items from listname`
Removes all items from the list named `listname`. Parameters: `duration`

`remove item from beginning of listname`
Removes the item at the front of the list named `listname`. Parameters: `duration`

`remove item from end of listname`
Removes the item at the end of the list named `listname`. Parameters: `duration`

`remove item from position index of listname`
Removes the item at position `index` from the list named `listname`. Parameters: `duration`

 **List Functions**

`first index of item`
Returns the index value of the first occurrence of the specified `item` in the current list.

`first item from list`
Returns the first item in the current list.

`is list empty`
Returns true if the current list is empty, false otherwise.

`ith item from list`
Returns the `ith` item from the current list.

`last index of item`
Returns the index value of the last occurrence of the specified `item` in the current list.

`last item from list`
Returns the last item in the current list.

`list contains item`
Returns true if the current list contains the specified `item`, false otherwise.

`random item from list`
Returns a random item from the current list.

`size of list`
Returns the size of the current list.

B.7 Method and Function Parameters

The following parameters are used throughout the `object` and `world` methods and functions.

`affectPosition`
A Boolean value which toggles if the `set point of view` method will modify the position of the current object as a result of the change in the object's point of view.

`affectQuaternion`
A Boolean value which toggles if the `set point of view` method will modify the quaternion (orientation) of the current object as a result of the change in the object's point of view.

`asSeenBy`
Specifies another object whose orientation is used to affect a method or function's movement on the current object.

`bubbleColor`
Sets the background color of the bubbles used to display a string that an object is saying or thinking.

`dimension`
Specifies a particular direction in which an object resize occurs (all, top to bottom, left to right, or front to back).

`duration`
The length of time in seconds the method or function will span.

`followHermiteCubic`
A Boolean value used to indicate whether a change in an object's point of view should follow a cubic hermite spline.

`fontName`
The name of the font used to display the string of text in an object's speech or thought bubble.

`fontSize`
The size in pixels of the display characters in an object's speech or thought bubble.

`fromMarker`
A characteristic of the `play sound` method that indicates the starting point of a sound (not necessarily the start of the sound file). Markers can be set using audio editing software (not Alice).

`howMuch`

A characteristic used to define the extent of a method or function's operation on an object (object only, object and parts, object and descendants).

`integerOnly`

A characteristic used to indicate whether the random number function should generate integer values (rather than the default floating point values). This characteristic is generally used with the `minimum` and/or `maximum` properties.

`isScaledBySize`

A Boolean value that indicates whether the amount to move an object should be scaled relative to the object's size.

`likeRubber`

A Boolean value that instructs the `resize` method to flatten the current object (as if it were a piece of rubber) during a front-to-back or left-to-right resizing.

`maximum`

Defines the maximum value the random number function can generate.

`minimum`

Defines the minimum value the random number function can generate.

`offset`

A position object that is used to modify (or offset) another location.

`onlyAffectYaw`

A characteristic indicating that execution of a method or function should only affect the object's yaw value, not the pitch (movement about the left/right axis) or roll (movement about the up/down axis).

`pointOfView`

Defines a point of view consisting of a position and quaternion (orientation).

`position`

Used to define a location in the world.

`quaternion`

Used to define an orientation in three-dimensional space.

`question`

A string value that is displayed when either the `ask user for a number` or `ask user for yes or no` functions are called.

`relativeToRenderTarget`

A Boolean parameter to the mouse functions that toggles whether the function returns a distance relative to the left/top edge of the screen (when set to false), or the rendering window (when set to true).

`style`

The characteristic used to describe the overall, starting, or ending animation approach (gentle or abrupt) and therefore how a given method or function's operation is perceived relative to the next animation effect on the same object.

title
>A string used as the title of a dialog box prompting the user to enter a string value.

textColor
>Sets the color of the text displayed in an object's speech or thought bubble.

toMarker
>A characteristic of the `play sound` method that indicates the ending point of a sound (not necessarily the end of the sound file). Markers can be set using audio editing software (not Alice).

upGuide
>`upGuide` is an undocumented parameter.

volumeLevel
>A numeric value indicating how loud a sound should be played. Values can range from 0.0 (muted) to 1.0 (loudest).

Appendix C
THE UNICODE CHARACTER SET

The Java programming language uses the Unicode character set for managing text. A *character set* is simply an ordered list of characters, each corresponding to a particular numeric value. Unicode is an international character set that contains letters, symbols, and ideograms for languages all over the world. Each character is represented as a 16-bit unsigned numeric value. Unicode, therefore, can support over 65,000 unique characters. Only about half of those values have characters assigned to them at this point. The Unicode character set continues to be refined as characters from various languages are included.

Many programming languages still use the ASCII character set. ASCII stands for the American Standard Code for Information Interchange. The 8-bit extended ASCII set is quite small, so the developers of Java opted to use Unicode in order to support international users. However, ASCII is essentially a subset of Unicode, including corresponding numeric values, so programmers used to ASCII should have no problems with Unicode.

Value	Char	Value	Char	Value	Char	Value	Char	Value	Char
32	space	51	3	70	F	89	Y	108	l
33	!	52	4	71	G	90	Z	109	m
34	"	53	5	72	H	91	[	110	n
35	#	54	6	73	I	92	\	111	o
36	$	55	7	74	J	93	]	112	p
37	%	56	8	75	K	94	^	113	q
38	&	57	9	76	L	95	_	114	r
39	'	58	:	77	M	96	`	115	s
40	(	59	;	78	N	97	a	116	t
41	)	60	<	79	O	98	b	117	u
42	*	61	=	80	P	99	c	118	v
43	+	62	>	81	Q	100	d	119	w
44	'	63	?	82	R	101	e	120	x
45	–	64	@	83	S	102	f	121	y
46	.	65	A	84	T	103	g	122	z
47	/	66	B	85	U	104	h	123	{
48	0	67	C	86	V	105	i	124	l
49	1	68	D	87	W	106	j	125	}
50	2	69	E	88	X	107	k	126	~

Table C.1

A small portion of the Unicode character set

Table C.1 shows a list of commonly used characters and their Unicode numeric values. These characters also happen to be ASCII characters. All of the characters in Table C.1 are called *printable characters* because they have a symbolic representation that can be displayed on a monitor or printed by a printer. Other characters are called *nonprintable characters* because they have no such symbolic representation. Note that the space character (numeric value 32) is considered a printable character, even though no symbol is printed when it is displayed. Nonprintable characters are sometimes called *control characters* because many of them can be generated by holding down the control key on a keyboard and pressing another key.

The Unicode characters with numeric values 0 through 31 are nonprintable characters. Also, the delete character, with numeric value 127, is a nonprintable character. All of these characters are ASCII characters as well. Many of them have fairly common and well-defined uses, while others are more general. The table in Table C.2 lists a small sample of the nonprintable characters.

Table C.2

Some nonprintable characters in the Unicode character set

Value	Character
0	null
7	bell
8	backspace
9	tab
10	line feed
12	form feed
13	carriage return
27	escape
127	delete

Nonprintable characters are used in many situations to represent special conditions. For example, certain nonprintable characters can be stored in a text document to indicate, among other things, the beginning of a new line. An editor will process these characters by starting the text that follows it on a new line, instead of printing a symbol to the screen. Various types of computer systems use different nonprintable characters to represent particular conditions.

Except for having no visible representation, nonprintable characters are essentially equivalent to printable characters. They can be stored in a Java character variable and be part of a character string. They are stored using 16 bits, can be converted to their numeric value, and can be compared using relational operators.

The first 128 characters of the Unicode character set correspond to the common ASCII character set. The first 256 characters correspond to the ISO-Latin-1 extended ASCII character set. Many operating systems and Web browsers will handle these characters, but they may not be able to print the other Unicode characters.

The Unicode character set contains most alphabets in use today, including Greek, Hebrew, Cyrillic, and various Asian ideographs. It also includes Braille, and several sets of symbols used in mathematics and music. Table C.3 shows a few characters from non-Western alphabets.

Value	Character	Source
1071	Я	Russian (Cyrillic)
3593	ฦ	Thai
5098	ꆚ	Cherokee
8478	℞	Letterlike Symbols
8652	⇌	Arrows
10287	⠭	Braille
13407	伥	Chinese/Japanese/Korean (Common)

Table C.3

Some non-Western characters in the Unicode character set

Appendix D JAVA OPERATORS

Java operators are evaluated according to the precedence hierarchy shown in Table D.1. Operators at low precedence levels are evaluated before operators at higher levels. Operators within the same precedence level are evaluated according to the specified association, either right to left (R to L) or left to right (L to R). Operators in the same precedence level are not listed in any particular order.

Precedence Level	Operator	Operation	Associates
1	[ ] . (*parameters*) ++ --	array indexing object member reference parameter evaluation and method invocation postfix increment postfix decrement	L to R
2	++ -- + - ~ !	prefix increment prefix decrement unary plus unary minus bitwise NOT logical NOT	R to L
3	new (*type*)	object instantiation cast	R to L
4	* / %	multiplication division remainder	L to R
5	+ + -	addition string concatenation subtraction	L to R
6	<< >> >>>	left shift right shift with sign right shift with zero	L to R
7	< <= > >= instanceof	less than less than or equal greater than greater than or equal type comparison	L to R
8	== !=	equal not equal	L to R

Table D.1

Java operator precedence

Table D.1 continued

Java operator precedence

Precedence Level	Operator	Operation	Associates
9	& &	bitwise AND boolean AND	L to R
10	^ ^	bitwise XOR boolean XOR	L to R
11	| |	bitwise OR boolean OR	L to R
12	&&	logical AND	L to R
13	||	logical OR	L to R
14	?:	conditional operator	R to L
15	= += += -= *= /= %= <<= >>= >>>= &= &= ^= ^= |= |=	assignment addition, then assignment string concatenation, then assignment subtraction, then assignment multiplication, then assignment division, then assignment remainder, then assignment left shift, then assignment right shift (sign), then assignment right shift (zero), then assignment bitwise AND, then assignment boolean AND, then assignment bitwise XOR, then assignment boolean XOR, then assignment bitwise OR, then assignment boolean OR, then assignment	R to L

The order of operator evaluation can always be forced by the use of parentheses. It is often a good idea to use parentheses even when they are not required, to make it explicitly clear to a human reader how an expression is evaluated.

For some operators, the operand types determine which operation is carried out. For instance, if the + operator is used on two strings, string concatenation is performed, but if it is applied to two numeric types, they are added in the arithmetic sense. If only one of the operands is a string, the other is converted to a string, and string concatenation is performed. Similarly, the operators &, ^, and | perform bitwise operations on numeric operands but boolean operations on boolean operands.

The boolean operators & and | differ from the logical operators && and || in a subtle way. The logical operators are "short-circuited" in that if the result of an expression can be determined by evaluating only the left operand, the right operand is not evaluated. The boolean versions always evaluate both sides of the expression. There is no logical operator that performs an exclusive OR (XOR) operation.

D.1 Java Bitwise Operators

The Java *bitwise operators* operate on individual bits within a primitive value. They are defined only for integers and characters. They are unique among all Java operators because they let us work at the lowest level of binary storage. Table D.2 lists the Java bitwise operators.

Operator	Description
~	bitwise NOT
&	bitwise AND
|	bitwise OR
^	bitwise XOR
<<	left shift
>>	right shift with sign
>>>	right shift with zero fill

Table D.2

Java bitwise operators

Three of the bitwise operators are similar to the logical operators !, &&, and ||. The bitwise NOT, AND, and OR operations work basically the same way as their logical counterparts, except they work on individual bits of a value. The rules are essentially the same. Table D.3 shows the results of bitwise operators on all combinations of two bits.

a	b	~ a	a & b	a | b	a ^ b
0	0	1	0	0	0
0	1	1	0	1	1
1	0	0	0	1	1
1	1	0	1	1	0

Table D.3

Bitwise operations on individual bits

The bitwise operators include the XOR operator, which stands for *exclusive OR*. The logical | | operator is an *inclusive OR* operation, which means it returns true if both operands are true. The | bitwise operator is also inclusive and yields a 1 if both corresponding bits are 1. However, the exclusive OR operator (^) yields a 0 if both operands are 1. There is no logical exclusive OR operator in Java.

When the bitwise operators are applied to integer values, the operation is performed individually on each bit in the value. For example, suppose the integer variable number is declared to be of type byte and currently holds the value 45. Stored as an 8-bit byte, it is represented in binary as 00101101. When the bitwise complement operator (~) is applied to number, each bit in the value is inverted, yielding `11010010`. Since integers are stored using two's complement representation, the value represented is now negative, specifically −46.

Similarly, for all bitwise operators, the operations are applied bit by bit, which is where the term "bitwise" comes from. For binary operators (with two operands), the operations are applied to corresponding bits in each operand. For example, assume `num1` and `num2` are `byte` integers, `num1` holds the value 45, and `num2` holds the value 14. Table D.4 shows the results of several bitwise operations.

Table D.4

Bitwise operations on bytes

num1 & num2	num1 | num2	num1 ^ num2
00101101	00101101	00101101
& 00001110	| 00001110	^ 00001110
= 00001100	= 00101111	= 00100011

The operators `&`, `|`, and `^` can also be applied to boolean values, and they have basically the same meaning as their logical counterparts. When used with boolean values, they are called *boolean operators*. However, unlike the operators `&&` and `||`, which are "short-circuited," the boolean operators are not short-circuited. Both sides of the expression are evaluated every time.

Like the other bitwise operators, the three bitwise shift operators manipulate the individual bits of an integer value. They all take two operands. The left operand is the value whose bits are shifted; the right operand specifies how many positions they should move. Prior to performing a shift, `byte` and `short` values are promoted to `int` for all shift operators. Furthermore, if either of the operands is `long`, the other operand is promoted to `long`. For readability, we use only 16 bits in the examples in this section, but the concepts are the same when carried out to 32- or 64-bit strings.

When bits are shifted, some bits are lost off one end, and others need to be filled in on the other. The *left-shift* operator (`<<`) shifts bits to the left, filling the right bits with zeros. For example, if the integer variable `number` currently has the value 13, then the statement

```
number = number << 2;
```

stores the value 52 into `number`. Initially, `number` contains the bit string `0000000000001101`. When shifted to the left, the value becomes `0000000000110100`, or 52. Notice that for each position shifted to the left, the original value is multiplied by 2.

The sign bit of a number is shifted along with all of the others. Therefore the sign of the value could change if enough bits are shifted to change the sign bit. For example, the value −8 is stored in binary two's complement form as `1111111111111000`. When shifted left two positions, it becomes `1111111111100000`, which is −32. However, if enough positions are shifted, a negative number can become positive and vice versa.

There are two forms of the right-shift operator: one that preserves the sign of the original value (>>) and one that fills the leftmost bits with zeros (>>>).

Let's examine two examples of the *right-shift-with-sign-fill* operator. If the int variable number currently has the value 39, the expression (number >> 2) results in the value 9. The original bit string stored in number is 0000000000100111, and the result of a right shift two positions is 0000000000001001. The leftmost sign bit, which in this case is a zero, is used to fill from the left.

If number has an original value of −16, or 1111111111110000, the right-shift (with sign fill) expression (number >> 3) results in the binary string 1111111111111110, or −2. The leftmost sign bit is a 1 in this case and is used to fill in the new left bits, maintaining the sign.

If maintaining the sign is not desirable, the *right-shift-with-zero-fill* operator (>>>) can be used. It operates similarly to the >> operator but fills with zero no matter what the sign of the original value is.

Appendix E JAVA MODIFIERS

This appendix summarizes the modifiers that give particular characteristics to Java classes, interfaces, methods, and variables. For discussion purposes, the set of all Java modifiers is divided into two groups: visibility modifiers and all others.

E.1 Java Visibility Modifiers

Table E.1 describes the effect of Java visibility modifiers on various constructs. Some relationships are not applicable (N/A). For instance, a class cannot be declared with protected visibility. Note that each visibility modifier operates in the same way on classes and interfaces and in the same way on methods and variables.

Modifier	Classes and interfaces	Methods and variables
default (no modifier)	Visible in its package.	Visible to any class in the same package as its class.
`public`	Visible anywhere.	Visible anywhere.
`protected`	N/A	Visible by any class in the same package as its class.
`private`	Visible to the enclosing class only.	Not visible by any other class.

Table E.1

Java visibility modifiers

Default visibility means that no visibility modifier was explicitly used. Default visibility is sometimes called *package visibility*, but you cannot use the reserved word `package` as a modifier. Classes and interfaces can have default or public visibility; this visibility determines whether a class or interface can be referenced outside of its package. Only an inner class can have private visibility, in which case only the enclosing class may access it.

E.2 A Visibility Example

Consider the situation depicted in the Figure E.1. Class P is the parent class that is used to derive child classes C1 and C2. Class C1 is in the same package as P, but C2 is not. Class P contains four methods, each with different visibility modifiers. One object has been instantiated from each of these classes.

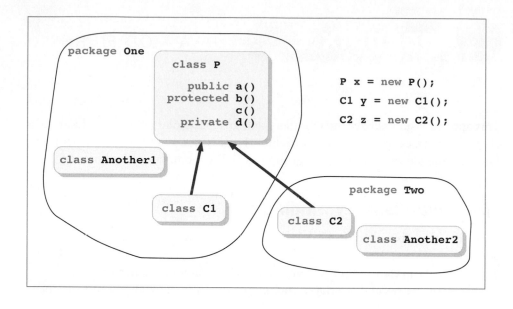

Figure E.1

A situation demonstrating Java visibility modifiers

The `public` method `a()` has been inherited by `C1` and `C2`, and any code with access to object `x` can invoke `x.a()`. The `private` method `d()` is not visible to `C1` or `C2`, so objects `y` and `z` have no such method available to them. Furthermore, `d()` is fully encapsulated and can only be invoked from within object `x`.

The `protected` method `b()` is visible in both `C1` and `C2`. A method in `y` could invoke `x.b()`, but a method in `z` could not. Furthermore, an object of any class in package `One` could invoke `x.b()`, even those that are not related to class `P` by inheritance, such as an object created from class `Another1`.

Method `c()` has default visibility, since no visibility modifier was used to declare it. Therefore object `y` can refer to the method `c()` as if it were declared locally, but object `z` cannot. Object `y` can invoke `x.c()`, as can an object instantiated from any class in package `One`, such as `Another1`. Object `z` cannot invoke `x.c()`.

These rules generalize in the same way for variables. The visibility rules may appear complicated initially, but they can be mastered with a little effort.

E.3 Other Java Modifiers

Table E.2 summarizes the rest of the Java modifiers, which address a variety of issues. Furthermore, a modifier has different effects on classes, interfaces, methods, and variables. Some modifiers cannot be used with certain constructs and therefore are listed as not applicable (N/A).

The transient modifier is used to indicate data that need not be stored in a persistent (serialized) object. That is, when an object is written to a serialized stream, the object representation will include all data that is not specified as transient.

Modifier	Class	Interface	Method	Variable
abstract	The class may contain abstract methods. It cannot be instantiated.	All interfaces are inherently abstract. The modifier is optional.	No method body is defined. The method requires implementation when inherited.	N/A
final	The class cannot be used to drive new classes.	N/A	The method cannot be overridden.	The variable is a constant, whose value cannot be changed once initially set.
native	N/A	N/A	No method body is necessary since implementation is in another language.	N/A
static	N/A	N/A	Defines a class method. It does not require an instantiated object to be invoked. It cannot reference non-static methods or variables. It is implicitly final.	Defines a class variable. It does not require an instantiated object to be referenced. It is shared (common memory space) among all instances of the class.
synchro-nized	N/A	N/A	The execution of the method is mutually exclusive among all threads.	N/A
transient	N/A	N/A	N/A	The variable will not be serialized.
volatile	N/A	N/A	N/A	The variable is changed asynchronously. The compiler should not perform optimizations on it.

Table E.2

The rest of the Java modifiers

Javadoc is a tool for creating documentation in HTML format from Java source code. The utility examines the source code, extracts specially marked information in the documentation, and then produces Web pages that summarize the software.

Documentation comments, also referred to as doc comments, specify the format for comments to be processed by the javadoc tool. Special labels called *tags* are also parsed by javadoc. Together, doc comments and tags can be used to construct a complete Java application programming interface (API) specification. A Java API is a specification of how to work with a class.

Javadoc can be run on packages or individual files (or both). It produces a well-structured, single document each time. However, javadoc does not support incremental additions.

Javadoc comes as a standard part of the Java Software Development Kit (SDK). The tool executable, javadoc.exe, resides in the bin folder of the installation directory along with the javac compiler and java execution tool. Therefore, if you are able to compile and execute your code using the command line, javadoc should also work.

Using javadoc is simple in its plain form; it is very much like compiling a java source file. For example:

```
javadoc myfile.java
```

The javadoc command may also specify options and package names. The source file name must contain the .java extension (similar to the javac compiler command).

F.1 Doc Comments

The document comments are subdivided into descriptions and tags. Descriptions should provide an overview of the functionality of the explained code. Tags address the specifics of the functionality such as code version (for classes or interfaces) or return types (for methods).

Javadoc processes code comments placed between /**, the beginning tag, and */, the end tag. The comments are allowed to span multiple lines where each line begins with a * character, which are, along with any white space before them, discarded by the tool. These comments are allowed to contain HTML tags. For example:

```
/**
 * This is an <strong>example</strong> document comment.
 */
```

Comment placement should be considered carefully. The javadoc tool automatically copies the first sentence from each doc to a summary at the top of the HTML document. The sentence begins after any white space following the * character and ends at the first period. The description that follows should be concise and complete. Document comments are recognized only if they are placed immediately before a class, constructor, method, interface, or field declaration.

The use of HTML inside the description should be limited to proper comment separation and display rather than styling. Javadoc automatically structures the document using certain tags, for example heading tags. Appropriate use of paragraph or list tags (ordered/unordered) should provide satisfactory formatting.

 ## Tags

Tags are included in a doc comment. Each tag must start on a separate line, hence it must be preceded by the * character. Tags are case sensitive and begin with the @ symbol.

Certain tags are required in some situations. The `@param` tag must be supplied for every parameter and is used to describe the purpose of the parameter. The `@return` tag must be supplied for every method that returns anything other than `void`, to describe what the method returns. The `@author` class and the `@version` tags are required for classes and interfaces only.

Table F.1 lists the various tags used in javadoc comments.

Note the two different types of tags listed in Table F.1. The *block tags*, which begin with the @ symbol (e.g., `@author`), must be placed in the tag section following the main description. The *inline tags*, enclosed in the { and } delimiters, can be placed anywhere in the description section or in the comments for block tags. For example:

```
/**
 * This is an <strong>example</strong> document comment.
 * The {@link Glossary} provides definitions of types used.
 *
 * @author Sebastian Niezgoda
 */
```

F.3 Files Generated

The javadoc tool analyzes a java source file or package and produces a three-part HTML document for each class. The HTML file is often referred to as a documentation file. It contains cleanly organized information about the class file derived from the doc comments included in the code.

The first part of the document contains an overall description of the class. The class name appears first followed by a graphical representation of the inheritance relationships. A general description is displayed next, which is extracted from the first sentence of each doc comment entity (as discussed previously).

Table F.1

Various tags used in
javadoc comments

Tag Name	Description
@author	Inserts an "Author" entry with the specified text.
{ @code}	Same as `<code>`{@literal}`</code>`.
@deprecated	Inserts a bold "Deprecated" entry with the specified text.
{ @docRoot}	Relative link to the root of the document.
@exception	See @throws.
{ @inheritDoc}	Copies documentation from the closest inherited class or implemented interface where used allowing for more general comments of hierarchically higher classes to be reused.
{ @link}	Inserts a hyperlink to an HTML document. Use: {@link name url}.
{ @linkPlain}	Same as { @link} but is displayed as plain text. Use: {@linkPlain link label}.
{ @literal}	Text enclosed in the tag is denoted literally, as containing any HTML. For example, {@literal <td> TouchDown} would be displayed as <td> TouchDown (<td> not interpreted as a table cell).
@param	Inserts a "Parameters" section, which lists and describes parameters for a particular constructor/method.
@return	Inserts a "Returns" section, which lists and describes any return values for a particular constructor/method. Use: @return description. An error will be thrown if included in a comment of a method with the void return type.
@see	Included a "See Also" comment with a link pointing to a document with more information. Use: @see link.
@serial	Used for a serializable field. Use: @serial text.
@serialData	Used to describe data written by the writeObject, readObject, writeExternal, and readExternal methods. Use: @serialdata text.
@serialField	Used to comment on the ObjectStreamField. Use: @serialField name type description.
@since	Inserts a new "Since" heading that is used to denote when particular features were first introduced. Use: @since text.
@throws	Includes a "Throws" heading. Use: @throws name description.
{ @value}	Returns the value of a code element it refers to. Use: @value code-member label.
@version	Add a "Version" heading when the –version command–line option is used. Use: @version text.

Next, a list of constructors and methods is provided. The signatures of all the constructors and methods included in the source file are listed along with one-sentence descriptions. The name of the constructor/method is a hyperlink to a more detailed description in the third part of the document.

Third, complete descriptions of the methods are provided. Again, the signature is provided first followed by an explanation of the entity, this time without the one-sentence limit, which is obtained from the doc comments. If applicable, a list of parameters and return values, along with their descriptions, is provided in the respective sections.

The HTML document makes extensive use of hyperlinks to provide necessary additional information, using the `@see` tag for example, and for navigational purposes. The header and the footer of the page are navigation bars, with the following links:

- *Package* provides a list of classes included in the package along with a short purpose and description of each class.

- *Tree* presents a visual hierarchy of the classes within the package. Each class name is a link to the appropriate documentation HTML file.

- *Deprecated* lists functionality that is considered deprecated that is used in any of the class files contained in the package.

- *Index* provides an alphabetical listing of classes, constructors, and methods in the package. The class name is also associated with a short purpose and description of the class. Each appearance of the class name is a link to the appropriate HTML documentation. The signature of every constructor and method is a link to the appropriate detailed description. A one-sentence description presented next to the signature listing associates the constructor/method with the appropriate class.

- *Help* loads a help page with how-to instructions for using and navigating the HTML documentation.

All pages could be viewed with or without frames. Each class summary has links that can be used to quickly access any of the parts of the document (as described above).

The output content could be somewhat generated by command-line options (see above) used when executing the javadoc tool. By default, if no options are specified, the output returned is equivalent to using the `-protected` option. The options include:

- `private` shows all classes, methods, and variables.

- `public` shows only public classes, methods, and variables.

- `protected` shows only protected and public classes, methods, and variables.

- `help` presents the online help.

- `keywords` includes HTML meta tags to the output file generated to assist with searching.

Index

Symbols

- − (NOT bitwise operator), 313
- ! (factorial function), 253–254
- ! (NOT logical operator), 105
- != (equality operator), 46, 105
- % (remainder operator), 105
- & (AND bitwise operator), 313
- & (boolean operator), 312, 315
- && (AND logical operator), 105
- // (slash marks), 8
- [ ] (square brackets), 160–161
- ^ (boolean operator), 315
- ^ (exclusive OR bitwise operator), 313
- {} (braces), 107
- | (boolean operator), 312, 315
- | (inclusive OR bitwise operator), 313
- || (OR logical operator), 105, 313
- ~ (complement bitwise operator), 313–314
- < (less than operator), 46, 47, 105
- << (left-shift operator), 314
- <= less than or equal to operator), 46, 105
- = (assignment operator), 104–105
- == (equality operator), 46, 105
- > (greater than operator), 46, 105
- >= (greater than or equal to operator), 46, 105
- >> and >>> (right-shift operators), 315

A

abstract classes, 184–185
abstract modifiers, 184, 317
Abstract Windowing Toolkit (AWT), 125
action events, 125–137
  ActionEvent, 128, 130
  ActionListener interface, 127–128, 133, 134
  buttons, 125–129
  check boxes, 130–131, 134
  controls, 130–137
  GUI components, 125–137

Java programming, 125–137
  Jbutton, 127
  labels, 126–127
  listener, 127–129, 130, 133
  push button, 127
  radio buttons, 131, 134
  text box, 130
  text field, 133
  ThunkIt program using, 129
add method, 126
Add Objects button, 12, 285–286
aggregate objects, 246–247
agile software development, 247
Alice, 1–122, 283–291, 293–305
  arrays, 87–89, 92–94
  Boolean conditions (true or false), 42–60
  comments (//) for, 8
  data in, 25–39, 104
  data structures, 87–98
  decisions and loops, 41–66
  environment reference, 283–291
  events, 67–85
  functions, 11, 31–32, 60, 91–92, 293–297, 299–305
  integrated development environment (IDE) of, 4–6
  introduction to, 2–4
  Java compared to, 2–4, 99–122
  lists, 87–92
  methods, 8–11, 13–15, 25–39, 91–92, 293, 297–299, 302–305
  objects, 1–23, 26–28, 34–35, 41–66, 67–85, 87–98
  operators, 46, 52–53, 104–105
  parameters, 9, 32–33
  world events, 69, 70–71
  worlds, 2–3, 284–285
animation, *see* movement of objects
API library, 103, 119, 154, 172, 225
  classes, 103, 154
  collections, 154, 172
  exceptions, 225
  methods, 119
ArrayList class, 154, 155–159
  methods of, 155–159

ThunkIt program using, 159
arrays, 87–89, 92–94, 160–172
  Alice, 87–89, 92–94
  bounds checking, 161–164
  characters in, 162–164
  data structures, as, 88–89
  declaring, 161
  element, 161
  fixed size of, 92
  index values, 92–94, 160–164
  initializer lists for, 164–167
  integers in, 160–161, 165–167
  Java, 160–172
  lists, as, 160–172
  lists compared to, 88–89
  multidimensional, 171–172
  obects, of, 168–169
  one-dimensional, 160–169
  parameters, as, 167–168
  square brackets [ ] for, 160–161
  String objects, 168–169
  ThunkIt grid class using, 170
  two-dimensional, 169–170
  variables, 160–161
assignment (=) operator, 104–105
assignment statements, 105

B

backtracking algorithm using recursion, 285–262
base case, 253
base class, 178
binding methods, 193
bitwise operators, 313–315
Blimps world example, 13–14
Boolean operators, 46, 312, 315
Boolean conditions (true or false), 42–60
  equality operators used for, 46
  If/Else statements, 42–48
  logical operators used for, 52–53
  Loop statements, 49–54
  programming decisions based on, 42–60
  relational operators used for, 46

Boolean conditions (*continued*)
 repetition statements, 49–60
 `While` statements, 49–54
Boolean logic functions, 293
bounding rectangle, 111
bounds checking, 161–164
 arrays in Java, 161–164
 index values, 161–164
 `length` constant, 162
 off-by-one errors, 161
`Bugs` world example, 14–15
built-in functions, 60
built-in methods, 10, 18, 91–92
 calling (invoking), 10
 lists, used for, 91–92
buttons, 125–129, 131, 134, 197–198
 check box as, 130–131, 134
 custom, 197–198
 GUI components, as, 125–129, 134
 `Jbutton`, 127
 listener, 127–129, 134
 push, 127
 radio, 131, 134
bytecode, 101

C
call stack trace, 207
calling (invoking), 8–11, 252,
  254–257, 287
 Alice, 8–11, 287
 comments (*///*) for, 8
 control statements and, 9–10
 Java, 252, 254–257
 methods, 8–11, 252, 254–257, 287
 `my first method` method, 8
 parameters and, 9
 recursion and, 252, 254–257
camera controls, 7–8, 291
`capture pose` button, 19, 290
case diagrams, 247
`catch` clauses, 207, 211
change events, 148–149
`ChangeEvent`, 130
characters, 162–164, 307–308
 arrays of, 162–164
 control, 308
 nonprintable, 308
 printable, 307–308
 Unicode set, 307–308
check box control, 130–131, 134
checked exceptions, 215–217
`Cheerleader` world example, 26–28
child class, 104, 178–182
 class hierarchies of, 181–182

constructors, 180
inheritance and, 104, 178–182
is-as relationship with parent class, 179
overriding methods, 181
`protected` modifier, 179–180
siblings, 181
subclass, as a, 178–181
`super` reference, 180
`choose true` function, 44
`Circle` class, 110–111
`circle` method, 33
class diagrams, 237–238, 246–247
classes, 12–13, 102–104, 106–112,
  131–133, 153–175, 177–192,
  198–199, 235–237, 239–247. *See
  also* inheritance
 abstract, 184–185
 aggregate objects in, 246–247
 Alice, 12–13
 API library for, 103, 154
 `ArrayList`, 154, 155–159
 assigning responsibilities in, 236–237
 base, 178
 braces {} in, 107
 child, 104, 178–182
 `Circle`, 110–111
 collections and, 153–175
 comparison of Alice and Java using,
  102–104
 dependency of, 240–246
 galleries of, 12–13
 generic (parameterized) types of,
  154–155
 `Graphics`, 112
 header, 107
 hierarchies of, 181–192
 identification of, 235–236
 importing, 103
 inheritance and, 104, 177–192
 inner, 133
 Java, 102–104, 106–112, 153–175,
  181–192
 `LinkedList`, 154
 listener, 131–133
 nesting, 131–133
 `Object`, 182–183
 objects and, 12–13, 102–104,
  106–112, 154–155, 240–247
 packages used for, 103
 parent, 104, 178–182
 programming with, 106–112
 relationships between, 239–247
 software design and, 235–237,
  239–247

subclasses, 178–181
superclass, 178
threads and, 198–199
`clone` method, 183
collections, 153–175
 API library for, 154, 172
 `ArrayList` class, 154–159
 arrays, 160–172
 data structures and, 154
 generic (parameterized) types,
  154–155
 `LinkedList` class, 154
 lists, 153–175
 ThunkIt program using, 159, 170
 types of, 172
`Collision` world example, 53–54
command-line arguments, 172
comments (*///*) in Alice, 8
compiler, 101–102
compile-time errors in Java, 102
`ComponentEvent`, 130
composite objects, 15–18
`Concert` world example, 77–78
concurrency of statements, *see*
  threads
condition events, 69, 77–80
 types of, 69
 `When a variable changes`, 79–80
 `When something becomes true`,
  78
 `While a something is true`,
  77–78
conditions, *see* Boolean conditions
constructors, 102, 110, 180
`ContainerEvent`, 130
content panes, 108
control characters, 308
control statements, 9–10, 13–15, 17,
  42–48, 105. *See also* statements
 adding to methods, 10
 Alice, 9–10, 13–15, 17, 42–48
 conditions for, 42, 44
 `do in order`, 14–15
 `do together`, 13–14, 17
 `If/Else`, 42–48
 Java, 105
 methods using, 9–10, 13–15, 17
 `wait`, 9
controls, 130–137
 check box, 130–131, 134
 Java event programming using,
  130–137
 listeners for, 133
 radio buttons, 131, 134

text box, 130
text field, 133
coordinate system, Java, 110–112
Cow world example, 79–80
create new event button, 68
custom buttons, 197–198
custom methods, 26–30

D
data, 25–39, 104–105. *See also*
    operators
    Alice, 25–39
    comparison between Alice and Java
        using, 104–105
    declared variables, 28–30
    expressions and, 28–32, 104
    Java, 104–105
    local, 29–30
    methods and, 25–39
    objects as, 34
    operators and, 104
    primitive types, 104
    random number function, 31–32
    variables, 28–30
data structures, 87–98, 154, 160–172
    Alice, 87–98
    arrays, 87–89, 92–94, 160–162
    collections and, 154
    Java, 154, 160–172
    lists, 89–92
    managing multiple objects using,
        88–89
declared variables, 28–31
default visibility, 317–318
dependency of classes and objects,
    240–246
details panel, Alice IDE, 6
dialogue, input for objects, 81
direct recursion, 257
distance variable, 30, 31
do in order statement, 14–15
do together statement, 13–14, 17, 55
    Loop statements, used in, 55
    methods using, 13–14, 17
    movement of objects using, 13–14,
        17, 55
Dragon world example, 54–55
drawing objects in Java, 106–112,
    112–115
    bounding rectangle, 111
    Circle class, 110–111
    coordinate system, 110–111
    for loops used for, 113–115
    frames for, 106, 108

graphical components, 112–115
    Graphics (gc) class, 112
    panels for, 106–109
drop dummy at camera button, 81
dummy objects, 81, 291
duplicating objects in Alice, 34

E
element type, 161
Else portion of If/Else statements,
    44–45
encapsulation, 109–110, 180
environments, 4–6, 101–102,
    283–291
    adding to, 285, 287, 289
    Alice, 4–6, 283–291
    bytecode, 101
    compiler, 101–102
    compile-time errors in, 102
    deleting from, 288
    installing, 283
    integrated developmental (IDE), 4–6,
        101–102
    Java, 101–102
    logical errors in, 102
    methods in, 286–289
    objects in, 285–286, 288,
        290–291
    parameters in, 289
    source code, 101
    statements in, 288
    syntax, 102
    variables in, 289–290
    worlds, 284–285
equality operators (== and !=), 46,
    105
equals method, 183
errors, 102, 161, 206
    compile-time, 102
    exceptions compared to, 206
    Java programming and, 102
    logical, 102
    off-by-one, 161
events, 67–85, 123–152
    Abstract Windowing Toolkit (AWT),
        125
    action, 125–137
    add method, 126
    Alice, 6, 67–85
    buttons for, 125–133
    change, 148–149
    condition, 69, 77–80
    create new event button, 68
    editor, Alice IDE, 6, 68–69

graphical user interface (GUI) for,
    68, 124–152
Java, 123–152
java.awt package, 125
javax.swing package, 125
keyboard, 69, 72–74, 144–148
labels for, 126–127, 129
listener objects, 124, 127–134,
    137–148, 149
loops compared to, 71
mouse, 69, 75–77, 137–144
my first method, 68
processing, 68–69
types of, 130
window, 149
world, 69, 70–71
exceptions, 205–229
    API library for, 225
    call stack trace, 207
    catch clause, 207, 211
    checked, 215–217
    creating your own, 225
    errors compared to, 206
    finally clause for, 211–212
    handling, 206–212
    hierarchy, 225
    I/O (input/output) and, 217–224
    IOException class, 219
    propagation, 212–215
    thrown, 207–209, 215–217
    throws clause, 215–217
    ThunkIt program using, 210–211
    try-catch statement for, 207–210
    uncaught, 207
    unchecked, 215–217
expressions, 28–32, 104
    data values as, 28–32, 104
    mathematical using variables, 30

F
factorial function (!), 253–254
files, 217–224
    input, 219–221
    Java I/O, 217–224
    output, 221–223
    reading, 219–221
    text, 219–223
    ThunkIt, processing in, 223–224
    writing, 221–223
fillingStyle property, 11
final modifiers, 181, 317
finally clause, 211–212
FocusEvent, 130
For all in order statement, 90–91

For all together statement, 89–90
for loops used for drawing objects,
        113–115
fractals example, 270–277
frame objects, 106, 108
Frog world example, 29–30, 31
functions, 11, 31–32, 60, 91–92,
        293–297, 299–301, 302–305
   Boolean logic, 293
   built-in, 60
   list, 91–92, 302–303
   math, 293–294, 296–297
   mouse, 294–295
   object, 299–301
   object methods as, 11
   parameters, 303–305
   point of view, 301
   proximity, 299–300
   random, 294
   random number, 31–32
   size, 300
   spatial relations, 300–301
   string, 294
   time, 295
   user-interaction, 294
   world, 293–297

G

galleries, classes and, 12–13
generic (parameterized) types,
        154–155
graphical user interface (GUI), 68,
        124–152
   action events using, 125–137
   Alice, 68
   buttons, 125–129
   check box control, 130–131, 134
   components, 124–129, 130–137,
        147–178
   event processing using, 68, 124–129
   Java, 124–152
   keyboard events using, 144–148
   keyboard focus of, 147–148
   labels, 126–127
   listener objects, 124, 127–134,
        137–149
   mouse events using, 137–144
   panels for components of, 125–127
   radio buttons, 131, 134
   text box control, 130
   text field, 133
Graphics class, 112, 119
grid class, ThunkIt, 170
groups of objects, 80

H

He Builder tool, 19
hierarchies, 181–192, 225,
        311–312
   abstract classes, 184–185
   child class, 181–182
   classes, 181–192
   exceptions, 225
   methods in, 183, 184–185
   Object class, 182–183
   operators, 311–312
   parent class, 181–182
   Shapemaker program, example of,
        185–191
   siblings, 181
   ThunkIt program using, 191–192
hop method, 14

I

I/O (input/output), 217–224
   exceptions and, 217–224
   files, 217–224
   IOException class, 219
   Java file, 217–224
   reading text files, 219–221
   streams in, 217–219
   text files in, 219–223
   ThunkIt file processing, 223–224
   writing text files, 221–223
IDE, see integrated development
        environment (IDE)
If/Else statements, 42–48, 50
   Alice use of, 42–48, 50
   choose true function, 44
   conditions for, 42, 44
   Else portion of, 44–45
   equality and relational operators for,
        46
   nested, 47–48
   While statement compared to, 50
if-else statements in Java, 105
implementation of software, 233
indentation of code, 108
index values, 92–94, 160–164
   Alice, 92–94
   arrays and, 92–94, 160–164
   bounds checking, 161–164
   Java, 160–164
   off-by-one errors, 161
indirect recursion, 257
infinite loops, 50–51, 53
infinite recursion, 253
inheritance, 104, 177–204
   abstract classes, 184–185

child class, 104, 178–179
   classes and, 104, 177–192
   hierarchies of classes, 181–192
   is-as relationship between classes,
        179
   methods in, 180–181
   modifiers in, 179–181, 184
   Object class, 182–183
   parent class, 104, 178–179
   polymorphism, 192–198
   reference variables in, 193–194
   Shapemaker program, example of,
        185–191, 194–198
   software reuse and, 178
   subclasses, 178–181
   threads, 198–199
   ThunkIt program using, 191–192,
        199
   visibility modifiers and, 179–180
initializer lists, 164–167
inner classes, 133
input streams, 217
input validation, 115
integers, arrays of, 160–161, 165–167
integrated development environment
        (IDE), 4–6, 101–102
   Alice animations using, 4–6
   details panel, 6
   events editor, 6
   Java environments compared to,
        101–102
   method editor, 6
   object tree, 5–6
   toolbar, 5–6
   world view, 5–6
Intersection world example,
        43–48
IOException class, 219
is-as relationships, 179
ItemEvent, 130
iteration, 51–52, 58–60, 234–235,
        256
   development process for software,
        234–235
   loops, 51–52, 58–60
   nested repetition statements and,
        58–60
   programming, 256
   recursion compared to, 256
   while statements and, 51–52

J

Java, 2–4, 99–282, 311–315, 317–319
   Alice compared to, 2–4, 99–122

API library, 103, 119, 154, 172, 225
ArrayList class, 155–159
arrays, 160–172
bitwise operators, 313–315
Boolean operators (&, |, and ^), 315
Circle class, 110–111
classes in, 102–104, 106–112,
　　131–133, 153–175, 177–192
collections, 153–175
command-line arguments, 172
coordinate system, 110–111
data in, 104–105
encapsulation, 109–110, 180
events, 123–152
exceptions, 205–229
general-purpose programming
　　language, as a, 3, 101
Graphics class, 112, 119
I/O (input/output), 217–224
inheritance, 104, 177–204
left-shift operator (<<), 314
listener objects, 124, 127–134,
　　137–148, 149
lists, 153–175
main method, 106–108
methods, 104, 106–118, 167–168,
　　180–181, 183–185, 193–194,
　　252, 254–257
modifiers, 109–110, 179–181, 184,
　　317–319
objects in, 102–104, 106–112
operators, 104–105, 119,
　　311–315
panels, 106–109, 125–127
parameters, 167–168, 172
polymorphism, 192–198
precedence of operators, 311–312
primitive data types, 104
programming using, 106–119,
　　123–152
recursion, 251–282
reserved words, 107, 109–110
right-shift operators (>> and >>>), 315
software design, 231–250
statements, 105–106, 112–118
subclasses, 178–181
threads, 105, 198–199, 278
ThunkIt program, 3–4, 118–119,
　　129, 142–144, 148, 159, 170,
　　191–192, 199, 210–211,
　　223–224
visibility modifiers, 109–110,
　　179–180, 317–318
java.awt package, 125

java.io package, 219
javax.swing package, 125
Jbutton, 127
Jet world example, 32–33
jump methods, 26–27

K

keyboard events, 69, 72–74, 130,
　　144–148
Alice, 69, 72–74
firing of actions using, 73
getKeyChar method, 147
getKeyCode method, 147
Java, 144–148
keyboard focus, 147–148
KeyEvent, 130
KeyListener interface, 144, 146–147
keyPressed method, 147
keyReleased method, 147
keyTyped method, 147
Let the arrow keys move an
　　object, 74
repetition, 147
switch statements used for, 147
ThunkIt program using, 148
types of, 69
When a key is typed, 72–73
While a key is pressed, 73–74
KochSnowflake program example,
　　270–277

L

label components, GUI, 126–127
late (dynamic) binding, 193
left-shift operator (<<), 314
length constant, 162
listener objects, 124, 127–134,
　　137–149
action events, 127–134
ActionListener interface,
　　127–128, 133, 134
adapter classes for, 149
check boxes and, 134
classes and, 131–133
controls and, 133
events and, 130
GUI components and, 124, 127–134
inner classes, as, 133
keyboard events, 144–148
KeyListener interface, 144, 146–147
mouse events, 137–144
MouseListener interface, 137, 140
MouseMotionListener interface,
　　137, 140

radio buttons and, 134
ThunkIt program using, 129,
　　142–144
types of, 130
lists, 87–92, 153–175, 302–303
Alice, 87–92
ArrayList class, 154–159
arrays as, 160–172
arrays compared to, 88–89, 160
built-in methods used for, 91–92
data structures, as, 88–89
For all in order statement for,
　　90–91
For all together statement for,
　　89–90
functions, 91–92, 302–303
initializer, 164–167
Java, 153–175
LinkedList class, 154
methods, 91–92, 302
ThunkIt program using, 159
variable-length, 172
local data, 29–30
logical errors in Java, 102
logical operators, 52–53, 105,
　　311–312
loop control variable, 56–57
Loop statements, 54–58
Do together statements in, 55
loop control variable for, 56–57
movement of objects using, 54–58
loops, 49–60, 114–116
Alice, 49–60
body, 49, 51
events compared to, 71
for, 113–115
infinite 50–51, 53
iteration of, 51–52, 58–60
Java programming and, 114–116
nested, 58–60
repetition statements as, 49–60
while, 116

M

main method, 106–108
mathematics, 30, 104–105,
　　253–254, 293–294, 296–297,
　　312
expressions, 30, 104–105
factorial function (!), 253–254
functions, 293–294, 296–297
operators, 46, 104–105, 312
recursion for, 253–254
variables, 30, 104–105

Maze class example of recursion, 258–262
method editor, Alice IDE, 6
methods, 8–11, 13–15, 25–39, 91–92, 104, 106–118, 119, 167–168, 180–181, 183–185, 193–194, 252, 254–257, 286–289, 293, 297–299, 302–305
  abstract, 184–185
  adding to objects, 26–28
  Alice, 8–11, 13–15, 25–39, 91–92, 286–289, 293, 297–299, 302–305
  API library for, 119
  arrays passed as parameters to, 167–168
  binding, 193
  built-in, 10, 18
  calling (invoking), 8–11, 252, 254–257, 287
  changing values passed to, 288
  classes and, 106–112
  constructors, 180
  control statements added to, 10
  creating, 286
  custom, 26–30
  data and, 25–39
  declared variables in, 28–30
  deleting, 288
  direct recursion, 257
  editing, 286
  expressions in, 30
  final modifier, 181
  functions and, 11, 287
  graphics, 112–115, 119
  header, 107
  hierarchies of classes and, 183, 184–185
  indentation used for, 108
  indirect recursion, 257
  inheritance and, 104, 180–181, 183–185, 194
  Java, 104, 106–118, 167–168, 180–181, 183–185, 193–194, 252, 254–257
  late (dynamic) binding, 193
  list, 91–92, 302
  local data in, 29–30
  local variables, adding to, 289
  main, 106–108
  messages to objects using, 17
  movement of objects using, 26–30
  my first method, 8, 68, 293
  objects and, 8–11, 13–15, 26–28, 106–112, 183, 297–299
  order of, 13–15
  overriding, 181
  parameters for, 9, 32–33, 167–168, 289, 303–305
  polymorphism and, 193, 194
  programming using, 108–111, 254–257
  public, 109
  random number function, 31–32
  recursion and, 252, 254–257
  statements and, 112–118, 287
  world, 293
models for software design, 233–234
modifiers, 109–110, 179–181, 184, 317–319
  abstract, 184, 317
  default visibility of, 317–318
  final, 181, 319
  inheritance and, 179–181, 184
  Java programming using, 109–110
  native, 317
  package visibility of, 317
  private, 109, 318
  protected, 179–180, 318
  public, 109, 318
  static, 319
  synchronized, 319
  visibility, 109–110, 179–180, 317–318
mouse events, 69, 75–77, 130, 137–144
  Alice, 69, 75–77
  GUI components and, 137
  Java, 137–144
  Let the mouse move objects, 77
  Let the mouse move the camera, 76
  Let the mouse orient the camera, 76
  listener objects in, 137–144
  mousedragged method, 140
  MouseEvent, 130
  MouseListener interface, 137, 140
  MouseMotionListener interface, 137, 140
  mousemoved method, 140
  mousepressed method, 141
  mousereleased method, 141
  ThunkIt program using, 142–144
  types of, 69
  When the mouse is clicked on something, 75–76
  When the mouse is pressed on something, 75
mouse functions, 294–295
move method, 14
movement of objects, 13–15, 17–19, 26–33, 41–85, 285
  circle method, 33
  condition events, 69, 77–80
  conditions for, 41–66
  control statements, 13–15, 42–48
  custom methods for, 26–30
  declared variables, 28–31
  distance variable, 30, 31
  do in order, 14–15
  do together, 13–14, 17
  events for, 69, 70–71
  hop method, 29–30
  jump methods, 26–27
  keyboard events, 69, 72–74
  mouse events, 69, 75–77
  move method, 14
  orientation (position) of, 18–19, 285
  parameters for, 32–33
  pivot points, 18–19
  proximity function for, 54
  random number function, 31
  repetition statements, 49–60
  rolling, 18–19
  turn method, 14
  turning, 14, 18–19
  world events, 69, 70–71
multidimensional arrays, 171–172
my first method method, 8, 68, 293

N

native modifiers, 317
nested statements, 47–48, 58–60
  control, 47–48
  If/Else, 47–48
  iteration of loops as, 58–60
  repetition, 58–60
nonprintable characters, Unicode, 308

O

Object class, 182–183
object-oriented programming (OOP), 2
object tree, Alice IDE, 5–6, 16
objects, 1–23, 26–28, 34–35, 41–85, 87–98, 102–104, 106–112, 118, 154–155, 168–198, 182–183, 235–236, 240–247, 285–286, 288, 290–291, 297–301. *See also* listener objects; movement of objects

aggregate, 246–247
Alice, 1–23, 26–28, 34–35, 41–85,
    87–98, 285–286, 288, 290–291
  arrays of, 168–169
  built-in functions, 60
  built-in methods, 10, 18
  calling methods, 8–11
  capture pose button, 19, 290
  classes and, 12–13, 102–104,
    106–112, 240–247
  comparison of Alice and Java using,
    102–104
  composite, 15–18
  constructors, 102, 110
  content panes, 108
  control statements for, 9–10, 42–48
  custom methods for, 26–28
  data, as, 35
  data structures for, 87–98
  deleting, 288
  dependency between, 240–246
  dialogue input for, 81
  do in order statement, 14–15
  do together statement, 13–14, 17
  drawing in Java, 106–115
  dummy, 81, 291
  duplicating, 35, 286
  encapsulation of, 109–110
  equals method for, 183
  events for, 69, 70–71
  frames, 106, 108
  functions, 60, 299–301
  galleries used for, 12–13
  generic classes of, 154–155
  graphical components for, 112–115
  groups of, 80–81
  He Builder tool, 19
  identification of, 235–236
  inheritance and, 182–183
  integrated development environment
    (IDE) for, 4–6
  Java, 102–104, 106–115, 118,
    154–155, 168–169, 182–183
  Let the arrow keys move an
    object event, 74
  Let the mouse move objects
    event, 77
  messages to using methods, 17
  methods, 8–11, 13–15, 26–28,
    106–112, 182–183, 297–299
  movement of in Alice, 13–15,
    17–19, 26–33, 41–85, 285
  multiple, 88–89

  opacity property, 11, 94
  order of methods for, 13–15
  orientation (position) of, 18–19, 285
  panels, 106–109
  posing, 290
  properties of, 11
  quad view of, 34
  renaming, 34
  repetition statements for, 49–60
  rolling, 18–19
  saving, 94
  She Builder tool, 19
  software design and, 235–236,
    240–247
  SpinningCubes world, example of,
    6–9
  String, 168–169
  texture maps, 94
  three-dimensional (3D) text, 60–61
  toString method for, 118, 183
  turn to face method, 14–15
  turning, 17, 18–19
  vehicle property, 60
  worlds, adding to, 285
off-by-one errors, 161
one-dimensional arrays, 160–169
opacity property, 11, 94
operators, 46, 52–53, 104–105, 119,
    311–315
  Alice, 46, 52–53
  assignment (=), 104–105
  bitwise, 313–315
  Boolean, 46, 312, 315
  comparison between Alice and Java
    using, 104–105
  data and, 104–105
  equality (==), 46, 105
  Java, 104–105, 119, 311–315
  left-shift (<<), 314
  logical, 52–53, 105, 311–312
  mathematical, 46, 104–105, 312
  precedence (hierarchy) of,
    311–312
  relational, 46, 105
  right-shift (>> and >>>), 315
orientation of objects, 18–19, 285
output streams, 217

P

packages, 103, 317
  classes, used for, 103
  visibility, 317
panels, 6, 106–109, 125–127

  details, in Alice, 6
  GUI elements in, 125–127
  Java, 106–109, 125–127
  objects drawn in, 106–109
parameters, 9, 32–33, 167–168, 172,
    303–305
  adding to methods, 33
  Alice, 9, 32–33, 303–305
  arrays as, 167–168
  command-line arguments, 172
  functions and, 303–305
  Java, 167–168, 172
  methods and, 9, 167–168,
    303–305
  variable-length lists, 172
  writing methods using, 32–33
parent class, 104, 178–182
  child class and, 104, 178–182
  class hierarchies of, 181–182
  constructors, 180
  final modifier, 181
  inheritance and, 104, 178–179
  methods, 179–181
  siblings, 181
  super reference, 180
pivot points, 18–19
play sound method, 61
point of view functions, 301
polymorphism, 192–198
  binding methods, 193
  inheritance and, 193–194
  late (dynamic) binding, 193
  methods, 193, 194
  objects and, 192–198
  reference variables, 192–194
  Shapemaker program, example of,
    194–198
precedence, see hierarchies
primitive data types, 104
print statement, 81, 105
printable characters, Unicode,
    307–308
println statement, 105
private visibility modifier, 109,
    318
programming, 41–66, 106–119,
    123–152, 254–257. See also envi-
    ronments
  Alice, decisions in, 41–66
  Boolean conditions (true or false),
    42–60
  braces {} for, 107
  class header, 107

programming (*continued*)
classes, with, 106–112
control statements, 42–48
controls in Java, 130–133
direct recursion methods, 257
drawing and, 111–112
driver, 107
events, 123–152
frame objects and, 106, 108
graphical components, 112–115
If/Else statements, 42–48
indentation, 108
indirect recursion methods, 257
input validation, 116
iterative, 256
Java, 106–119, 123–152, 254–257
Loop statements, 49–54
loops in, 114–116
main method, 106–108
method header, 107
methods, 108–119, 254–257
recursive, 254–257
repetition statements for, 49–60
reserved words, 107, 109–110
statements, using in Java, 112–119
visibility modifiers, 109–110
While statements, 49–54
propagation program for exceptions, 212–215
properties of objects, 11
protected visibility modifier, 179–180, 318
proximity functions, 54, 299–300
public visibility modifier, 109, 318
push button, 127

Q
quad view, 34

R
radio buttons, 131, 134
random functions, 294
random number function, 31–32, 46
reading text files, 219–221
recursion, 251–282
backtracking algorithm using, 285–262
base case in, 253
definition, 252–253
direct, 257
factorial function (!) and, 253–254
fractals, example of, 270–277
indirect, 257
infinite, 253

iteration compared to, 256
KochSnowflake program, example of, 270–277
mathematics using, 253–254
Maze class, example of, 258–262
methods and, 252, 254–257
programming, 254–257
TiledPictures program, example of, 267–270
Towers of Hanoi puzzle, example of, 262–267
tracing execution of, 255–256
use of, 257–277
reference variables, 192–194
relational operators, 46, 105
remainder (%) operator, 105
renaming objects, 34
repetition statements, 49–60
conditions for, 49, 54
infinite loops, 50–51, 53
iteration of loops, 51–52, 58–60
loop body, 49, 51
Loop, 54–58
loops in, 49–60
nested, 58–60
While, 49–54
reserved words in Java, 107, 109–110
right-shift operators (>> and >>>), 315
Rocker world example, 75–76
Rockette world example, 72–74
rolling objects, 18–19
rubberbanding technique, 186
Runnable interface, 199

S
Safe world example, 58–60
saving objects in Alice, 94
SchoolOfFish world example, 89–90
sequence diagrams, 238–238
Shapemaker program example, 185–191, 194–198
Shark world example, 50–53
She Builder tool, 19
siblings, 181
size functions, 300
software design, 231–250
agile software development, 247
assigning responsibilities in, 236–237
case diagrams, 247
class diagrams, 237–238
classes and, 235–237, 239–247
creation of, 232–233

development process for, 232–237
identification of classes and objects, 235–236
implementation of, 233
iterative development, 234–235
models, 233–234
objects, identification of, 235–236
requirements for, 232
sequence diagrams, 238–238
test-driven software development, 247
testing, 233
unified modeling language (UML), 237–239, 247
software reuse, 178
sounds, importing in Alice, 61
source code, 101
spatial relation functions, 300–301
SpeedingCar world example, 56–57
SpinningCubes world example, 6–9
standard I/O streams, 218
statements, 9–10, 13–15, 17, 42–60, 105–106, 112–118, 198–199, 278, 287
Alice, 9–10, 13–15, 17, 42–60, 287–289
adding to methods, 287
assignment, 105
concurrency of, 105
control, 9–10, 13–15, 17, 42–48, 105
deleting, 288
do in order, 14–15
do together, 13–14, 17, 55
for loops, 113–115
graphic methods in, 112–115
If/Else, 42–48, 50
if-else, 105
Java, 105–106, 112–118, 198–199, 278
methods for, 112–118
nested, 47–48, 58–60
repetition, 49–60
threads as, 105, 198–199, 278
while loops, 116
While, 49–54
static modifiers, 317
streams, 217–219
input, 217
java.io package, 219
output, 217
standard I/O, 218
System class, 218
string functions, 294

String objects, 168–169, 172
subclasses, 178–181. *See also*
    child class
    constructors, 180
    inheritance and, 178–181
    overriding methods in, 181
    protected modifier, 179–180
    super reference, 180
super reference, 180
superclass, 178
SurferWave world example, 15–17
switch statement, 147
synchronization of threads, 200
synchronized modifiers, 317
syntax, 102
System class streams, 218

T

test-driven software development, 247
testing software, 233
text box control, 130
text field, 133
text files, 219–223
    reading, 219–221
    writing, 221–223
texture maps, 94
threads, 105, 198–200, 278
    class definition and, 198–199
    concurrency of statements using,
        105, 198
    creation of, 198–199
    inheritance and, 198–199
    Runnable interface for, 199
    synchronization of, 200
    ThunkIt program using, 199
three-dimensional (3D) text objects,
    60–61
throws clause, 215–217
ThunkIt program, 3–4, 118–119, 129,
    142–144, 148, 159, 170,
    191–192, 199, 210–211,
    223–224
    action events, 129
    ArrayList class in, 159
    arrays and, 170
    collections and, 159, 171
    exception handling in, 210–211
    file processing, 223–224
    grid class, 170
    hierarchies of classes, 191–192
    inheritance and, 191–192, 199
    introduction to, 3–4, 118–119
    keyboard events, 148
    listeners in, 129, 142–144, 148

mouse events, 142–144
    try-catch statements in, 210–211
TiledPictures program example,
    267–270
time functions, 295
toolbar, Alice, 5–6
toString method, 118, 183
Towers of Hanoi puzzle example,
    262–267
tracing execution of recursion,
    255–256
transient modifiers, 317
try blocks, 207, 209–212
try-catch statements, 207–212
    catch clauses, 207, 211
    exception handling with, 207–212
    finally clause for, 211–212
    throwing exceptions using, 207–209
    ThunkIt program using, 210–211
    try blocks, 207, 209–212
turn method, 14
turn to face method, 14–15
turning objects in Alice, 17–19
two-dimensional arrays, 169–170

U

UML, *see* unified modeling
    language (UML)
uncaught exceptions, 207
unchecked exceptions, 215–217
Unicode character set, 307–308
unified modeling language (UML),
    237–239, 246–247
    aggregation represented by, 246–247
    case diagrams, 247
    class diagrams, 237–238, 246–247
    software design and, 237–239,
        246–247
uniform resource locators (URLs), 219
user-interaction functions, 294

V

variable-length lists, 172
variables, 28–31, 79–80, 104–105,
    160–161, 192–194, 289, 290
    adding to methods, 289
    Alice, 28–30, 79–80, 289, 290
    arrays and, 160–161
    assignment (=) operator used for,
        104–105
    condition events for, 79–80
    declared, 28–31
    distance, 30, 31
    expressions using, 30, 104

Java, 104–105, 160–161, 192–194
    local data as, 29–30
    methods, used in, 28–30, 298
    polymorphism and, 192–194
    random number function, 31
    reference, 192–194
    setting the value of, 290
    When a variable changes event,
        79–80
vehicle property, 60
visibility modifiers, 109–110,
    179–180, 317–318
    default visibility of, 317–318
    inheritance and, 179–180
    Java programming using, 109–110
    package visibility of, 317
    private, 109, 318
    protected, 179–180, 318
    public, 109, 318
volatile modifiers, 317

W

WackAMole world example, 92–94
while loops, input validation using,
    116
While statements, 49–54
    conditions for, 49, 54
    If/Else statement compared to, 50
    infinite loops in, 50–51, 53
    iteration of loops, 51–52
    logical operators for, 52–53
    loop body, 49, 51
    proximity function for, 54
Windmill world example, 70–71
window events, 130, 149
world events, 69–71
    Begin section, 70
    During section, 70–71
    End section, 70
    types of, 69
    When the world starts, 70
    While the world is running, 70–71
world view, 5–6
worlds in Alice, 5–8, 284–285,
    293–297
    adding objects to, 285
    camera controls in, 7–8
    creating, 284
    functions, 293–297
    integrated development environment
        (IDE), 5–6
    methods, 293
    vitual, use of, 5–8
writing text files, 221–223